GW00676353

*Finding Meaning
and Direction
Amidst Today's
World Crisis*

WORLDSTORM

ROY S. NEUBERGER

WORLD

Finding Meaning and Direction
Amidst Today's World Crisis

ISRAEL BOOKSHOP
LAKEWOOD, NJ

STORM

Roy S. Neuberger

DISTRIBUTED BY:
ISRAEL BOOKSHOP
501 PROSPECT STREET
LAKEWOOD, NJ 08701
732.901.3009
FAX: 732.901.4012
EMAIL: ISRBSHP@AOL.COM

COVER AND BOOK DESIGN:
DC DESIGN

TYPOGRAPHY, PRINTING AND BINDING:

© Copyright 2003 Roy Neuberger

All rights reserved.

This book, or any part thereof, may not be reproduced, stored in a retrieval system or
transmitted in any form or by any means, electronic, mechanical, photocopying,
recording or otherwise, without the express written permission of the copyright holder.

ISBN 1-931681-49-X

PRINTED IN THE UNITED STATES OF AMERICA

בס"ד

שמואל קמנצקי
Rabbi S. Kamenetsky

2018 Upland Way
Philadelphia, Pa 19131

Home: 215-473-2798
Study: 215-473-1212

[Handwritten Hebrew letter]

דברי מלו"ה
[signature]

To the honored and esteemed Torah personality, R' Yisroel Neuberger,

I received your manuscript "Nation Alone,"* whose purpose resembles the purpose of your first book, which brought great benefit to the many Jews who are estranged and bereft of the will of G-d. Undoubtedly, this book, too, will serve as a vehicle to fortify and arouse the thoughts of those who strive to listen to the words of G-d.

I saw in the Pesikta of Rav Kahana commenting on the parasha of V'zos HaB'racha– "don't read it 'b'racha' – blessing; rather read it 'b'reicha' – wellspring. For just as a well-spring spiritually cleanses the impure, so too, Moshe drew close the distanced; previously, Basya [by being a vehicle of merit for her] and now again by "may Reuven live [in this world] and not die [in the next]. So it says explicitly in the Midrash "blessed are you on your arrival and blessed are you at your departure – this verse refers to Moshe [who saved others from his birth to the time of his death]." You have merited to draw close the estranged Jews who have now been awakened, and so may you merit to continue attracting hearts and to publicly sanctify G-d's name.

May you merit to be counted among those who bring merit to the masses, whose righteousness stands by them eternally, and may you see much nachas from your honored family.

With heartfelt blessings,
Shmuel Kamenetsky

* Previous book title.

HASKAMA

ב"ה

Rabbi Y. Belsky
506 EAST 7th STREET
BROOKLYN NEW YORK 1218

ישראל הלוי בעלסקי

941   0112

I am fascinated by the original ideas expressed so sparkingly by Reb Yisroel Neuberger in this intriguing and insightful volume.

The creative concepts presented here are a tribute to the deep and abiding faith of the author, whose life's odyssey is related in his other equally fascinating work, *"From Central Park to Sinai: How I Found My Jewish Soul."* Reb Yisroel's personal story reads like fiction, albeit somewhat stranger and more exciting. One can discover in those pages whence stems the dynamic force that drives the author to such heights of imaginative interpretation found in this current opus, adding new vistas of thoughts - spurring ideas to the classical understanding of the Holy Writings and Traditions.

I wish Reb Yisroel well and look forward to future volumes written by him in the same spirit as this one. May *Hashem Yisborach* reward him and his wife with a fulfilling visionary life and the attaining of his dreams of great achievement as evident from his writings.

28 Iyar 5763
Brooklyn, New York

ישראל הלוי ב' בעלסקי

Yisroel ha Levi Belsky

בס"ד אור ליום ה' לסדר כי תצא חדש אלול ה' תנש"א
ישלח יד"ש ל'כבוד
ידידי הרב החשוב ר' ישראל נ"י!

בנים ובנותם גדתי את ספרו לי ואני
אמן, כי ספר חשוב מאוד ורב תועלת.
יופע עיונים חדוד ונבוע ותרבה דעת,
עד אשר הארץ דעה את ה' כמים לים מכסים,
במהרה בימינו.

ותזכה לעסוק בתורה ובעבודת ה' מתוך ישוב
הדעת ולעלות במהרה עם כלל ישראל
להר הבית במהרה ביומינו

המוקירו ומכבדו,

אביגדר נבנצל
[ירושלים]

In honor of R' Yisroel Neuberger,

I read your book with interest and amazement. Truly, this is a book that is thought provoking and most purposeful. May your wellsprings spread ever outward, may the masses immerse in them, increasing knowledge "until the world is full of knowledge," speedily in our days.

May you merit to focus on Torah and service of Hashem with tranquility and peace of mind, and to soon ascend, along with the rest of the Jewish nation, to the Temple Mount.

I who value and honor him,
Avigdor Nebenzahl
Jerusalem

HASKAMA

YESHIVA OF FAR ROCKAWAY · DERECH AYSON RABBINICAL SEMINARY
802 HICKSVILLE ROAD · FAR ROCKAWAY, NEW YORK 11691 · 718.327.7600 · FAX:718.327.1430

Rabbi Yechiel I. Perr
Rosh HaYeshiva

Rabbi Aaron M.Brafman
Menahel

Rabbi Eli Goldgrab
General Studies Principal

Rabbi Shmuel Kohn
Executive Director

I have been spellbound by the manuscript of R' Yisroel Neuberger. His writing is so compelling and poetic that we cannot help but be swept along into an other-worldly experience.

One cannot know whether his scenario is prophetic or fantasy. But it certainly shakes me out of the state of complacency.

There are certainly adequate sources that could substantiate his vision and thesis, but one would have to have ruach hakodesh to speak with certainty. However, anyone who feels, as I do, that we are living in extraordinary times, and the events taking place are of Tanachik monumental proportions, should read this book.

Rabbi Aaron M. Brafman

IN LOVING AND GRACIANA MELOHN BUILDING MEMORY OF REB JOSEPH MELOHN

לזכר נשמת ר' אהרן בן קדוש סיני ר' אברהם מרים פנחו

YESHIVA DARCHEI TORAH ישיבה דרכי תורה

YAAKOV & ILANA MELOHN CAMPUS, IN MEMORY OF REB YOSEF MELOHN ז״ל

Rabbi Yaakov Bender
Rosh HaYeshiva

Mr. Richard Altabe
Dean of Secular Studies

Rabbi Shmuel Strickman
Menahel, Elementary School

Rabbi Dovid Morgenstern
S'gan Menahel

Rabbi Refael Skaist
Menahel, Junior High School

Rabbi Yitzchok Brailofsky
S'gan Menahel

Rabbi Yehuda Harbater
Executive Director

Rabbi Zev Bald
Administrator

Mr. Ronald Lowinger
President

Mr. Lloyd Keilson
Chairman, Board of Trustees

Mr. Motty Klein
Chairman, Board of Directors

Mr. Adam Mirzoeff
Mr. Dovid Scharf
Co-Chairmen, Executive Board

Sivan 5763
June 2003

It has been my sincere privilege to be a close friend and confidante of Rabbi Yisroel Neuberger since he registered his son in our yeshiva over twenty-two years ago. We have been in close contact ever since.

I have watched Reb Yisroel and his wife interact with their Rebbeim and with Gedolei Yisroel and use this influence to be *mechanech* their wonderful children, their son Ari and their daughters. They are *mekabel* what they learn in both Torah and Yiras Shomayim, inculcating that Torah they have learned from their many mentors into their entire beings.

Through intense research and studying, and especially learning from the esteemed Rebbetzin Esther Jungreis, Reb Yisroel has used his oratorical splendor and excellent writing capabilities to produce a work from which all of Klal Yisroel can benefit.

As a close personal friend, I am sincerely yours,

Rabbi Yaakov Bender
Rosh HaYeshiva

257 Beach 17th Street, Far Rockaway, NY 11691   Tel: 718-868-2300   Fax: 718-868-4450

Rebbetzin Esther Jungreis
PRESIDENT

This is the second time I have had the privilege of endorsing a book wrtitten by Yisroel Neuberger. There can be no greater satisfaction in *kiruv* - outreach than to know that the person to whom you have reached out is now reaching out to others. I first encountered Yisroel over thirty years ago at the inception of our Hineni movement. Since then, he has traveled light years and has become a vital part of our Hineni family. He immersed himself in Torah and *mitzvos* - and the rest is history, His first book described his odyssey as a Jew, and in this, his second book, he shares the insights that he has gleaned from his Torah studies. This thought-provoking book is bound to ignite the imagination of the reader and awaken him to greater Jewish commitment.

Rebbetzin Esther Jungreis
President, Hineni

The Hineni Heritage Center
232 West End Avenue, New York, NY 10023   tel: 212 496 1660   fax: 212 496 1908
email: rebbetzin@hineni.org

DEDICATION

This book is dedicated to my wife Leah. G-d introduced us to each other in our teenage years. We knew even then that we were two parts of one entity. I have the privilege of sharing life with an angelic partner. May she succeed in all her holy work and may we continue to see unlimited *nachas* from our exalted children!

My gratitude to Leah does not lessen my gratitude toward my parents, my spiritual parent, Rebbetzin Esther Jungreis, and to G-d, Who rescued and continues to rescue me from my mistakes and inadequacies. I hope to justify all their hopes in me. May our family and all who trust in G-d and hope for the Redemption soon see the day when *"the earth will be filled with the knowledge of G-d as the sea fills the ocean bed."* [1]

TABLE OF CONTENTS

INTRODUCTION

We are living in frightening and dangerous times. How do we understand these days? How do we protect ourselves and our families from forces that seem greater and stronger than we are? How do we navigate these unfamiliar and stormy seas?

The title of this book is, "Worldstorm: Finding Meaning and Direction Amidst Today's World Crisis."

The "world crisis" I am referring to is certainly the world against Israel. It is also the world against itself, specifically the war between the Arab World and the Western world.

In my first book, "From Central Park to Sinai: How I Found My Jewish Soul," (Jonathan David Publishers) I tell the story of how I grew up "allergic" to my Jewishness. I was never inside a synagogue until I was thirty years old. I found out, after many adventures on the sea of life, that the only way to navigate was to fix my sights on G-d.

But how do we go beyond the personal? How do we translate our discovery of G-d into a search for a way out of the personal, national and world sufferings that are besetting us today?

I discovered that we can learn nothing useful from the

media. We may learn that a bomb exploded somewhere, but we cannot learn how to defuse the bomb or the bomber. For that we need to refer to the only reliable source of Truth in the entire world, the Torah*, the Bible dictated by G-d at Mount Sinai to Moses and the Jewish People, and through us to the world.

I decided to open that Book and return to the beginning of time, to search for the clues and keys to redemption at the very Creation of the world. I went back to the days of Ishmael and Esau and explored the ancient rivalries that are being played out today in the worldwide war against Israel and the Jewish People, as well as the current battle between the Moslems and the Western World.

Today we are ready for answers to big questions; we are ready to reassess our lives in order to make this world safe for us and our children.

We are living amidst a Worldstorm, but we are the nation to whom the Prophet Isaiah said, "O afflicted, storm-tossed, unconsoled ones, behold. I shall lay your floor stones upon pearls and make your foundation of sapphires... All your children will be students of G-d and abundant will be your children's peace."

---

* The word "Torah" refers to the Written and Oral Law handed down by G-d to Moses at Mount Sinai. Moses taught it to the children of Israel, through whom the Written Torah (The Bible) became known to the entire world.

ACKNOWLEDGMENTS

If you have read "From Central Park to Sinai: How I Found My Jewish Soul," you will have discovered that I am not a Torah Scholar. I never entered a synagogue before the age of thirty and I had no Jewish education whatsoever until that time. I am still trying to catch up.

I thank G-d and the wonderful people who have helped us so much over the years. We have been fortunate to meet many great and kind people who have nurtured us on the road of life.

My friend Rob Rosenthal pointed out to me an appropriate passage from the classic work, Duties of the Heart,[2] which describes my feelings about this book. *"When I considered acting on my decision to write the book, I realized that a man like myself was unworthy of authoring such a work. I thought my powers too limited..."*

In my case it is true.

On the other hand (to continue quoting), *"if everyone who intended to perform some good act ... kept silent and stood still until he felt perfectly qualified, not a word would have been spoken by any man since the prophets..."*

I am not qualified, but my desire outweighs my caution.

"How can I repay G-d for all His kindness to me? I will raise the

cup of salvations and invoke the name of G-d."[3]

I would like to do something for G-d. Every time the Children and the Land of Israel are denigrated or insulted or are the objects of violence, G-d's Name – which is associated with the Children and the Land of Israel – is also demeaned. I cannot sit by; I cannot refrain from writing and speaking.

I have learned friends and advisers who are helping to ensure that what I say is correct and proper according to the Torah. I am fortunate beyond comprehension!

I am happy to thank the following people. Some are mentioned in the Dedication, but here I may speak at greater length.

My wife is the greatest gift I have been given beyond life itself, but, since we share life, it is all one. She has enabled me to survive my own weaknesses and vanities and steer toward something meaningful. She reads every word I write and constantly guides and encourages me, always with patience and a smile. May she be rewarded for all her holy acts, both known and unknown to me. May she see *nachas* from me and all the members of our family and may we merit to live together forever in the world of Messiah the son of David along with our family and the righteous people of the world.

We have wonderful children, sons-in-law and a daughter-in-law, and grandchildren who light up the world and act in such a righteous and honorable way that they make us realize our lives have achieved something meaningful. I want to thank our children and grandchildren for giving us this priceless gift. We feel that our children have given us life. May we and our children and their children through the generations see only righteousness in a world filled with the knowledge of G-d.

Our parents have bequeathed to us the most basic attitude of reverence for life and moral behavior. We Jews have a saying, *"derech eretz kadma l'Torah," proper behavior precedes the Torah.*

Our parents, by teaching our family proper behavior and deep ethical concerns as well as personal modesty and self-sacrifice, gave us the foundation for the Torah life.

Our Rebbetzin, Esther Jungreis, the Founder and President of the Hineni Organization, introduced us to the Torah way of life and guides us to this day. Rebbetzin Jungreis is one of a handful of people who pioneered the Teshuva Movement, the return of the Jewish People to our ancient heritage, in the days when she was a voice in the wilderness. Her courage, dedication and articulate brilliance in the service of G-d and her People are beyond measure. She is responsible not only for the uncountable numbers of souls she has touched through her writing and speaking over the years, but for giving birth to the movement of Return to G-d that is now sweeping through the Jewish and non-Jewish worlds. Rebbetzin Jungreis' words, ideas and influence can be felt in countless ways throughout this manuscript, even when her name is not specifically cited.

I want to thank all those distinguished leaders of our People who have been kind enough to read my manuscript and give letters of rabbinical approbation, which you will see in the early pages of this volume. I am honored by their support and caring guidance. In spite of their prodigious schedules and responsibilities they took time to help me with this book.

Rabbi Avigdor Nebenzahl read my manuscript carefully (although neither he nor any other rabbi bears responsibility for my mistakes or for sections of the text that I may have changed after the initial reading and which I may have inadvertently forgotten to show them in revised form). Rabbi Nebenzahl made page after page of corrections and suggestions, and in addition gave me over an hour of his precious time.

Rabbi Shmuel Kaminetsky gave much precious time and the benefit of his exalted guidance on many subjects.

Rabbi Aaron Brafman has been a friend and devoted mentor for years. His belief in me has sustained me and aided me greatly in writing this book.

Rabbi Eliezer Ginsburg has added tremendous strength to this book and has given me much guidance and encouragement.

Rabbi Yisroel Belsky spent much time with me and inspired me with his beautiful words and wise guidance.

Rabbi Yaakov Bender has been and continues to be the rosh yeshiva of our children and grandchildren and a continuing source of strength, encouragement and blessing to our family.

Rabbi Dovid Cohen has been a constant source of halachic and intellectual guidance, a font of endless goodness and good humor and a wonderful source of encouragement.

I want to acknowledge the privilege of having received blessings from Rabbi Avraham Pam, may his memory be a blessing, Rabbi Shmuel Berenbaum, Rabbi Zelig Epstein, Rabbi Yitzchak Feigelstock, Rabbi Elya Jurkonski, Rabbi Chaim Kanievsky, Rabbi Nesanel Quinn and Rabbi Aharon Leib Shteinman.

Rabbi Yeshaya Klor is a close personal friend who has opened up countless doors through which we could never have passed without him. Our meeting was nothing short of miraculous and is a story that begs to be told, because it illustrates how everything is for the best in the world that G-d has created. That, however, is for another place.

Rabbi Moshe Grossman, with whom it has been my privilege to study Torah for many years, has opened the door for me to many great rabbis and has been a constant source of guidance and wisdom.

Rabbi Shaul Dov Miller, my brilliantly talented editor, has challenged me on practically every page. He has made this book much better than it was before, but is not responsible if I have made errors, although he has saved me from many.

Deenee Cohen and Henshy Barash, and their associates at DC Design are responsible for the powerful and beautiful cover and book design. Rabbi Yosef Dovid Rosemarin, who patiently and expertly shepherded this book through the technical aspects of production, has become a good friend.

I am extremely grateful to Rabbi Zev Paretsky, the brilliant and patient Torah scholar who so kindly assisted me in locating the sources of many quotes and concepts mentioned in the book.

Two precious friends, Tsemach Glenn and Shuey Rhine, have become part of our family and have brought us great blessings. Without them, my first book would not have touched the thousands of hearts it did and is continuing to do. G-d has given these two young men unusual talents. May they flourish in every way and live lives of spiritual satisfaction and great accomplishment.

I want to thank Moshe Kaufman and the staff at the Israel Book Shop. Moshe's calm wisdom, wise counsel and trustworthiness have endeared him to me. I also want to thank the Kolatch Family and Marvin Sekler of Jonathan David Publishers, the publishers of "From Central Park to Sinai." I am proud to be associated with such fine people.

I want to thank Mr. Aaron Goldstein for sage advice, friendship and support, and for introducing me to Moshe Kaufman, and Rabbi Yechezkel Kaminsky for his friendship, encouragement, his many introductions, and for arranging publicity and speaking tours. I also want to thank Rabbis Joshua Fishman, Zvi Bloom and Nate Segal of Torah Umesorah and Rabbi Eli Gewirtz of Partners in Torah for arranging many exciting and inspirational speaking tours.

I also must pay tribute to my web site designer and computer guru, Gene Mastropieri, Jr., a gentleman if there ever was one, and a constant pleasure to work with, along with his wife, Allison.

I want to thank Mrs. Sara Averick and Mr. Jose Rosenfeld, my devoted representatives in Israel, and Mr. Abba Goldblatt of Shvut Ami, who is responsible for the excellent Russian translation of "From Central Park to Sinai." Kim Cherovsky, Malky Lowinger, Don Softness and Herbie Saltzman, who believed in the value of my first book, all aided with their talents and dedication in bringing it to the public.

I want to thank in addition the following people, who have helped me with this manuscript and in countless other ways, including in some cases inspiring me with Torah concepts which I used in this book: Yocheved Amrami, Rabbi Zvi Bajnon, Rabbi Aharon Bina, Mr. Stanley Blumenstein, Rabbi Moshe Eisemann, Rabbi Yaakov Feitman, Yosef Dov Feldhamer, Rabbi Yissacher Frand, Rabbi Eli Friedman, Mr. Larry Gordon, Rabbi Avraham Halpern, Mr. Eric Herman, Mr. Richie Herman, Mr. Steven Hill, Rabbi Shmuel Hiller, Rabbi Naftali Jaeger, Yaakov Jungreis, Rabbi Zev Kahn, Rabbi Yehoshua Kalish, Rabbi Mattis Kantor, James Kaufman, Esq., Rabbi Baruch Lovett, Rabbi Menachem Nissel, Mr. Paul Packer, Mr. Moshe Pilevsky, Rabbi Yisroel Reisman, Mr. Raphael Rosenberg, Rabbi Shlomo Rottenberg zt"l, Mr. Henoch Satt, Rabbi Efraim Wachsman, Rabbi Dovid Weinberger, Rabbi Avi Weinrib. I also want to thank the Roshei Kollel and Rabbis in numerous cities in the U. S., Canada and Israel who have been so kind in setting up speaking programs.

I want to thank the Mesorah Heritage Foundation, publisher of the Artscroll Series, for many of the fine English translations of Torah sources that I have used.

My apologies to anyone I may have neglected to mention. There must be many, since so many people have helped with this book, even prior to its conception, and with the previous book. I have tried to remember everyone. G-d will remember you even if I have not, but I hope there will be future editions in which to print your names.

The ultimate expression of gratitude is to *"hamalach ha go-ail osi mikol ra,"* the angel who redeemed me from all evil, and the One Who sent him, the *Ribono shel Olam*, the Master of the World. On January 10, 1966 (as you may read in "From Central Park to Sinai: How I Found My Jewish Soul") I realized for the first time that G-d is real, just as my life was about to unravel completely. He sent His angel to rescue me, and from then on I hope that each day has been one rung (or more) up on the ladder of Torah. My gratitude to G-d is endless. He saved and continues to save my life in infinite ways every day, He has rescued me from forces stronger than I am, and He has sent to me blessed friends to teach me Torah and guide me through this world.

These books are part of my attempt to express my gratitude to Him.

May the Father of the world have *nachas* from all His children!

CHAPTER ONE

THE GARDEN

"Blessed are You, Our G-d, King of the Universe, Who forms light and creates darkness..."[4]

Even darkness is created by G-d. Everything He creates is good. It is important to remember that, because all of us, at one time or another, walk through darkness. We desire to be in the presence of light, but if we must walk through darkness, it is so important to remember that even there G-d is with us.

In the beginning of time, when the earth was fresh, G-d created a man in a Garden. This was an almost-perfect world. G-d could have created it perfect, but He wanted the man to be His partner, so he left the finishing touches to the man.

"Almost perfect" may sound inappropriate in describing G-d's work, because everything G-d does is by definition perfect. But the world's very incompleteness was intentional on the part of G-d. Why, for example, is man born uncircumcised? Because *"G-d desired to perfect the [physical] character of the Chosen People; and He wished that this perfection be effected by man."* [4a]

He gave the man a gift called free will. This gift put man on a high spiritual level, in some ways higher than the angels, because man could decide whether to obey G-d or not. If he obeyed G-d, his reward would be endless, because he had over-come temptation and by his own will placed himself on a high plateau. But, if he disobeyed, his punishment was deserved, because he had of his own accord gone against his Creator.

G-d established rules for mankind[5] in the beginning of time. There were limitations on man: just as he had not made himself, so he also did not make the rules. The One Who made him also made the rules.

Most of the rules seem to have been designed to give moral guidelines for the conduct of life. But there was one rule that referred specifically to the Garden of Eden. There was a tree in the Garden, called the Tree of the Knowledge of Good and Evil. The man was not to eat from the fruit of the tree.

Free will meant that the man had the choice: follow the rule or reject it. That was his test. As King David says, *"The heavens are G-d's, but the earth He has given to mankind."*[6]

The first man was named Adam, which means "dust," because he was created from dust. G-d "breathed into" his body a spiritual essence, an eternal soul.* The soul could speak with G-d and hear G-d speaking.

As G-d had made the world incomplete, so was Adam incomplete. Part of him was missing; he was only a half. When Adam felt alone, G-d formed from his flesh another human being, the part he needed to be complete. The two people were different but similar, two halves of a whole. Spiritually and physically they were designed to complete each other. Eve completed Adam, but because she had been created from his living flesh, she was on a higher level than he, who had been created from lifeless dust.[7]

---

* The Bible says, "G-d blew into his nostrils the soul of life" (Genesis 2:7). The significance of the fact that the soul enters through the nostrils is discussed in Chapter Six.

They were created to help each other, two people sharing one life, one fate, one future. Before Eve, there had been no one "across from" Adam to advise and guide him. But now he was no longer alone. If he lived in accordance with G-d's will, she was there to encourage him. If he strayed, it was her job to oppose him, and by so doing help him cleave to the path of life.*

Two beautiful human beings in an unspoiled world. There was nothing to mar their spiritual or physical happiness. Sickness, death and conflict were unknown. G-d, the Creator and Ruler of the universe, was immediately accessible to them. There was no barrier between them and G-d, because – by following G-d's will — they lived in perfect spiritual innocence. Because they were innocent before G-d, they had no wish to hide from Him.

Today, looking back on that distant era, men might say, "I would not have wanted to live in that Garden because of boredom." But Adam and Eve did not know what boredom was. They did not desire distractions to take their minds off the troubles of life. They had no troubles. What could they want? They were happy in their world. They had everything. Today we are told** that we are unfulfilled, that we need more in order to be happy. But Adam and Eve (at least before the serpent influenced them) were completely satisfied. They desired nothing. That is the essence of life in the Garden of Eden: completeness.

In their world, every animal and plant, all the clouds in the sky and the stars and planets, existed in harmonious unity. All life was nourished without pain to any other living thing. Plants were the food of all living creatures; flesh was not consumed. There was no killing, animosity or competition. G-d

---

* Eve is described in the Bible as "*ezer kenegdo*" (Genesis 2:18), meaning "a helper against him." When Adam was on the right path she was his "helper"; when he was on the wrong path she was "against him." (Talmud Tractate Yevamos 63a, Rashi)
** By the advertising industry, for example.

had made a world of beauty for the enjoyment of His creatures.

Why would a horse have stripes? For the enjoyment of man. When Adam and Eve looked at the zebra they could bless G-d because He had made such an extraordinarily beautiful animal for them to admire and delight in. The flashing colors of exotic fish, the leap of a gazelle, the song of the birds, the Northern lights in a starlit sky, a distant thunderstorm…all this was created just for them.

Why did G-d make such a beautiful universe? Only for us, His beloved children, so that we should have a world to delight in.[8] When you take your child to the zoo, are you not delighted by the look on his face? So too, G-d delights in our happiness at the beautiful world He created.

WHAT WENT WRONG?

Something went wrong. We know something went wrong, because we are living in the world that resulted from it.

Remember free will? Remember that powerful ability G-d gave us, through which we could rise toward Him? Have you heard the expression "two-edged sword"? Everything could go two ways: the greater the opportunity, the greater the risk. G-d gave us this great gift in order to enable us to rise toward Him, but there would be no meaning to it if we did not have the corresponding ability to descend away from Him and sink in the bottomless abyss, G-d forbid! Having this tremendous power to rise close to G-d involves responsibility: we have to use it in the right way. If we use our power to come close to G-d by subordinating ourselves to His will, there is nothing to bar us from the ultimate Good. If we use it the wrong way by rebelling against Him, there is nothing to prevent the ultimate downfall. That is why the Bible says, *"choose life."*[9]

So G-d, in His love, gave us this most precious and powerful of all gifts, the two-edged sword of free will. He did not desire that His beloved children should be automatons. A robot is neither good nor bad; there is no *nachas* from a robot.

Parents desire a child who by his own free will chooses to live in a way that brings credit to them. Being a parent is the ultimate joy and in some cases the ultimate tragedy. Is there a tragedy deeper than the death of a child? What if a child's life is filled with pain, sickness or despair? What if a child rejects the parent who raised him with love? What if a child rejects the life-giving truths a parent tried to instill and demonstrate by personal example? Is there a greater tragedy for parents?

Can you imagine the pain of G-d, Who gave His children a perfect world and the ability to exist in intimate proximity to Him? Can you imagine His pain when His children reject Him? Can you imagine His pain when He sees His children in such desperate trouble?

"An ox knows his owner, and a donkey his master's trough; but Israel does not know, My people does not comprehend. [They are] a sinful nation, a people weighed down by iniquity, evil offspring, destructive children. They have forsaken G-d; they have angered the Holy One of Israel, and have turned their back [to Him]."[10]

"O Israel, if you would but listen to Me...."[11]

G-d did not need us. He is complete without us. He created us so we could bask happily in His presence and the beauty of His universe. Yet we, for whom He created all this, have rebelled against Him!

What suffering we brought into a perfect world!

And who suffers? We suffer!

Yes, there was a snake. He was not blameless, but his poison entered our system only because Eve permitted him to tempt her.

What did the snake say?

Are you really happy here? Do you think everything is perfect in the Garden? If so, why does G-d limit you? If you made the rules, or at least influenced the rules, then you could be on a level with G-d!

Thus doubt was introduced into a perfect world.

Doubt, the other edge of the two-edged sword. Free will is a powerful weapon if it is combined with trust in G-d, Who provided it. Then it overcomes all obstacles in the way of spiritual elevation.[12] If it is not combined with trust in G-d, it wounds the bearer.

Eve – who was entrusted with the moral guidance of her husband – was the first to use the wrong edge of the two-edged sword.

Perhaps I know as much as G-d. I also know what is right and wrong. Why should G-d make up all the rules?

That little thought is all it took. That drop poisoned the wine. The fruit she ate rotted in her mouth,* a perfect world spoiled by a tiny, insidious thought. Today, is our trouble anything else? Is there really anything more than that? Do we have to look anywhere else? Search through thousands of years of history and you will find nothing more troublesome than that little thought.

From that little thought came all sickness, death, mental and physical pain, tragedy, violence, perversion and war. Closeness to G-d is spiritual and physical health and serenity; separation from G-d is chaos, the greater the distance the greater the chaos.

LIFE OUTSIDE THE GARDEN

How could Adam and Eve live with the burden they had introduced into the world?

How, I ask, <u>did</u> they live?

For quickly they knew. Quickly they sought clothing because sud-

---

* In a spiritual sense.

denly their innocence was not good enough for them. Before
their rebellion they had nothing to hide because they had no
guilt. But now no amount of clothing could cover their guilt.
Where could they run to escape from G-d?

Nowhere! It is G-d's world!

So the banishment was self-inflicted; they had sealed their
own doom. Can you imagine their burden on that day, the hot
tears flowing as their feet walked out of that perfect world and
passed the sword of the angel guarding the entrance through
which no man has ever returned? Can you imagine what rested
upon their shoulders? Already then they must have felt the guilt
of thousands of future generations of their own children, the
accumulated pain which was to befall every individual who
would ever exist in the future world. It would all come about as
a result of their one "tiny" error in the Garden of Eden.* How
could they bear it? How could anyone bear the responsibility for
such untold suffering?

The truly amazing thing is that they did bear it. Their greatness is shown perhaps more by the way they bore their exile than
by their actions inside the Garden. Adam and Eve did not commit suicide. That same Adam and Eve – whose introduction to
life outside the Garden included the murder of one son by
another – walked onward through life. They did not give up!
They lived to become the parents of yet another son, Seth, who
carried the knowledge of G-d onward to the next generation
and through whom the hope of the world was to survive.

"*A righteous man can fall seven times and rise, but the wicked
shall stumble upon evil.*"[13]

An evil man is defeated by his sin.

A righteous man does not give up. Despite the deepest of

---

* It is a remarkable lesson for all of us, in every generation. Every microscopic deviation from
G-d's will leads to infinite suffering in the future world. Every microscopic movement toward
G-d and devotion to His Law leads to infinite blessing in the future world.

calamities, he keeps moving forward, acknowledging his inadequacies and asking G-d to heal him, fighting both against his failures and the tendency to be depressed by them. He will not permit these often-huge burdens to weigh him down to the point that he stops. He asks G-d for strength and moves on, knowing His Creator is watching over him. *"Cast your burden on the L-rd, and He will bear you; He shall never allow a righteous man to falter."*[14]

A righteous man knows that G-d will never abandon him nor allow him to face a test that he is unable to pass.[15]

At first, Adam and Eve had borne two sons, Cain and Abel. Cain was a tiller of the soil, Abel a shepherd. There were four people in the entire world, and trouble was brewing. Once the door is open to rebellion against G-d, it is very hard to shut. Rebellion is insidious and contagious. After all, when you hide from G-d, you are hiding from your own protection.

G-d blessed both sons with success in their work, but each reacted differently. Abel realized that his increase and success came only from G-d, and so he expressed his gratitude by giving back to G-d the best of his crop, a better portion than his own. If he gave G-d the best, what was he losing? It all came from G-d anyway.

Cain, on the contrary, wanted to keep the best for himself. Yes, he also offered a sacrifice to G-d, but since it was not from the best of his increase, the implication is clear that Cain saw himself as the prime cause of the success, not G-d. It seems there was a deficiency in Cain's appreciation of the fact that his ENTIRE success came from G-d. By keeping the best for himself, he declined to acknowledge that G-d was the sole Source of his success. He apparently did not see with sufficient clarity that everything had come from G-d in the first place.

Cain's attitude can be summed up as, *"from the strength of my own hand I achieved this."*[16]

Why do I owe so much to G-d? I toiled and produced this increase. G-d helped me, but I did the work!

But if the increase fails, and sometimes – in this world outside the Garden – it will, whom do you blame? Cain could have blamed himself, but he was not that type of person. Usually, the one who does not thank G-d with a full heart when things go well is the one who blames G-d when things go badly.*

The one who thanks G-d when things go well is the one who blames himself when things go badly. *"Surely I am deficient in my relationship with G-d."* Such is the route to self-improvement.

The one who believes that all his good fortune comes from the work of his own hand must then compete with his neighbor. If my hand is to prevail upon earth then my neighbor's hand must be weakened. This is the beginning of competition. The Bible tells us *"you shall not covet your neighbor's house...your neighbor's wife... his manservant, his maidservant, his ox, his donkey or whatever belongs to your neighbor."*[17] But if you are not to covet what belongs to your neighbor, then you must believe that all comes from G-d, from Whose largesse all men are sustained. If you don't believe that, then you must destroy other men in order to prosper upon the earth.

Cain made a "deal" with Abel, the original swindle. Between them, they owned the entire world; let Abel own all the animals and Cain all the land. Abel agreed. Usually, the innocent man trusts the crooked man, because the innocent man believes the world is as innocent as he is. But now Cain, according to the deal, "owned" the land, and demanded that Abel vacate "his premises." Abel was standing on Cain's land! For the trespass that he could not correct, Abel must be punished, and so it was

---

* Rebbetzin Jungreis gives the example of a sick person who complains, "G-d why did You do this to me?" But that same person never asked G-d when he was healthy, "What did I do to deserve my health?" [16a]

that the first murder occurred in this once pristine world.*

It wasn't just that Cain killed Abel; it was that brother killed brother. Every murder since then has really been the same, for Biblical history clearly shows that we are all one family. Every murder is the murder of a brother or a sister, and every murder destroys the fabric of the world.

In fact, when you get to the bottom of it, every crime stems from jealousy. A person who understands that G-d apportions all things is happy with what he has. He does not need what belongs to someone else.

So we had a pristine world, in which two people lived in harmony with each other and G-d, and in a very short time this pristine world descended into chaos. Why? All because Eve was a little jealous of G-d, and wanted to claim that she was also able to make the rules. Then Adam, who was made from dust, exhibited the weakness of dust in that his material side prevailed. He failed to reach upward toward spiritual strength. He did not ask G-d to help him and his wife pass this test. He failed to stop Eve, joining her and falling into the same sin.

It is clear that rebellion against G-d is the basis of all trouble.

Life went on. Generations passed. There were other men in the world by now. The children of Adam and Eve had multiplied, and there were those who knew only what they saw with their eyes. They were not interested in stories about reality beyond the physical world. There were those who made tools and those who made war with the tools. Men hurt each other

---

* Some say that this Medrash (Genesis Rabbah 22:7) is not to be believed literally, only a fable designed to illustrate a point. Could Abel have been such a fool? But the fact is that innocent people are victimized by swindlers because of their very innocence, their inability to comprehend duplicity. This story is a paradigm for the future history of Israel. The Children of Israel have been killed for centuries by such hypocrites, and in today's world nothing has changed. The sons of Ishmael say every day, "Get off my land or I will kill you!"

with the tools they made. Because the knowledge of G-d was receding into the misty past, their trust in the benevolent Ruler of the universe was fading away. They didn't know that G-d would provide for them, so a phenomenon called "competition" began. They worried about their livelihood, so they thought they had to fight with other men to earn their bread.

Let the other man die so I can live.

Men struggled against men to eke out their bread from the earth. The bitterness of competition made enemies out of brothers, like Cain and Abel.

"*G-d saw that the wickedness of Man was great upon the earth, and that every product of the thoughts of his heart was but evil always. And G-d reconsidered having made Man upon the earth and He was pained in His heart.*"[18]

MEN WHO REMEMBER; MEN WHO FORGET

At the same time as men were fighting each other for bread, there were quiet, private men who gripped tightly the thread of the knowledge of G-d. Adam had passed on the story to his son Seth; Seth had passed it on to his son Enosh and so on, through the generations.

And this was a story! Can you imagine what Adam had to tell! A tragic story, but one that ended with the certainty that some day, perhaps far in the future, mankind would once again walk with G-d in that perfect Garden.

It was the story of how G-d had created the world with mankind as its crown, how G-d and man could speak, and how that relationship had been compromised by man's disobedience. It was the story of the perfect Garden in which mankind had been born, and how man had been expelled from that Garden and was now a prisoner in a world bound by pain, fear, jealousy and death.

Seth understood the story told by his parents. The entire key to Truth is transmitted through stories passed from one generation to the next. Although Seth lived outside it, he knew that somewhere the Garden existed; therefore he lived with hope. He knew there was a place of purity in the world in which G-d was accessible, and he knew that somehow the purpose and goal of mankind would be to re-enter that Garden, no matter how many millennia that might take.*

"For G-d comforts Zion. He comforts her ruins, and He will make her wilderness like Eden, and her wastes like a garden...Gladness and joy shall be found there, thanksgiving and the sound of music."[19]

But to return to that Garden would take work now, and Seth knew what the work entailed. Somehow mankind would have to purify its soul. Somehow man would have to deserve to re-enter the Garden. But how? How to come close to G-d? Seth had only the tradition of his parents to go on, but that was a start. He knew there is a G-d. He knew G-d makes rules. He knew that G-d is all-powerful and the embodiment of morality.

There is a story[20] about a man who used to build a fire at a certain spot in the forest. At that fire he would worship G-d. His son also built a fire and worshipped G-d, but he couldn't find the exact spot in the forest where his father had worshipped. The grandson also built a fire, but he couldn't find the forest. His son forgot how to build the fire but he still worshipped G-d. His son forgot how to worship G-d, but he told the story of how his

---

* I am using the concept of re-entering the Garden of Eden as the goal of mankind. If living in the Garden of Eden is the original state of man, the state from which we lost our closeness to G-d, then it is certainly logical to assume that when we regain our closeness to G-d and our original purity, we will once again dwell in that Garden. The time of Messiah will be the Eternal Shabbos. The place of the Eternal Shabbos will presumably be the Garden to which we hope to return, may it be soon in our days!

fathers had worshipped G-d in the forest by the fire. But in the next generation, his son forgot the story.

THE ADVENT OF IDOL WORSHIP

This is what happened in the days after the expulsion from the Garden. Among the sons of men, battling each other and the material world, the story of the beginning of mankind was gradually being swallowed up in the mists of time. The pattern for the rest of history was being established: the mass of men were aware of nothing but the material. In contrast to them, the few men who remembered that there is a G-d were quiet, not "grabbing for the headlines." Their goal was to preserve the knowledge of the existence of G-d, not to enhance their own prestige. They knew that G-d would reveal His existence at the moment He desired to do so, but He is hidden from those who know only the material world. Just as Adam and Eve had tried to hide from Him after their rebellion, so the majority of men flee from knowledge of the Truth, trying to hide among theories, rationalizations and delusions of their own making.*

It's not only that rebellious men don't see G-d, it's that they don't want to see G-d, because G-d makes rules that they don't want to follow. Remember what Eve said in the Garden? *"Perhaps I know as much as G-d. I also know what is right and wrong.*

---

* What, for example, is the "Theory of Evolution," if not a massive intellectual fig leaf? The theory of evolution assumes a world in which life evolves out of other life and nature is an independent force. There is no place in their theories for G-d Who has created nature; there is no need or place for G-d in the world imagined by Darwin. I would venture to say that Darwin and his ilk NEEDED to create a theory of evolution in order to rationalize their refusal to admit that G-d is real. If G-d is real, then mankind cannot act the way it pleases; it must adhere to the laws promulgated by G-d. But if "nature" – a mechanical system that has no moral or spiritual component – is in control, and there is no wellspring of life beyond the material universe, then mankind is apparently free to act without restraint. That is exactly what has happened. Fantasies like the theory of evolution are both symptom and cause of the amoral chaos we find in the world today.

Why should G-d make up all the rules?" That tiny rebellious thought, the drop of poison that destroys the wine!

When corrupt men rule the earth, G-d must hide His light in order to protect it from them. Otherwise they would try to destroy it. In other words, people who are close to G-d are in danger in this world. That is why holy people are frequently found in the most unlikely places, as if a king would dress in rags so that nobody would recognize him. G-d places those who are devoted to Him in places where people do not recognize them, in order to protect them.

In the case of Judah and Tamar,[21] the light of G-d was hidden within a relationship that had to be shielded from the eyes of men. In the days of Ruth, the light of G-d was hidden in the fields of Moab, the most corrupt nation in the world.[22] In our own days, the light of G-d is also hidden. We do not know from where the Messiah will come, but surely his presence is hidden in a place we would not think of looking. In Chapter Six, with G-d's help, we will try to find it, but G-d must protect His holy ones. If they were well known, then the corrupt world would attack and endanger them. As it is, the world is always attacking the children of Israel, and this is because the majority of men cannot bear to acknowledge the truth that we carry with us the light of G-d.

"You, G-d, will guard [your servants], You will preserve each one forever from such a generation, [in which] the wicked walk on every side, when baseness is exalted among the sons of men."[23]

In the years after the expulsion from the Garden, an error arose that has pervaded and confused the world to this very day.

"During the times of Enosh [the grandson of Adam], mankind made a great mistake, and the wise men of that generation gave thoughtless counsel... Their mistake was as follows: they said G-d created stars and spheres with which to control the world. He placed

them on high and treated them with honor, making them servants who minister before Him. Accordingly, it is fitting to praise and glorify them and to treat them with honor. [They perceived] this to be the will of G-d, blessed be He, that they magnify and honor those whom He magnified and honored just as a king desires that the servants who stand before him be honored. Indeed, doing so is an expression of honor to the king. After conceiving of this notion, they began to construct temples to the stars and offer sacrifices to them. They would praise and glorify them with words, and prostrate themselves before them, because by doing so, they would – according to their conception – be fulfilling the will of G-d. This was the essence of the worship of false gods, and this was the rationale of those who worshiped them."[24]

In contrast to those who worshipped false gods, there were in those times just a few men who held the thread of Truth in their hands and carried it forward in lonely courage through the ten generations from Adam to Noah. That thread has passed unbroken through every generation since the beginning of time, which is amazing considering how many thousands of years have passed and how hostile the rest of the world has been to spirituality, sanctity and morality.

Throughout the entire history of mankind, loud and brazen men may be successful in material things, but the ones who keep the world alive are quiet, sometimes even hidden men who dedicate their entire lives to serving G-d. They don't need to make noise; they are aware that G-d is listening.

THE GENERATION OF NOAH

What happened in the generation of Noah?
Competition led to conflict, which introduced theft into the world. Theft destabilizes the world and destroys society.

How does theft destroy the world?

If I take your possession, I demonstrate that I consider your existence unimportant. I don't care about your feelings. I don't care whether your possession is precious to you or your wife or your children. I don't care if your dignity or your home has been violated. I don't care if you worked for years to acquire what I took from you. It doesn't matter to me if you cry.

When people don't care about each other's feelings, the fragile thread that binds the world together comes unraveled. Theft is a message that I have no respect for you or for the Creator Who gave you your possessions.

Society is built upon mutual trust and respect. If there were no moral law from Above to keep order in the world, then mankind would kill each other, leaving a chaotic and bloody scene behind. When only four people existed in the world, Cain killed Abel. The two brothers could have lived in harmony! What prevented it? Cain felt entitled to Abel's possessions, so murder was introduced into the world!

G-d is a giver. A thief is a taker, the opposite of G-d. The entire point of existence is to imitate G-d. A taker destroys the entire basis upon which the world was created.[25] Theft is not just taking your possession; theft destroys life itself by attempting to nullify G-d's purpose in creating the universe *"The generation of the Flood transgressed everything, yet the decree of their punishment was not sealed upon them until they stretched forth their hands in robbery."*[26]

At the time of Noah, men also started to engage in sexual practices that deviated from the intentions of their Creator and the design of their souls and bodies.[27]

Adam and Eve were each half of one whole, opposites created to complete each other. There is a Biblical basis for the common saying, "opposites attract." G-d designed and created a fertile world, in which every living thing produces seed that enables it to perpetuate itself. *"G-d said let the earth sprout vegetation of plants bringing forth seed, trees of fruit yielding fruit each after its kind, which have their seed in them..."*[28] The physical process of male and female uniting to produce life echoes the spiritual process of man uniting with G-d to produce spiritual life that never ends.

When man rejects G-d's design of the universe the Presence of G-d is "pushed away," just as Adam and Eve's rebellion had "pushed" G-d out of their lives. The sinless world inside the Garden was bright, but the world outside was dark. We have a tradition[29] that when G-d created light on the First Day, some of it was placed in the sun, but most of it was hidden, to be saved for the righteous in the future. But this primeval light was not put away immediately; it shone in the Garden of Eden until Adam and Eve sinned. Only after that was it removed, to be stored away for the days of the Messiah.

The days of the Messiah are described as follows: *"Arise! Shine! For your light has arrived and the glory of G-d shines upon you. For behold, darkness may cover the earth... but upon you G-d will shine and His glory will be seen."*[30]

This was the darkened state of the world in the time of Noah. After ten generations, the thread of spiritual continuity, the unbroken line of those who carried with them the knowledge of G-d, was in Noah's hands. Noah must have had tremendous strength to withstand the influence and charms of a world that tried to lure him away from loyalty to his Creator. After all, he was one of the tiny minority in his generation to have inherited this precious gift and he was building an ark in full view of all those who had caused the world to descend to this dangerous state. The world was jealous and angry, just as in later centuries they would be angry at the Jews, because inwardly they knew their own guilt. They knew they were rebelling against G-d.[31]

The world wanted to pressure Noah, to mock him, to corrupt him, possibly to kill him.* Such is the fate of the man of G-d in every generation. As Noah worked on the ark, the world mocked him. *"What is this fool wasting his time on?"* This was a preview of later centuries, in which the world was to mock and attack the children of Israel, as we were to labor on our "ark" in full view of those who hate us. Do you remember the Nazi car-toon caricatures of Jews? Do you see and hear the hatred of our enemies to this very day, what they teach their children about us? What has changed since the days of Noah? Is anything new under the sun?

When Noah saw a culture steeped in theft and sexual corrup-tion, he understood that the world could not survive. He knew the rules of the universe.[32] Life is not arbitrary; it's simply logical that men cannot survive if they are destroying each other and flouting the rules through which their world was created and is sustained.

Is it possible to understand what Noah faced at this time? The Flood that came upon the world is a striking illustration of the way the world is run. We ignorant men think that the doings of "Mother Nature" are purely physical phenomena. We assume there is no moral reason for a flood or an earthquake or a storm. The Torah[33] shows us that life is not at all that way. Everything that occurs in the world is a moral phenomenon. G-d gives us messages continuously through the events of nature and histo-ry.** To say that there is no moral cause for events is to live in blindness. Like Pharaoh, we persuade ourselves that G-d does

---

* According to Rashi on Genesis 7:16, G-d surrounded the ark with wild beasts so that people would not attack Noah. Why did they want to attack him? What had he done to them by building an ark? He had aroused their guilt. It is the paradigm for the recurring scenario: kill the one who tells you the truth.

** During times when we are close to G-d, we know directly from Him when we sin. But when we push Him out of our lives and close our ears to His voice, then we can only learn of His messages indirectly. In our dark era, communications from G-d are cloaked behind the veil of what we think of as "natural events." If the world seems chaotic, is it not a reflection of our rebellion?

not control the world. Why? It is inconvenient to know the Truth. To say the least, it would disrupt our lifestyle! Either G-d makes the rules or I make the rules; it can't be both ways.

Here is just one more striking illustration. On Yom Kippur afternoon we read the Book of Jonah, which says, *"Then G-d cast a mighty wind toward the sea and it became such a mighty tempest in the sea that the ship threatened to be broken up."*[34] Do you think any storm is different? Do you think any wind blows that is not specifically created by G-d for some purpose? The result may not seem as monumental as Jonah's storm or the Biblical Flood, but nothing happens in the universe by accident, not even the prick of a finger.[35]

I am reminded of the story of the rabbi who fell down the steps. His students crowded around him: *"Rebbe, are you all right?"*

"I am not hurt. I am sitting here on the floor because I want to try to understand why I fell. What did I do wrong?"

The rabbi saw that his fall was not an accident, but rather a message from G-d designed to help him elevate his life.

If we would see the world that way, then we could start back on the road toward re-entering the Garden. The events in the world are not haphazard; there is no event, small or large, individual or cosmic, which does not occur for a reason. G-d is giving us signals that tell us how closely we are following the rules He has set down for the operation of the universe.

Adam and Eve's expulsion from the Garden of Eden should have been a lesson for their descendants. Alas, we have not learned. We have repeated their rebellion in every generation, and each repetition has taken us further away from G-d. Adam and Eve at least realized that they were naked. We don't realize we are naked! We are so far away that we forget we are hiding; we forget there is a G-d altogether. We are like the son who forgot the story his fathers had told about worshipping G-d by a fire in the forest.

Noah in his greatness did not forget that the universe is ruled by moral standards, that G-d stands above the history of individuals and nations, and judges us by the laws which He has established and taught us.[36] Yes, Noah also had to battle his own humanness,* his desire for pleasure, the passions that arise from being a creature of flesh and blood. He was depressed after the Flood, and "drowned his sorrows" in wine.[37] His drunkenness led to a test for his three sons. Their response was an indication of the destiny of their progeny and indeed the future history of the world (because every person in the world is descended from them). The character of the nations who descended from them reflects the character shown by their progenitor at that crucial moment in the history of the world.**

The story of Noah, from his actions before the Flood to the actions of his children after the Flood, is remarkable because it shows so starkly how every action and event is a moral test and every test has repercussions that echo throughout history. Noah knew the world was on a fatal course. People were not asking, "What does G-d want?" They were asking, "How can I get what I want?" Is today any different? Can't we see that today the world is heading for catastrophe? Most people do not link the possibility of changes in their own behavior to solving the problems of the world. We would rather join a committee to combat global warming, for example, than start keeping the commandments of G-d.

Noah worked constructively to correct the situation. He

---

* This, of course, is part of the greatness of the Torah, which tells the story of real people, who battle real weaknesses, just the way we do. That is why those people described by the Torah are guides for us in our struggles. This is in accord with the famous principle enunciated by the Ramban (Nachmanides), "Whatever happened to the patriarchs is a sign for the children."

** This is reminiscent of the famous story about the Chofetz Chaim, who reportedly asked a visitor, "Do you know why I am a Kohen? Because when Moses Called out, 'Whoever is for G-d, come to me!' (Exodus 32:26) my ancestors ran to Moses. As a result they were rewarded with the eternal Priesthood." Each action ia s bequest to our descendants forever!

realized that he was a part of this depraved world. Noah's life was spent building a way to survive the coming catastrophe, which to any clear-eyed person was inevitable unless the inhabitants of the world changed their way of life. The very act of building the ark was so monumental that people could not help but observe and question him. They didn't get the point, but that was their own choice; Noah, however, did his work in full view of the world.

Noah is a hero because he so clearly stood against the moral vacuum of his time and followed G-d's will even in the face of universal ridicule. In this he was like our Father Abraham. He was unlike Abraham in that his efforts to reach out to the world were passive (he built the ark in public), rather than active (he did not go out to the people with an explicit message), but he was a hero nonetheless.[38]

Anyone who stands with G-d against the darkness of the world is a hero. It may seem that he is alone, yet he is not alone. He perceives G-d, while those who ridicule him do not perceive G-d. Consider those holy ones who perished in the Nazi inferno: their eyes were focused on eternity; they were not alone. Those who murdered them, who believed that they were in the majority, are eternally alone because they divorced themselves from the Source of life!

Those who are alone are the hordes groping through life without thinking; they are doomed to an eternity of darkness. The man of G-d walks with G-d, with his eyes open, in eternal splendor.

A TURNING POINT

The life of Noah marks a major turning point in history. G-d created the world in a simple way, a way in which access to Him was natural and our restrictions were minimal. G-d gave one Commandment that was specific to the Garden of Eden: do not eat from the fruit of the Tree of the Knowledge of Good and Evil. The other rules were easily understood and logical to the human mind. Perhaps we would all live as good children and the world would remain forever a paradise.

It was not to be.

We failed!

It was not just Adam and Eve who failed; it was each succeeding generation, building failure upon failure to the point at which they "forgot the story their fathers had told." By Noah's generation, theft, sexual aberration and moral corruption were so widespread that we had forgotten how to return to our point of origin.

When Noah stood before the world building the ark, there was no one except his wife and their children's families who understood him, no one whose free will prompted him to rise above the push and shove of material existence to embrace a life of eternity. There were only the dumb animals, creatures of no free will, who follow G-d's laws only because obedience to those laws is built into their system. Do not give an animal credit for being good, kind or obedient; animals are only what they have been programmed to be by their Creator. We humans are the only creatures in this world with free will.

The first period in history, the great experiment in which free-willed creatures were given the opportunity to live as partners with G-d in a perfect world ended in a deluge, a deluge which hinted at the flood of tears to be shed by mankind throughout creation, an ocean of tears that never had to be.

We could have prevented it!

G-d made two building blocks in the physical world, fire and water. Each is beneficial and each is dangerous.

The fire that emanates from the sun warms the earth and keeps us alive, but if the sun were only slightly closer, the earth would burn! The fire that emanates from the soul of a holy man can incinerate objects at which he looks,[39] but through its warmth the world survives and the presence of G-d is manifest. Fire is our salvation and our enemy. Controlled fire is our salvation and uncontrolled fire is our enemy.

It is said that there are three partners in a marriage: a man, a woman and G-d. How do we know? The word for "man" in Hebrew is "ish." The word for "woman" in Hebrew is "ishah." The word "ish" contains the Hebrew letter "yud." The word "ishah" contains the Hebrew letter "hey." "Yud" and "hey" together spell the Name of G-d, and that is how we know that if a man and woman truly desire to build an eternal home, they must become partners with G-d, and become aware that through their unity the presence of G-d is brought into the world and into their home. But if the letters "yud" and "hey" are taken out of "ish" and "ishah," they become different words. "Ish" without "yud" becomes "aish," and "ishah" without "hey" also becomes "aish." What is "aish"? Fire! Marriage without G-d is fire, which rages out of control and can destroy everything in its path.[40]

The principal manifestation of G-d's control over fire in the marriage is the commandment concerning mikveh, the ritual bath in which the Jewish wife immerses herself each month. The water of the mikveh controls the fire!

Which leads us to the question of …

Water.

Water is the other basic element in G-d's creation, apparently the opposite of fire.[41]

Water is also potentially beneficial and potentially dangerous.

When G-d created the earth, the first element that emerged from the void was apparently water. The Bible tells us that "the *breath of G-d was hovering upon the surface of the waters"*[42] even before G-d had created light. In order, however, for life to exist upon the earth, G-d had to control and contain the waters. So, on the Second Day, "G-d said, *'Let there be a firmament between the waters and let it separate between water and water."*[43]

"And G-d called the firmament 'Heavens.'"[44]

In order to control water, G-d separated it into compartments. When water overflows its compartments, however, it floods the earth and destroys everything.* That is why we praise G-d every morning, because He "spreads out the earth upon the waters."[45] If He failed to maintain the separation of the waters for even one microsecond, we and our world would drown.

The waters of the *mikveh*, which reflect the purity of the original days of creation, are the vehicle by which Jewish women and men purify themselves. The Torah gives us this method of trying to regain the purity that prevailed at the beginning of time.

Water sustains life. The man of G-d is *"like a tree standing by streams of water."*[46] Torah is compared to water,[47] and Torah is life. Without water a man cannot live; without Torah a man cannot live in this world or the Next World.[48]

I mentioned earlier that G-d made men and women as opposites. "Opposites attract" seems to be a universal law. Through the union of opposites, seed is fertilized, life is perpetuated, and the world continues to exist. Only by the union of opposites! It seems that fire and water, two opposites brought together by G-d, also reflect this principle. The G-d-imposed union of fire and water brings about the condition of "*shalom*," peace in the world. As we say about G-d, "*He Who makes peace [between fire and*

---

* We are concerned about this today, as a result of "the effects of global warming." For example, it was reported in the New York Sun on September 17, 2002 that London real estate is in danger because of rising waters attributed to global warming.

water] in His heights, may He make peace upon us, and upon all Israel..."[49] Plants do not grow under the hot desert sun; rain is needed for growth, the thunderstorm as well as the sunshine![50] When sun and rain coexist, the sign of the rainbow is seen, the sign of peace between G-d and all living creatures.

In a Jewish home, there are two symbols of peace and abundance: the *Shabbos* candles and the waters of the *mikveh*, fire and water, husband and wife, opposites held in balance by G-d.

But water is also dangerous. A flash flood in the dust-dry desert can drown you almost before you know it is upon you.

At the time of Noah, the boundaries holding back the waters were removed. G-d reversed the decree of Creation; water flowed up from the deep and down from the heavens. But really, G-d did not do it; people did it. In their blindness they chose to exercise their "knowledge of good and evil." They wanted to create their own laws, rather than adhere to G-d's obviously beneficial commandments. They paid the price. They had not learned from the expulsion of their ancestors, Adam and Eve, from the Garden. As a result, they "expelled" themselves from their own world; they brought the flood upon themselves by destroying the boundaries that G-d had set for them. Therefore the boundaries that had protected them were also broken, and the waters engulfed them.

The story of self-inflicted pain has been repeated again and again in the world. Why did no one learn from what had happened in the Garden of Eden? Perhaps no one was thinking. If we would just think, our lives would be so different!

But at least one can think after the fact. G-d gives us all second chances, and even sometimes third chances, and more....

Adam and Eve had repented, understood their sin and given birth to a child named Seth, who had understood the implications of his parents' life. Seth transmitted the lessons of the past to his children and grandchildren. Not all of them absorbed the meaning of the story, but a line of children who knew G-d extended from Adam and Eve, through Seth, as we have said above. Noah received the tradition in the tenth-generation from Adam and Eve.

This is what saved Noah!

It is so simple!

Only the transmission and comprehension of the story; that is what saves us! Noah absorbed and understood. He, his wife, their children and their spouses were spiritually alone on a hostile planet, yet their courageous fidelity to G-d saved them, and they floated above the destruction in their Ark.

What is an Ark?

An ark is a container that floats upon the water and sustains life. Moses as an infant was also saved in an Ark. Throughout history, when conditions seemed hopeless, G-d has always sent an ark to save us. In English (although the word in Hebrew is different) we term the container that holds the Torah Scroll in our synagogues an ark. Just as the ark saved Noah and Moses, so the ark has saved the children of Israel throughout the centuries. The ark continues to save us to this day.

After the Flood, a new era began. Up to that time, the world had still been relatively innocent, even after the failure of Adam and Eve in the Garden. G-d had given us continual opportunities to return to Him, but mankind as a whole had trampled the boundaries of His simple rules. G-d did not destroy the world; we destroyed the world.*

This had been the childhood of the world, the innocent years. G-d said to Israel centuries later, *"I remember for your sake the kind-*

---

* Rabbi Chaim of Volozhin in Nefesh Hachaim (1:4) says that, in essence, we destroyed the Second Temple, not the Romans. As Rebbetzin Jungreis says, those who ask, "Where was G-d during the Holocaust?" are asking the wrong question. The question should be, "Where was man during the Holocaust?"

ness of your youth, the love of your bridal days, how you followed Me in the Wilderness in an unsown land."[51] The days before the Flood could have been the Bridal Days of all mankind. We had discarded the opportunity to enjoy the beauty of this innocent happiness.

Now things were going to get tougher. After the Flood, the lifespan of mankind became shorter. Instead of living for centuries, man now succumbed to the difficult world of his own making by perishing at a much earlier age. For those fewer years, we would require greater strength.

Up to now, mankind had sustained itself through vegetable food. Now killing for food became a part of life, and that hardened us. We became different people, tougher and more brutal. The world was no longer the same.

THE WORLD AFTER THE FLOOD

G-d always gives us a second chance! At Mount Sinai he gave us a second set of tablets. If we miss Passover we have Pesach Shaini. If we fall short during the year, G-d gives us Yom Kippur to cleanse our souls. If our life is deficient, G-d gives us a gift called *teshuvah*, the ability to return to Him. We can always start anew if we so desire.

The world after the Flood had lost its freshness. Eternal spring was replaced by seasons. Spring was not destroyed, but it was forced to share the world with extremes of frigid winter and broiling summer. *"Seedtime and harvest, cold and heat, summer and winter, and day and night, shall not cease."*[52]

Life became more challenging. In the Garden, life had been perfect. Now man had to build secure shelter against heat and cold. He had to struggle against other men as well as nature itself to provide himself and his family with food and clothing. Survival itself could not be taken for granted. Life after the

Flood always has a particle of fear in it; spiritual contentment in the presence of G-d became much more difficult to attain. Can we understand how much we have lost?

With each passing year, as the memory of the Garden receded into the past, the dwellers on earth were further removed from closeness to G-d; the children of men "forgot the story" their fathers had told. With additional layers of murky forgetfulness, additional rules were needed for those people who desired to return to the ways of their fathers. In the Garden, following just a few simple commandments were sufficient to elevate a man's soul. If only a man could master *"do not eat of the fruit of the tree of the knowledge of good and evil"* — *do not think that you can make up your own rules, do not think that you are G-d* – that would have been sufficient to ensure an eternal bond with G-d.

But in the world after the Flood, life became much more complicated. The waters of the Flood covered not only the surface of the earth, but also they covered as it were the history of the earth. The memory of the pristine world that had existed at the beginning of time was no longer readily accessible to those who walked upon the land. Man, separated from G-d by more layers of sin; became ever more concerned with making a living. As the seasons became a feature of the world after the Flood, man seemed to be in a war with nature to eke out his living. It appeared that the controlling influence on the world was "nature," not nature's Creator.

When man's lifetime was reduced, we needed greater strength to toil upon the challenging earth. To provide sufficient strength for our labors under the sun, we were permitted to eat animals, but this also endowed us with some of their qualities; we became heavy, brutish and – for those who ate the meat of carnivores – cruel and vicious.* As we said above, the very

---

* As the contemporary saying goes, "You are what you eat."

killing of animals familiarized us with a new level of violence.*

Noah's children were responsible to fulfill the commandments that had originally been given to Adam and Eve in the
Garden, to which was added a commandment prohibiting the
consumption of flesh from a living animal. These commandments are binding upon his descendants – that is to say, all
mankind – to this day. If the nations of the world want to
come close to G-d, all they need do is follow these seven commandments.[53]

What commandments are applicable to all mankind?[54] Six
are negative: do not 1) worship idols, 2) murder, 3) steal, 4) eat
the limbs of animals that were removed when the animal was
alive (this is the "new" commandment given after the Flood), 5)
curse G-d, or 6) engage in prohibited sexual relationships. One
is positive: 7) set up a judicial system.

With the addition of the commandment concerning meat,
the generalized rules for the world became seven rather than
six.[55] There is something elemental about the number seven.
Seven is the number of days of creation, the number of days of
the week. Even though the observance of the Sabbath is
reserved for the children of Israel, still the world knows that
there is a Sabbath and that the seven-day week is built into the
pattern of creation.[56]

The number six represents this world: the six directions
(north, east, south, west, up and down) represent the limits of

---

* This does not imply that we should be vegetarians. The reality of the post-Flood world is that
we need the strength derived from meat. Since G-d has permitted it, He has also defined the
limits within which we may slaughter animals and eat their meat. That is how we guard ourselves from potential negative consequences and in fact make a blessing out of our weakness.
Thus the children of Israel have been given elaborate dietary regulations, through which we
eat only that which is permitted to us. Mankind in general have been restricted from eating
the flesh of a living animal (one of the Seven Commandments applicable to all men). To go a
step higher, on Shabbos and Holidays it is considered a merit to rejoice with "meat and fish
and tasty foods." [52a]

the material world. Those are the directions in which we wave the *lulav* and *esrog* on *Sukkos*, and they represent the directions from which our blessings come in this world. The number seven represents the Presence of G-d in this world, and that is why the Sabbath is the culmination of life in this world. Seven is the number that connects the material with the spiritual, ascending beyond the world of nature, work, competition, time and space. Seven is the number that connects us to G-d.[57] Just as one day differs from the other six, so there is one commandment that differs from the other six commandments. There is one day that is all positive and there is one commandment in the Seven given to the children of Noah that is positive. We toil on six days; six commandments tell us we must observe boundaries and restrictions as we toil. We must constantly restrict ourselves on those six days in order not to fall into sin as we struggle to earn our bread under the sun.

There is one day on which our heart is at peace, one day in which we do not have to fight. But the Seven Commandments were not enough. Even in the world after the Flood men continued to rebel. What good are the reminders if those who need them do not choose to listen? Why in fact would G-d expect us to obey these commandments now, after the Flood, any more than we had obeyed them before the Flood? Had we not shown that we ignored the lesson of the Garden of Eden? Why should we not ignore the lesson of the Flood as well?

Well, we did ignore the lessons of the Flood.

Yes, G-d helps us and is willing to rescue us at every moment if we so desire, but our task becomes more difficult and complicated with each additional deviation from His will. For Adam and Eve, return would have been relatively simple; they had violated only one commandment. By Noah's era it was much more difficult. For us who live after the Flood, the road Home is much

longer and harder. After the Flood, an additional commandment was added.[58] For the children of Abraham, Isaac and
Jacob another 606 commandments were added.[59] Yes, we can
come back, but we have made our job so much more difficult!

The shortest of all chapters in the Bible is, *"Praise G-d, all
nations, praise Him all the states! For His kindness has overwhelmed
us, and the truth of G-d is eternal!"*[60]

Our commentators tell us that the shortness of this chapter
hints at the simplicity of the world in the time of the Messiah.[61]
I would venture to say that the same was true of the world before
the Flood. After the Flood, we needed more commandments to
handle a much wider range of problems and challenges than
existed before. It was a chastened and darker world that greet-
ed Noah as he stepped off the ark, and we can understand that
one of his first acts was to "drown his sorrows" in wine. His act
was self-defeating, but we can understand it.

Noah and his wife had three sons, Shem, Cham and Yafes.
Just as Seth was the one who chose to carry on the story of
Adam and Eve to the next generation, so Shem, the first son of
Noah and his wife, was the one to carry on the thread of the
knowledge of the existence of G-d through his generation to the
next.

Noah taught his sons the story of his ancestors Adam and
Eve. Not everyone understood. This is true in every generation
and is a paradigm for the future. It is quite clear that only the
tiniest minority in each generation understands the realities of
creation. So it has been throughout history.* In our world the
"tiny minority" that has been assigned that responsibility is
specifically the children of Israel, plus those who recognize and
respect our unique mission in the world. Tragically, even among

---

* It is not impossible for a majority to understand; that is what we expect after the coming of the
Messiah. But in practice most men go through life without thinking or trying to understand.

the children of Israel at many times in our history only a minority chose to remember the story and carry on the heritage. Even before we left Egypt eighty percent of our people had perished in the Plague of Darkness.[62] Even under Moses' leadership we rebelled many times; the Bible recounts these tragic episodes.[63] Today, again tragically, many among the children of Israel still do not acknowledge the existence of the Creator and live by His laws.

Over the course of history, those among the children of Israel who did not choose to recognize the reality of G-d have been lost to us. I am not referring to those who die; everyone in this world dies. I am referring to those who have rejected G-d. Over the centuries some have detached themselves from the Tree of Life.[64]

Shem, the son of Noah, clung to the Tree of Life.

"*Blessed is... the G-d of Shem,*" said Noah.[65] It is not that G-d rejected Cham and Yafes; it is rather that they rejected Him.[66] They had other priorities, just as free-willed men have had since the beginning of time. They were free to choose their fate and they did so.

"*Cursed is Canaan (the son of Cham)... May [Yafes] dwell in the tents of Shem, and Canaan shall be a slave to them.*"[67] Every man chooses his own destiny.

What had Canaan (Cham) done to deserve a curse? Yafes may not have had the relationship with G-d that Shem had, but why did Cham deserve to be cursed with the destiny of a slave?

"*Cham ... saw his father's nakedness.*"[68] The Talmud tells us that this is a euphemism for the act of emasculating his father.[69] A rationale advanced for this is that Cham was afraid his father would have more children and thus diminish his own inheritance.

Do you see why Cham is cursed with the destiny of a slave?

Nobody made him a slave. Someone who believes that his destiny can be good only if he destroys someone else's destiny is by nature a slave. He is a slave to the mistaken idea that there is no G-d Who regulates the affairs of the world. He believes that he must ensure his fortune by destroying others. This, as we mentioned earlier in discussing Cain, is the origin of strife in the world. If we are to live in peace in G-d's world, we must live with the knowledge of His beneficent rule. We were supposed to dwell in a Garden; we dwell in a jungle only if we live by the laws of the jungle.

So Cham cursed himself; through his violence he became lower than a beast. But no one is beyond redemption, because there is always free will. The curse of slavery that Cham brought upon himself can become a blessing, because if he acknowledges that he has debased himself, he can rise and overcome his debased condition. If he really becomes a slave in "the tents of Shem" – in other words if he subordinates himself to those who serve G-d – he has a chance to free himself from his debasement.

Eliezer, the servant of Abraham, is an example of a descendant of Cham who became great by subordinating himself to a person whose entire life was dedicated to the service of G-d.[70] The worst situation for Cham would be if he never recognized his debased status, for then his defilement would be complete and there would be no redemption. In effect, he would have nullified his soul, and without an elevating soul, he would be simply a material creature like an animal, a clod of earth never to be remembered again in the final disappearance of all material things. An animal at least has the merit of having followed the dictates of its Maker, albeit without the free will to do otherwise. But a rebel has used his free will to separate himself from G-d, and thus he has forfeited his gift of life.

Tragically, the rebel has also poisoned society in general. Is there such a thing as a private act that affects nobody? Nothing is private. *"A bird of the air will carry the sound."*[71] What transpired "secretly" within the tent of Noah – his humiliation at the hands of Cham – became public knowledge in the most widely circulated book ever written! Similarly, what transpired generations later between Lot and his daughters in the darkness of a mountain cave[72] is memorialized in the same book. The names of the two nations — Ammon and Mo-av – who emerged from that darkness, are eternal testimony to what took place there.

THE GENERATION OF THE TOWER OF BABEL

And yet, somewhere in every generation, there are those who cling to the knowledge of G-d's existence. One end of the thread of holiness is rooted in the soil of the Garden of Eden; the other end is held in the hand of G-d's faithful children in every generation throughout history. Like the phases of the moon, these faithful children are sometimes visible like blazing fire in the eyes of the entire world (like Moses at Mount Sinai) and sometimes hidden in the most unlikely places (like Ruth in the fields of Moab). From Noah's time, the tradition was maintained through ten generations by the following bearers of the thread: Shem, Arpachshad, Shelah, Eber, Peleg, Reu, Seug, Nahor, Terach, and Abraham.

In the dark aftermath of the Flood, G-d gave Noah a sign of hope, the rainbow.[73] Why is the rainbow a sign of hope? Because it contains every color in the spectrum. When the world looks dark, it is only because we do not see the entirety of

Creation. The rainbow symbolizes the entirety of creation, including the presence of G-d. When we view G-d standing over it, then we have hope.[74] That is possibly a reason why Jewish law mandates that we not mention to others when we see a rainbow: it is dangerous in this world to reveal too much. Those who hate G-d are always standing ready with their weapons of destruction, so when storm clouds darken the world, we must hide our knowledge to protect it. When the sun shines in the days of the Messiah, everything will be revealed.

Before we meet Abraham, who changed the course of history, we must deal with a major occurrence that preceded his life.

In the generations after the Flood, idol worship led to new forms of rebellion against G-d. Now man put himself on a high level, a level on which he tried to compete with G-d.

G-d creates many creatures, each of whom He has given certain powers.

Lions are physically powerful.

The sun has power; it radiates life-giving warmth and light as it glides across the heavens.

Certain men seem very powerful.

G-d gives powers to His creations, but their power emanates only from Him. If He so desired, the sun would disappear in an instant. We would either continue to live with a different source of warmth and light or we would disappear with the sun. It's all up to G-d.

But what if we tell ourselves that the sun rules independently? Then we make it into a "god," an idol. Or a lion? Or a cow? Or a man? Then we forget about G-d, Who created these objects. The objects themselves become our idols, our substitutes for G-d.

What is wrong with treating creations as if they were the Creator? It is false; they have no power, only the power that has been granted them from G-d. So it is a fundamental error to worship a creation as if it had independent power.

Why do men worship idols?

The answer is amazingly simple: they do not want to be subservient to G-d. They see there is a power above them in the world, and they want to connect with it, yet they want to be their own boss; they don't want to be ruled by anyone else.

Idols have no power; they cannot formulate a way of life for us. They don't tell us what to do. The "rules" that idol worshippers follow are created by the idol worshippers themselves and then put into the "mouths" of the idols. The rules do not come from Above, from the Power that created us; they are formulated by men. Then we pretend that the idol instituted the rules and imposed them upon us. That is what makes idols so alluring. A stick, a stone, a lion or cow, the sun or moon makes no rules, does not reward or punish, does not know what we do. It is not alive.

Speaking about man-made idols, King David says, *"They have a mouth, but cannot speak; they have eyes, but cannot see. They have ears, but cannot hear; they have a nose, but cannot smell. Their hands – they cannot feel; their feet – they cannot walk; they cannot utter a sound from their throat. Those who make them should become like them, whoever trusts in them!"*[75]

A stick or stone cannot rule over us, but if we say, "the stick told me to stand on my head," or "the stick told me to steal or kill" there is not much to argue with. Idol worship is a rationale for doing anything you want to do while still claiming to believe that there is a G-d.

We cannot have it both ways. Either there is a G-d and He rules over us, or we deny Him completely. Idol worship – attributing power to one of G-d's creations – is simply a cover-up for pretending that we are G-d and making our own rules.

The ultimate example of this was the Biblical Pharaoh, who believed that he had made himself.

Pharaoh did not have a good end. His world-vision was an illusion, and in the end the illusion was washed away by the waters of the Red Sea. Self-delusion always ends in disaster.

The late dictator of Germany, may his memory be obliterated, built a world of illusion, which disappeared in the implosion of the Third Reich.

The late dictator of Communist Russia, may his memory be obliterated, also built a world of illusion. When its end came, it evaporated in a blink.

And yet, millions believed in these illusions, like the emperor's new clothes. The children of men create havoc and unimaginable suffering on the earth as a result of their fantasies.

It is not only murderous dictators, however, who indulge in idolatrous fantasies. Society as a whole is susceptible to potentially fatal delusions that become accepted as if the world had been built upon them. We have already cited political theories like Marxism or communism and fascism, but what about democracy itself? To question its value is considered heresy in the contemporary Western World, but who says the majority vote of the people is correct? Have we not seen that the knowledge of good and evil lies with G-d, not man?

What about cosmic theories like Darwinism or the "Big Bang"? The Western contemporary world accepts them unquestioningly. Those who believe that these concepts are based on absolute truth or that they have the power to save mankind, are suffering from a delusion.

What about the obsession with money or power? That can also be idolatry.

In the generations after the Flood, men joined together not only to worship idols, but to try to slay G-d in order that they should never again have to listen to a Voice from above. It was one step beyond *"you shall not eat from the fruit of the tree of the knowledge of good and evil."* There man had taken into his own hands the distinction between good and evil, deciding what law he would follow. Here he tried to build on that foundation of rebellion a structure that reached to the sky and challenged the reign of G-d over His own creation. Can you imagine a watch telling the watchmaker, "I'm taking over," or a painting telling the painter, "You're out. I'm in charge"?

Here indeed was chutzpah to the ultimate degree. Since idolaters do not see beyond the material world, they believe that they could fight and kill G-d as if He were a mortal. They could not imagine an Existence that created the material, a "world" beyond the material.

"Why leave the governing to G-d? If G-d is material and I am material, why can't I be G-d? Let me fight Him!"

So they built a platform from which they could fight G-d and try to take over the universe! If Cain could kill Abel, maybe Cain's descendants could kill G-d! This was the generation that built the Tower of Babel, an edifice on which people thought they could stand in order to fight G-d. But it doesn't make sense to fight the Creator of all material and spiritual things. They didn't understand Who G-d is.

Today we also have tall buildings that stretch up into the sky. The Tower of Babel stretched as far as men could build it. It must have been a dizzying height, and taken days if not weeks for a man to reach the top. Someone falling from up there would never survive. A brick dropped from the tower would be a lethal weapon, and many who worked on this edifice lost their lives,[76] but for what? It was one of the greatest feats of construction in the history of the world, a project almost beyond comprehension. From its windy heights, men on the earth must have appeared as mere specks, and so they were, for this Tower made man into a minuscule thing, a machine, a soul-less laborer in the "cause."

What, in the end, was the "cause"?

Isn't it clearly futile to attack G-d? Well, yes, but you only realize it if you think about it. What happens if you don't think about it?[77] Ah, that was a generation that didn't think about what they were doing. G-d has given us all brains, but do we use them? *"From heaven G-d gazed down upon mankind, to see if there exists a reflective person who seeks out G-d."*[77a]

Here was a generation that was sacrificing itself to an idea that had no substance. If they had thought about it, they would never have built it, but they never thought about it. That's why, when they looked at their brothers from the summit, they only saw specks. They had reduced themselves to specks because man's greatness is manifest only if he lives by the instructions G-d gives him. If he doesn't, then he reduces himself to a speck, a dot upon the earth that has no significance when it is "alive," and is forgotten forever when it is dead.

Man without awareness of G-d is dangerous to himself and to others, especially to those who are aware of Him. Sometimes G-d has to hide His followers because of the dangerous men ruling the earth in that generation. If the dangerous men would be aware of the great people living in their times, then they would kill them, as Cain killed Abel, and the knowledge of G-d could disappear from the face of the earth. In later generations, we will find that G-d has always hidden His most loyal servants until the time was ripe for their appearance. We see this most clearly in the case of King David (who was hidden from his own generation) and his descendant, King Messiah, *may we soon see him!* But more of that in its place.

A poet once said, "most men lead lives of quiet desperation."

So it is, when man goes through life without knowing there is a world beyond the material. What is the purpose of my life? What is the purpose of all my toiling beneath the sun?[78]

In the long run, men do not succeed when they unite to become more powerful. When most of mankind united to build the Tower of Babel, it was like a group of men who tried to form a world government, based on their own ideas of who should rule the earth. Did they ask G-d? No, they came up with their own principles of unity. Nobody asked the Ruler of the Universe whether He wanted them to unite and under what principles. So their efforts were doomed, because man without G-d is stupid. If he turns to G-d he is smart, because man's puny brain does not comprehend the rules that govern the universe. If he bases his life on emptiness and builds a structure out of sand, eventually the waves will wash away his sand castle, even if it stretches miles into the sky.

G-d has many ways to remind us of His presence. The Roman general Titus, who oversaw the destruction of the Second Temple, was himself destroyed by a barely-visible gnat that entered his nostril and hammered on his brain until he went mad.[79] The human gnats who built the Tower of Babel were destroyed because G-d "confused" their language.[80] Imagine men who each spoke a different language constructing a skyscraper. No one would know what the other was saying. Before long, they would be fighting with each other on beams thousands of feet above the earth, and bodies would be falling through the sky until they became mere specks on the earth below.

Do you think it is a fairy tale? When man disregards G-d, the entire principle of unity in the world is destroyed. Of course man cannot communicate. Do you know how many millions of documents the United Nations has produced? Do you see the peace that has come to the earth from these millions of documents? Where is the peace? Where is the salvation? Where is the new Garden of Eden? Where is the unifying world government that was going to save us? The world was never so dangerous as it is now!

When the Ruler of the world is ignored, then the men who try to rule in His place are only fooling themselves. It is only a matter of time until their sand castles are washed away.

The Tower of Babel was the end of an era. Up to that time, all mankind spoke one language, and that unity could not be sustained without allegiance to   G-d. Today, man has still not learned the lesson. The World Wide Web, the Internet, is potentially our new Tower of Babel, because today the Internet unites the world as one language united the world in those distant days. The Internet could be an instrument of holiness, were it not for the fact that *the soul of man is continually running to do evil.*[81]

To fight G-d it would not be necessary to bring guns up the top of the Tower of Babel and fire at Him; just building the Tower was sufficient. Just believing that you are as high as G-d is sufficient to doom you to self-destruction. It's not that G-d is "taking revenge." He doesn't need to. Our own stupidity can kill us. Once the sand castle reaches high enough in the air, it falls of its own weight. Once the conglomerate gets too big, the boss at the top doesn't even know what's going on at the bottom, what he's standing on or why he's there.

Why am I here? What am I controlling? Can I control myself, let alone the structure I am standing on? What was the purpose of swallowing all those companies? What is the purpose of my life? When the speck that I am is swallowed up in the passage of time, will there have been any meaning to my toil under the sun?

When the ancient Egyptian empire reached the pinnacle of

its powers, a tiny nation of slaves who obeyed the Highest Power revealed the weakness of its foundation.

When the ancient Roman culture reached the pinnacle of its expansion, its moral weakness undermined its internal structure and it crumbled.

When the recent German dictator allowed his hatred of the children of Israel to overcome all other desires, then the hatred turned upon itself and destroyed him and his plans.

When any desire other than the desire to serve G-d prevails, the culture in which that desire has taken root will eventually be destroyed from within.

So the world was divided and separate nations arose. They did not arise by chance. Man brought this upon himself when he tried to unite the world according to his own ideas rather than the principles emanating from his Creator.

ABRAHAM APPEARS UPON THE WORLD'S STAGE

At this moment a unique figure, a man who changed life here forever, entered upon the stage of history. Abraham was the son of an idol worshipper, but he was also a descendant of Shem, the son of Noah who had carried the tradition forward. Abraham marked a new departure for the human race.

Abraham knew by tradition the commandments given in the Garden and the additional commandment given to the children of Noah, but he apparently saw that a more intensive level of closeness to G-d was needed in a world that was in a constant state of open rebellion against its Creator. How do you educate a world? How do you make an impact on a world that has gone mad?

We learn from the Bible that the most powerful force in the world is words. G-d created the world with words, and words remain the repository of overriding power. This may surprise you, for most people believe that a gun or a bomb, a tank or military aircraft is the source of power, and that is where they invest their hope. But it is not true. King David says in the Psalms, *"some [fight] with chariots and some with horses but we call out in the Name of G-d."*[82] The children of Israel have outlasted every other nation, and all of those nations were abundantly armed with the most modern weapons of their day. How did we outlast them? Because we "called out in the name of G-d."

The Father of our nation, Abraham, taught us to call out in the name of G-d.

Let us imagine what he was like. First of all, he was very much alone. He had received a tradition from his ancestors that G-d had created the world 1948 years before his birth. He knew that G-d had established commandments and that his ancestors had violated those commandments with horrendous results. He knew that Adam and Eve had repented for their rebellion but their repentance clearly was not sufficient to gain re-entry to the Garden. He knew that Adam and Eve had given birth to a son named Seth, who had carried on his parents' story and legacy. He knew that the men of the pre-Flood world had continued to rebel against G-d and that only a tiny minority had preserved the legacy carried on through Seth. He knew that the rebellion had made life on earth unsustainable in the time of Noah, and that Noah had listened to G-d and enabled a tiny remnant to escape the devastation of the earth and carry through to the next generation. He knew that G-d had established an additional commandment for the descendants of Noah. And he knew that men who toil beneath the sun had also rebelled against the Seven Commandments, and that their Tower, which was designed to provide a platform from which to fight G-d, had failed them because of disunity among the builders.

According to Rashi,[83] the generation of the Tower was less wicked than the generation of the Flood. The sin of the generation of the Tower was greater but the punishment of the generation of the Flood was greater. The proof is that the generation of the Flood died, which is a worse punishment than being scattered across the earth, which was the fate of the generation of the Tower. Rashi states that the generation of the Flood died because there was hostility among them and that *"conflict is hateful."* Even though the sin of the generation of the Tower was greater because they tried directly to attack G-d, they were spared the death penalty because they were unified.

Millennia later, the children of Israel were exiled after the destruction of the Second Temple amidst terrible anguish because of *"sinas chinom,"* causeless hatred between Jew and Jew, in other words lack of unity.[84] It must be deeply contemplated by all of us how conflict destroys life upon the earth. Abraham established the basis for true unity and peace among his children, and in the world in general, by discovering the laws through which G-d runs the world.

Abraham looked upon the mischief done in the world. Why should one not learn from the mistakes of the past? Has G-d not given us eyes, ears and brains for precisely that purpose? He had inherited the tradition from his ancestors, but he applied it in a way no one had done before him.

He saw that the "powerful real estate interests" of his day had constructed a stupendous tower that had collapsed. He saw that those who had sponsored this project had had their language turned to babble and had been scattered to the ends of the earth. He saw that his own father, Terach, not only sold but manufactured idols* and was one of the principal entrepreneurs in this business. He saw that there is a discrepancy between recognizing the Ruler of the Universe and making a business out of claiming that sticks and stones have power over us. Terach, after all, reported his son to the authorities when he insisted upon rejecting idol worship. Is that the character trait of one who is following the path of truth? Does a father attack a son?

I am reminded of a scene I witnessed. Many years ago, a young woman found a wonderful husband at Rebbetzin Esther Jungreis' Hineni organization. This woman's parents were furious that their daughter was returning to the Torah life. They refused to have anything to do with their daughter's wedding, so Rebbetzin Jungreis and her family arranged and paid for it. I was there. I saw the mother of the bride enter, wearing a black dress, walk up to Rebbetzin Jungreis and slap her face in front of all the guests!

Such is the hatred of parents who cannot tolerate it when their children embrace the service of their Creator. Such was the hatred of Terach toward Abraham, and that is why he sought to have his son killed.

How did Abraham defend himself? He did not rely upon the weapons used against him. Instead, he relied upon his closeness to G-d, the "weapon" that has saved his children to this very day.

Please, my dear friends, note this well: that knowledge alone saved him.

Obviously, since our Nation has survived against all odds and

---

* My wife pointed out that, as I write these words (just before Passover in the year 2003), the Iraqi people are looting their museums in the aftermath of the United States attack. These museums contain objects of idol worship from both the geographical location and the historical era of Abraham's father. The contemporary Iraqi people, rather than trying to sell these ancient objects, are smashing them! At least three times a day, we Jews pray that we may soon see the day when G-d will *remove detestable idolatry from the earth.* Could these contemporary events be a sign of the imminent coming of the day "when all humanity will call upon your name"?

logic, G-d's protection must be effective! If only we, in this generation – who are now coming constantly under attack – if only
we would remember how our Father Abraham survived in the
face of worldwide antagonism and condemnation, we could
instantly turn degradation into exaltation. *"If only My people
would heed Me, if Israel would walk in My ways, in an instant I
would subdue their foes and turn my hand against their tormentors."*[85]

Our Father was named "Abraham the Ivri." From "Ivri"
comes the term "Hebrew," which is applied to us until today. *Ivri*
means "across,"[86] because Abraham came from *"across the river."*

What does the Torah mean by "across the river"?

Geographically "the river" refers to the Euphrates River; spiritually it refers to the "waters" that separate those who cleave to
G-d from those who do not see beyond the material world.

Abraham was called *Ivri* literally because he crossed the
Euphrates River when G-d called him,[87] and he settled in the
Land of Canaan, later to be called the Land of Israel. Spiritually, Abraham was alone on one side and the rest of the world
on the other side.[88] The entire world worshipped idols; Abraham worshipped G-d. Abraham was not afraid to stand opposite the entire world. He did not follow the herd of men who
worship sticks and stones. If Abraham had been acting in
accordance with the world's values, there never would have
been such a nation as Israel.

Because he was willing to cling to G-d in lonely allegiance,
his children have had the courage (and the destiny) of being a
nation alone, a nation that is constantly isolated and ostracized
in a world that continues to worship sticks and stones. Like our
Father Abraham, we stay close to our G-d; we refuse to associate ourselves with those who worship idols. It was not that he
wanted to dissociate himself from other people, but he wanted
to dissociate himself from idol worship.

We children of Abraham have inherited both his personality and his destiny. At the same time as we are the envy and admiration of the world, we are the most isolated and reviled nation in the world, a nation alone, a nation apart.*

Our enemy, Balaam the non-Jewish prophet, described this condition in the most graphic and stark terms: "*It is a nation that will dwell in solitude and not be reckoned among the nations.*"[89] In the eyes the material world, this is a curse. In the eyes of G-d, this is a blessing, the unique blessing of the children of Israel.

We inherited all this from our Father Abraham.

The fear of standing in opposition to the rest of the world comes about when one judges oneself through the eyes of the rest of the world. In other words, if you want to look good in other people's eyes then you will try to please them. If you want to look good in the eyes of G-d, then you will try to please Him. It depends on what standards you are trying to fulfill. Your perspective on the world depends completely on this. If you realize that the ultimate judge of your actions is G-d – *What does G-d think of what I'm doing?* – you will act differently than if you think man is the ultimate judge.

This reminds me of a remarkable passage in the Bible. The ill-fated spies who went to inspect the Land of Israel say about the inhabitants of the land, "*we were as grasshoppers in their eyes, and we were as grasshoppers in our own eyes.*"[90] In other words, they looked upon themselves with the eyes of their potential enemies. This is why they were afraid! Of course they lost their courage!

They sacrificed the clear vision that emanates from stick-

---

* Granted that we are not on Abraham's level, but the ironic duality of the world's attitude toward him has been inherited by us. At the same time as the world honors us for our spiritual attainments and the fact that we have spread the knowledge of G-d, they envy us for our special relationship with G-d. This is the original "love-hate relationship." Our only defense is to rely on G-d to protect us, through strengthening our bond with Him.

ing close to G-d; they believed themselves to be powerless because they did not look at themselves the way G-d looked at them. He who forgets his Creator feels like a grasshopper; he who remembers his Creator possesses limitless strength, strength beyond nature. The "minority" among the spies, Joshua and Calev, had learned from our Father Abraham. They looked upon themselves as made *"in the image of G-d."*[91] Thus they were able to stand against the majority who were *"on the other side"* of the river.

At the inception of our history, then, the very name of our founder contains within it the concept that we are separated from the rest of the world because we cling to the One G-d. We do not need the world's approbation; we are willing to travel through history without it, as long as we have the approbation of G-d and live by His commandments. That is the very basis of our existence as a nation, and it was thus from the beginning.

Today, thousands of years later, as we experience the "birth pangs of the Messiah," this issue is in the forefront of our consciousness, as the children of Israel weigh whether to act like the children of Abraham or like the children of the rest of the world.

Upon which bank of the river shall we stand?

The modern state of Israel is a touchstone. When we live by the standards of the rest of the world, Israel is subjected to almost universal condemnation. When we live by our eternal values, we survive and thrive in spite of whatever is thrown against us.

This is why the story must be re-told.

The continued existence of the children of Israel will be guaranteed only by adherence to the laws of the G-d of our Fathers, Abraham, Isaac and Jacob. Once again, we recall the heart-rending, prophetic words, *"If only My people would heed*

Me, *if Israel would walk in My ways, in an instant I would subdue their foes and turn My hand against their tormentors."*[92]

Why do we flail uselessly and embarrassingly, like grasshoppers facing an insurmountable tidal wave of troubles, when G-d is standing and waiting to help us?

Have we learned nothing over the centuries?

And yet, there is always hope for the children of Israel. We are the nation that, like the moon, renews itself constantly.

Let us now, with G-d's help, travel onward through time, and discover the nature of the new nation that arose from Father Abraham.

CHAPTER TWO

THE FAMILY:
ABRAHAM TO MOSES

*...because He loved your forefathers, and He chose
[their] offspring after [them], and He took you out
before Him with His great strength from Egypt, to
drive away from before you nations that are greater
and mightier than you, to bring you, to give you their
land as an inheritance...*[92a]

Terach, Abraham's father, was a descendant of Shem, part of
the lineage of those who remembered the story of Adam and
Eve. As we learned in the previous chapter, although Terach knew there is a Ruler in the universe, he became not only
an idol worshipper and manufacturer, but even an enemy of his
own son, who had discarded idols and found G-d. The opposition of his father, however, was not to deter Abraham from
searching for Truth.

Abraham lived in a chaotic era, the generation of the Tower
of Babel. How did he find a way to get closer to G-d than anyone since Adam? How did he discover* more commandments

---

* Yes, the commandments are commanded, but that does not mean that they cannot be discovered. Just as Abraham discovered the existence of G-d by looking logically at the world, he
also discovered the commandments by looking logically at the world. How is this possible?
Because G-d created the world "by looking in the Torah." (Medrash Bereishis Rabbah 1:2)
Thus it is logical to assume that there is evidence for the commandments in the world.

than the seven given to Noah? How did he manage to construct a foundation on which his descendants, until the end of time, would build an everlasting way of life, a spiritual edifice that would withstand the fiercest assaults throughout the centuries?

There are certain people who are not satisfied when they see a world that seems to be running on automatic pilot, a world without rules, in which the King is not acknowledged. Such people cannot rest. I myself remember, as a child, how frightening it was to believe I was living in a world that seemed to have no direction, no guidance. It was like being in a car that was running out of control at high speed. One knows there must be a "Driver" of the universe. The question is, how and where does one start to look?

Of course, Abraham had a tradition handed down to him from Adam.[93] He knew that G-d exists. He knew that a Driverless world will ultimately crash; after all, the world had self-destructed in the time of Noah. But that vague knowledge is not concrete enough to provide a structure for an enduring lifestyle. Obviously, he also felt the need to find the Guiding Principle himself, to establish a direct relationship with the Source of all life, to comprehend what G-d wanted of him. A person such as Abraham looks for clues and evidence everywhere, and if he looks, he will find the evidence, perhaps beginning in the most obvious place, the world of nature.

But first, he will feel the presence of a spiritual element in himself. He will realize that the very fact that he is thinking about these things indicates that there is a part of him that can think, a part of him that is not physical! If he has within him a non-physical aspect, then clearly there is a world beyond the physical. So he starts to explore that world.

He understands that he did not make himself, either physically or spiritually. There must a Creator Who made him. But the Creator is not in the physical world, since obviously – although he came biologically from his parents – his parents did not create his spiritual part. So the Creator is outside the material world. Since he has discovered the spiritual world, he will try to communicate with the One Who created him.

How does he start that process? He will pray, because prayer means speaking with the Creator. He calls out from his soul, his spiritual self, *"Is there anyone here with me in this world?"* If he is humble, he will try to subordinate himself to the Creator and learn to ask the Creator to help him, to guide him, and provide illumination to him. And when his eyes are opened, he will look out at the world in a different way. He will see that, just as he was created from the spiritual world, so was all of nature created from the spiritual world.

Abraham confronted a world in which the original commandments given at the inception of the world were still being ignored. It became urgent that the Creator be recognized by the mass of men. How otherwise could he or anyone else live in a world that threatened to destroy itself once again?

But how was he to find the details of what G-d wanted? How did Abraham discover 613 laws in a world that did not yet know them?

"G-d looked in the Torah and designed the world."[94]

If G-d designed the world according to the Torah, then the world should contain clues to the Torah. The search should work in reverse. Today you can search for a person's phone number if you know his name, but, if you know where to look, you can also search in reverse; you can find a person's name and address if you know his phone number. Abraham had to look in reverse. If you are perceptive, honest and humble enough, you should be able to look in the world and discover the Torah, even the commandments that are not obvious or apparently logical.[95]

The existence of the Creator is indicated by the nature of the world.[96] Practically everyone has heard the analogy to the construction of a watch. We know the watch did not build itself. How much more so is this clear when we look at the body of a human being, or beyond that to the countless facets of a natural world that interact with incomprehensibly perfect precision: the course of the sun, which travels across the sky in a set pattern on a daily and a yearly basis; the phases of the moon; the paths of the stars; the seasons, always returning, always in a cycle of life, death, rebirth and life again. Those are the "big" creations, but what about the life of a honeybee? An ant? The breeze that brushes your cheek: where did it come from?

"The heavens declare the glory of G-d and the firmament tells of His handiwork. Day following day utters speech, and night following night declares knowledge. There is no speech and there are no words; their sound is not heard. [But] their precision goes forth throughout the earth and their words reach the end of the inhabited world. In their midst He has set up a tent for the sun, which is like a groom emerging from his bridal chamber; it rejoices like a powerful warrior to run the course. Its source is the end of the heavens and its circuit is to their end; nothing escapes its heat. The Torah of G-d is perfect; it restores the soul."[97]

Do you notice here how King David learns from observing G-d's world that there is a G-d? And do you see how he learns from that observation that *"the Torah of G-d is perfect"*?

Anyone who thinks will understand from observing nature that there is a G-d.

But who thinks?

Abraham thought. That is not to say that G-d did not speak to him. G-d speaks to all of us, but how many listen?

How can we understand the process by which Abraham came to find G-d and His laws? How can we understand what Abraham went through? How does it make sense?

For one thing, Abraham saw the effects of man's arrogance at the Tower of Babel. He saw what happens when man tries to become like G-d, when he imagines that G-d is material, and tries to reach Him by building physical structures. Through the Tower of Babel, destruction, dissension and turmoil came into the world. Abraham, the keen observer, must have seen that man does not bring about a better world by building physical structures. True building for man is scaling the spiritual heights, the internal battle to master one's negative traits and incorporate the will of G-d into one's life.

"Your children ("banaich") will be students of G-d and your children will have abundant peace. Do not read 'banaich' [your children] but 'bonaich' [your builders]."[98]

Who are the true builders? Students of G-d.

G-d is not material; he is not at the top of a mountain. Those who climb Mount Everest do not come closer to Him. If you try to reach G-d by building a physical platform high into the sky you are making a mistake; you are not coming close to Him. Abraham saw that men who attempt to reach G-d by physical accomplishments succeed only in destroying themselves and their institutions. Man's fate is not accidental.

The world is positively influenced by righteous people and negatively influenced by evil people, but Abraham also saw that people who rebel against G-d can return to Him in repentance and that their rebellions can be atoned for and the breaches repaired.[99] All these things are evident from looking at the world.

LEARNING COMMANDMENTS BY EXAMINING NATURE

One can learn the existence of G-d by looking at nature. If one contemplates the incalculably complex intricacies of the natural world, it is clear that there is an Intelligence and Power beyond what we can fathom. Clearly, an Intelligence that has created the universe must be able to communicate with us. But how can I communicate with the Creator?

Well, how could the Creator not be able to communicate? The question is: how to do it?

Abraham knew that G-d had spoken to Adam and Eve, and He had established commandments in their time. There had been terrible consequences for failure to observe those commandments. Abraham also knew that G-d had spoken to Noah. Noah and his children had received the commandments originally given in the Garden,[100] and the world had been destroyed for rebellion against those commandments.

But Abraham also must have seen the *"chessed,"* the kindness in the universe. Not only did G-d allow those who obeyed His commandments to survive, but He also had made the world such a beautiful place for those of us who live in it. As we asked in Chapter One, why for example did G-d make such a variety of apparently "unnecessary" creatures in the world, and create such a magnificent array of trees and flowers, butterflies, geological formations, weather, sky and so on? The world does not have to be beautiful. G-d made it beautiful so that His creatures would have a beautiful place to live. From this we learn His *chessed.*

We also learn from the fact that G-d put us into a beautiful world that G-d desires us to live in an attractive place. We learn from this that one's home should be decorated and adorned so that one can live an honorable existence in this world, as befits one who serves the King. G-d made a pleasant world for us. If it has become unpleasant, it is only through our faults. This is part of His *chessed,* the kindness of G-d.

Nature, G-d's creation, simulates and hints at the spiritual world. The physical world is a pattern based on the spiritual world.[101] As we said above, we know that G-d "looked into the

Torah and designed the world." Abraham discovered details of the Torah to supplement what he had received through tradition.[102] Later on, at Mount Sinai, all of it was directly revealed by G-d, but apparently Abraham was great enough to discover it himself. If a G-d-fearing person looks at the world, he can see in it patterns that will indicate the nature of the Creator and what the Creator intends His creations to learn from the material world.

What else can we learn from nature? As we said, it is clear from nature that G-d is full of kindness, but are there other lessons to be learned? Can we learn specific laws and commandments?

What can we learn from the seasons?

Nature apparently dies in the winter; the elements become "unfriendly" and the natural world seems to shut down. But in the spring a miracle occurs; the world warms up; plants come back to life; hibernating animals reappear and the entire world becomes a garden. Flowers of every color appear and the trees are adorned with fragrant blossoms. Each leaf is a different shade of green, sparkling with the dew of new life. The entire world is filled with hope. It seems that new life is possible after the death of winter.

As spring becomes summer, we learn to feed ourselves from this abundant earth. The beauty of spring becomes the means of preserving life. The idyll of spring does not last forever. The world becomes hot and the freshness of spring turns to the heat of summer. We cannot simply contemplate the beauty; we have to work to make the most of it, so that we will have food to eat for the summer, the autumn and especially the brutal winter, which we know will return as long as *seedtime and harvest, cold and heat, summer and winter, day and night shall not cease.*[103] So we plant seeds in the spring and cultivate them in order to harvest them during the summer and autumn.

Summer is another test, because – especially in the Land of Israel – the heat becomes intense and the land dry. Too much "goodness," too much sunshine is also a test. Just as we can die in the winter during the "death" of nature, we can die in the summer during nature's most intense period of heat and light. Summer can be a time of overconfidence and extreme danger; in order to survive, one must think very clearly about preserving life.

Autumn is a time when the fruits of the year's work are harvested, and we prepare for winter.

What can we learn from the yearly cycle?

Is it not amazing that there is a spring after winter? Is it not amazing that the earth blooms again after "death"?

Can we not learn the existence of the World to Come from the fact that spring follows winter? Can we not see that life comes after death?[104] Abraham observed that.

G-d created the world starting with night and ending with day. Abraham learned that from the legacy passed down from Adam, because the world was created with the formula, "it was evening and it was morning."[105] Does that not also instruct us that darkness precedes light? Our entire view of history is that difficulties always precede triumph. *"In the evening one lies down weeping, but with dawn – a cry of joy!"*[106]

That also has spiritual implications. Why, for example, did Abraham and Sarah have so much difficulty conceiving a baby?[107] Nothing important comes without struggle, toil, and prayer. Day follows night as "joy follows weeping." Abraham learned from nature and from his own life.

What else can we learn?

Purim and Passover are holidays of the spring. There are no more joyous occasions than Purim and Passover, because we are full of hope at the beginning of life. Sukkos is "the time of our happiness," because the harvest is in and we have passed the test of the yearly cycle. It is like the saying that *the day of death is better than the day of birth.*[108] Sukkos, with its mature satisfaction, represents the happiness of a successfully completed cycle. But Purim and Passover are at the beginning of the cycle, "the time of our freedom," the time of our liberation from death, the time of greatest hope. What greater joy is there than to find out that death has forever been defeated (as we say at the very end of the Passover Seder[109]), when despair blossoms into hope and the dead earth explodes into an ecstasy of life?

Is it difficult to understand why spring should be the moment for the holiday of the redemption from slavery, the time when the children of Israel emerged from an iron fortress from which no prisoner had ever hoped to escape? Is it difficult to understand why Purim should have come about at this time? The events of Purim also involve the miraculous escape from a catastrophic situation that appeared to be completely hopeless.

COMMANDMENTS THAT APPEAR TO HAVE NO BASIS IN NATURE

What about commandments that appear to have no basis in nature? We have seen that certain commandments are derived by logical deduction from patterns in nature, but what about others that seem to have no reflection in the natural world, or some that seem even to go against what nature or logic would dictate? We know that Abraham and Sarah and their descendants kept the commandments in all their details, even before their descendants were formally commanded at Mount Sinai.[110] How did they learn these commandments and these details?

They had the tradition from Adam and Eve and they had the lessons they learned from observing the world. What did they see in the world, however, that could teach them to say *Shema Yisroel*[111] or to wear *tzitzis*[112]? They certainly could not have learned to wear *tzitzis* on four-cornered garments from Adam and Eve or Noah, for no such requirement was in effect in their times.

How does one learn laws that are not passed down from previous generations, directly observable in nature or linked to natural or historical facts?

Let's examine a commandment that is not readily apparent in nature, for example *tzitzis*. How would a thinking person who understands that there is a G-d in the world Who establishes moral regulations, how would such a person discover the commandment of *tzitzis*?

In the physical world (which we said is a "mask"[113] that hints at the spiritual world), we wear clothing to protect ourselves from the elements, to shield ourselves from the sun or the cold or the rain.

To a sensitive, thinking person, the process of going through life causes one to feel spiritually vulnerable, under attack, under duress. If we feel a need to protect our physical selves from the "attack" of nature, don't we also feel a need for spiritual "clothing" to protect us from the spiritual pain we encounter in this world?

When we encounter difficulties, tragedy, sickness, anguish, pain, loneliness, betrayal, sadness, embarrassment... any situation which seems beyond our ability to tolerate, we want protection, we want to enwrap ourselves in a protective spiritual "garment" in order to get through the pain, just as we enwrap ourselves in a protective physical garment to get through the rain. A G-d fearing person wants to enwrap his soul in something that protects him spiritually from the dangers lurking everywhere in this world.

That's what *tzitzis* represent. We want to wrap holiness around us to protect us and to keep our soul pure in this dangerous world. *Tzitzis* stands for the commandments.[114] When we enwrap ourselves in the *tzitzis* we are enwrapping ourselves in the protection of the commandments. Those commandments are what protect us in this world. That is the concept of *tzitzis*. We are enwrapping ourselves in something that symbolizes the Torah as a protection and as a constant reminder that *"[you should not] explore after your heart and after your eyes after which you go astray,"*[115] but rather follow G-d's instructions.

So we take a garment that we frequently wear, a garment with four "corners"[116] and we attach strings to each corner[117] in order to remind us of the commandments.

Life comes with "strings attached." The strings remind us of the number of commandments that we have to perform. So the *tzitzis* is constructed with the purpose of reminding us. It's not just that when we wear a four-cornered garment we have to put strings on it; it's that we make a four-cornered garment specifically so that we can attach strings to it to serve as a source of spiritual protection. We know that we are vulnerable, and so we desire ways to ensure that we will live as G-d wants us to live. This is our incentive to look for such commandments as *tzitzis*. We Jews walk and talk and eat and carry out our responsibilities as all men do, but we do all these things in special ways that are designed to remind us of the presence of G-d. As King David says, *"I have set G-d before me always..."*[118] Even our garments are designed to remind us of the presence of G-d.

One could also say that the four-cornered garment we wear reminds us of the "four corners" of the earth.[119] We are trying to recall that the entire world was created by G-d and only exists because He wills it to exist. So we remind ourselves that G-d's presence is everywhere in the "four corners" of the world by wearing a four-cornered garment with strings tied in a certain way that reminds us of His presence and our obligations to Him.

We are weak. We need reminders on our body (circumcision) and reminders in our home (*mezuzos*[120]) and reminders in general (which is why we speak to G-d three times a day in prayer) and so on.

Mezuzos bear a resemblance to *tzitzis*. How is this?

A house is a physical protection against the elements. We live in a house because otherwise we would be exposed to the rain, the snow, the wind, the bitterness of winter. What about protecting our soul from spiritual "weather"? Don't we desire to construct a sanctuary for our souls, to protect us against exposure to harmful spiritual emanations? So in additional to our physical home, we must build a spiritual home. *Mezuzos* enable our physical home to become in addition a spiritual home, a protection against inclement spiritual weather. Our physical home thus becomes a spiritual protection for those who dwell there. The physical house in which our bodies are sheltered is, in addition to being a physical protection, a symbol of the spiritual house in which we would like our souls to be sheltered. So we make our physical house spiritual by attaching *mezuzos* to the doorposts.[121] Every time we walk through a doorway, we are reminded that our essence – the soul that communicates with G-d – lies beyond the material realm.

Let's go further: how would Abraham, for example, have discovered some of the details of these commandments? How, for example, would Abraham have discovered that there are four strings doubled over in each of the *tzitzis* that hang from each corner of a four-cornered garment? The answer to this is truly amazing, but when you think about it, you can understand how our Father Abraham could have discovered all the details of these commandments even before G-d revealed them at Mount Sinai.

Remember what Abraham was doing. He was aware that there is a G-d and that G-d is actively ruling every aspect of creation. Abraham knew that the commandments would demonstrate that and keep us in the proper relationship with G-d.

The number "representing" eternity is eight.[122] Why is that? Because there are seven days in the week. Abraham knew that the week consists of seven days, and that the Seventh Day is the Sabbath. So six represents nature as we know it within the limitations of this world. There are six weekdays and six directions (north, south, east, west, up and down, the directions in which we shake the *lulav* on Sukkos). Those six days and six directions represent the material world.

Seven represents the world in its highest state, the material world in which G-d is ruling, the perfection of the material world, as we know it on the Sabbath. Seven is the material world with the presence of G-d manifest in it, the material world in which the presence of the Eternal World is acknowledged and perceived.

Eight is the spiritual world, the world beyond the material, the Eternal World from which the material world was created by G-d.

How would you symbolize the presence of the Eternal World in the material world? You would take the number eight and you would "insert" it into the material world. Now the material world is represented by six, but the earth itself is represented by four, because there are four directions, or *"four corners of the earth."* So the "insertion" of eight into four would symbolize the presence of G-d in the world.

What are the *tzitzis?* The garment hangs down over the body;

on each of four corners eight strings hang down. This is a representation of the world: the Presence of G-d, the Infinite, is covering us and extending down from His realm, throughout our entire material world. The "strings" from Above extend into this world and it is up to us to remind ourselves of that fact. *Tzitzis* is one of the ways we remember. This is how the details of *tzitzis* could have been discovered by Abraham.

What about the details of the *mezuzah*? How, for example, could Abraham have discovered what should be written on the scroll that we attach to our doorposts and gates?

This is also quite remarkable, because it is clear that this also could have been deduced by Abraham.

Our Father Abraham not only rediscovered the fact that G-d made the world, but he also rediscovered that G-d has legislated rules for us. The prayer that we say every day, the prayer that G-d tells us to bind *"upon your arm"*[123] and *"between your eyes,"*[124] and place *"on your doorposts"*[125] and *"your gates,"*[126] would logically emphasize this fundamental concept.

What is that prayer? *"Hear O Israel: Hashem*[127] *is our G-d, Hashem is One."*

This is truly remarkable.

What should Israel "hear"? Israel should hear that the Creator and the Lawgiver is One!

Isn't that[128] what our Father Abraham spent his entire life explaining to the world? The very fact that G-d is One, that the same G-d Who created the world also governs the world and governs us – that is what our Father Abraham was explaining to the world! And that is what the *Shema* prayer says! Is it any wonder that the contents of the *mezuzah* and the *tefillin* and the primary prayer mentioned in the Torah could have been discovered by Abraham? That was in fact what concerned Abraham his entire life and constituted the basis of his teachings!

So here again the exact details, including the wording, of several commandments (*mezuzah, tefillin* and "*Shema Yisroel*") could clearly have been discovered by Abraham by examining the world and thinking clearly about what had to be true.

Here we have seen several examples in which Abraham could have discovered commandments by thinking about life from the perspective of someone who knows that G-d exists. These are logical commandments for a person who is searching for a way to get close to G-d. Abraham discovered them and took them upon himself so he could come closer to G-d.

KOSHER FOOD

What about other commandments? What about kosher food? Abraham was the tenth generation after Noah. He could look back in history and know that a Flood in Noah's time had destroyed the world. Following the Flood, man was re-constituted in a new world, a world that had lost its primeval purity, a world of compromise in which man's lifestyle and lifespan were diminished. After the Flood, man was subject to the depredations of nature; he needed more strength. G-d had given permission to Noah and his descendants to eat meat, which had not been the case before the Flood.[129] When that happened, a distinction arose between the kind of food man had been permitted before the Flood, and the type that man was permitted to eat after the Flood. The laws of separating meat and milk hinted at the two states of man, before and after the Flood.

A cow, for example, provides two types of food, milk and its own meat. Are they similar? Before the Flood, man was permitted to drink the milk; after the Flood man was permitted to eat the cow itself! But think of the difference!

When we drink the milk, the cow lives.

When we eat the meat, the cow dies.

The very act of eating meat involves a compromise, because we have to kill in order to eat this food.[130] In order to sustain ourselves, we take a life. It is permitted, but it is not ideal. Since it was not permitted according to the way the world was originally constituted it is obviously a compromise. It was permitted only as a result of conditions which arose as a result of man's rebellion, which brought about the Flood and the new world after the Flood. That world was not as pure as the world before the Flood.

The necessity of killing one of G-d's creations in order to sustain ourselves, although permitted, reflects the growing gap between G-d and man. Furthermore, killing to sustain ourselves, while it strengthens us physically, does something negative to our soul. It is not good for our soul to kill. (Some people have a twinge of conscience even when killing a fly, let alone larger animals.)*

Before the Flood, we sustained ourselves without harming the earth or its inhabitants. We ate vegetables and fruit** and drank milk, water and juices … sustenance that would not diminish the world. Our sustenance and growth did not come at the expense of other life.

We should not think that meat and milk are the same type of food. Just as we should not fool ourselves into thinking that New York is the same as Jerusalem or that Wednesday is the same as the Sabbath, we should not think that life after the Flood is the same as life before the Flood.

---

* This reminds me of the well-known saying, "There may come a day when we can forgive our enemies for killing us, but we can never forgive them for forcing us to kill them."

** Interestingly, I have heard that fruit is on a higher level than vegetables, because eating fruit does not destroy the tree, but eating vegetables usually destroys the plant, for example in the case of a carrot or onion or lettuce.

We can see that from these considerations that Abraham could have deduced logically the commandment to separate meat and milk from contemplating the history of the world and the tradition that had been passed down to him from previous generations.

Interestingly, the details of the commandment echo the history of the world. According to Torah law, milk "comes first." If you eat milk, you may follow it with meat, but if you eat meat, you must wait before you eat milk products. This would seem to indicate the milk naturally precedes meat, which it does in the history of the world. Torah law also reflects the fact that there was a "break" (the Flood) between the period of milk and the period when meat is permitted.[131]

So it would seem that by contemplating nature and the history of the world a person with a great soul could discover the laws of kashrus.

A commandment like studying Torah would appear to be completely self-evident, if one may say such a thing. If G-d rules the world then it seems clear that we should study His laws in order to know how to follow His will. If the whole purpose of our life in this world is to discover what G-d wants of us, then how could we not study the Torah? The whole purpose of life is studying Torah.

But what about a commandment like saying *"Shema Yisroel"* twice a day? How would Abraham have "deduced" the existence of that?

Again, it seems evident that since we are material/spiritual beings in a material universe that was created by a Spiritual Power, it would be logical to say a "pledge of allegiance" to G-d twice a day. The presence of the spiritual world is not obvious when we look with our eyes, listen with our ears and perceive the world around us with our other senses. So it would make sense that we remind ourselves every day that "G-d is One[132]." Being weak mortals, we need constant reminders, like *mezuzos* on every doorpost and *tzitzis* on our garments.

But why twice a day? Why not once a day or twenty four times a day?

Life is divided into waking and sleep. In sleep, our soul returns to a spiritual world; in the waking hours, our soul perceives a physical world. We say *Shema* when we wake up in the morning so that, during the time our soul perceives the material world, we will remember that G-d exists and that material things are not to be confused with G-d. We remind ourselves of this in order to get through the day without becoming confused and deluded by the material entities that surround us.

What about at night?

It is possible, at the moment we go to sleep, that we may have the wrong intentions, and not direct our soul to the heavenly realms, especially after having been so influenced during the entire day by material objects. We therefore want to give our soul a correct "send-off" for its nightly trip by directing it to the spiritual realms. If that were not the case, then sleep would not yield its proper effect, because we would have only a physical sleep without the nightly renewal of the soul that occurs through its contact with G-d.[133]

Just as everything in nature reflects the existence of the spiritual world, so sleep is not simply physical but also spiritual. Sleep is not simply the body refreshing itself, but it is a chance for the soul to regain its strength by contact with the Creator. In our terms, we might think of the analogy of recharging a battery by plugging it into a power source.

A person who knows that G-d exists sleeps differently from another person. That is why the sleep on the Sabbath is different from the sleep on a weekday. The Sabbath is called *Yom*

Menucha, the Day of Rest, partly because the soul's natural condition on the Sabbath is to be very close to G-d, as it is during sleep. Perhaps that is why holy people often can train themselves to require very little sleep, because their souls are close to the Creator even when they are awake.

APPARENTLY ILLOGICAL COMMANDMENTS

What about the most apparently illogical of all commandments, the commandment concerning the red heifer? [134]

When one becomes impure through contact with a dead body, the only way to eliminate the impurity is through the sprinkling of the ashes of a red heifer that has been slaughtered and burned. While those upon whom the ashes are sprinkled become pure, those who slaughter and handle the red heifer become impure. This is the aspect of the red heifer that seems so illogical and for which the nations have ridiculed us.[135] King Solomon, the wisest man who ever lived, stated that he could not completely comprehend this commandment.

But amazingly enough there is a hint of the red heifer in nature.

I recently heard[136] that one of the most potent new drugs for fighting certain forms of cancer is actually not a new drug at all, but a plant that has been known for centuries as a deadly poison, arsenic. Medical researchers have found doctors in China using arsenic as a cure for cancer.

How can a poison be used as a cure?

But doesn't it make sense? If you have sickness threatening your body, then you have to kill it before it kills you. So you administer poison in a controlled manner in order to poison what is threatening to kill you. But anyone handling this poison endangers himself. You would not take the poison if you were not sick, because the medicine could kill you. Only the one who is so sick that his life is in danger will use these extreme measures; he will swallow the poison because that is his only chance for life. Anyone who is not in mortal danger is not going to swallow the poison.

So with the red heifer. The ashes of the red heifer are poison because they represent the pure animal instinct in us, which is the opposite of the spiritual. They also are connected to the golden calf, which is the symbol of idol worship. Idol worship and the animal instinct kill us because they cancel out adherence to the Source of life. Ideally, as we were originally created, we were supposed to live forever; indeed our souls are eternal. But a person who is subject to death has endangered his connection with G-d. He has become so infected by corruption that his soul is in danger of expiring because it has been cut off from the Source of eternal existence.

He must save himself, so he takes a poison that weakens his soul to such an extent that he also weakens his power to rebel against G-d. He brings himself so close to death that he "kills" his power of rebellion. That is his only hope for saving himself! But this extreme measure is dangerous, because he can kill himself, so he only does it if he is already very sick.

This is a way to explain how even the details concerning the red heifer, apparently the most inexplicable of all commandments, could be found in nature. Even though Abraham preceded the generation in which Israel sinned with the Golden Calf, for which the red heifer is an atonement, it is possible to believe that he discovered this atonement even before the sin made its use necessary. After all, he is our father, and a loving father understands his children's needs.

THE FIRST GENERATION:
THE CHALLENGE OF ISHMAEL

Abraham discovered the commandments, but what was he to do with his discovery? If that discovery were to end with him then what value would it have? Part of Abraham's greatness was that he desired to discover the commandments in order to elevate mankind so we could all reconnect with our Creator. Abraham was not simply enhancing his own life; he was giving the greatest possible gift to all future generations. His discovery was designed to be passed down through the generations so that it could enable the world to return to its pristine state, to show mankind a path by which it could stop running away from G-d and reunite with Him.

We can try to imagine how G-d viewed the world. He had created man with free will. But with that free will, almost all men had forgotten about their Creator and were trying to run the world as if G-d did not exist. That is a recipe for disaster. We had already seen disaster in the Garden of Eden and during the Flood, as well as in other, less dramatic ways. How was G-d going to help man heal himself in a way that was consistent with free will?

A solution was to have a special relationship with a man who would cleave to Him and teach his children to cleave to Him. He and his children would teach the world that G-d exists. Was there such a man on earth? Abraham, who sought and found G-d, was the man who could accomplish that mission, and Abraham was to become the father and founder of this family. But of course, Abraham would then have to pass on his knowledge of G-d to descendants who would never forget that knowledge, and who would in turn pass it on to the entire world. So in order to carry out this mission, Abraham and Sarah had to have children through whom the tradition of service to G-d would be carried out.

But like everything else that is holy and important in life, the process of having children was not easy for Abraham and Sarah. For people whose children would alter the entire future of mankind, bringing those children into the world was not a simple or easy process. Holy people often have the most difficult time. It seems that every important thing in life is difficult.[137] I like the analogy of the forest, which takes hundreds of years to grow. Each giant tree starts as a tiny, almost invisible seed, and is challenged constantly as it grows and attains its lofty stature. But to knock down that tree takes only a few minutes. To destroy is easy; to build is difficult, time consuming, and constantly challenging.

The world does not understand this.

When Sarah saw that she was having difficulty conceiving, she gave her Egyptian maidservant, Hagar, to her husband in order that he should bear children through Hagar. Hagar had no difficulty conceiving and giving birth, but she made a serious error. She assumed that because she had had no difficulty conceiving and because Sarah was having great difficulty conceiving, that she (Hagar) was blessed by G-d and that Sarah was not blessed.[138] This was Hagar's rationale for acting arrogantly toward Sarah.

But Hagar misunderstood the way the world is run. Those who have an easy life are not the ones who are close to G-d; it is usually precisely the opposite. Who, after all, but the children of Israel – the nation closest to G-d – have suffered the most pain in this world? Who but the children of Israel is the lamb that has been surrounded by seventy wolves throughout the centuries? Don't we often see holy and pure people undergoing severe trials and troubles?[139] Don't we often see arrogant people apparently gliding through life without a problem?

Great rabbis have discussed for millennia the question of why apparently "bad" things happen to good people and why apparently "good" things happen to evil people. How can we explain that? Moses had difficulty understanding this phenomenon, and asked G-d to explain it to him.[140] This is a subject that in itself requires many books. Suffice it to say here that the complete picture of our lives can only be comprehended by understanding that there is a spiritual world from which our souls come and to which they will return. One who looks at the material world alone does not see the complete picture. The reward for righteousness and the punishment for evil are not seen until the soul has re-entered the spiritual realm.

Hagar did not see the whole picture. She interpreted her success in childbearing as an indication that G-d favored her over Sarah.[141]

We cannot take someone's apparent success as an indication of whether or not that person is blessed. We do not know. If someone is elected president of the United States or General Motors it is not necessarily a sign of G-d's blessing.[142] As we said, sometimes the most righteous people have the least apparent success and the evil ones have the most.

Hagar made a basic mistake when she assumed that Sarah was not blessed by G-d. That emboldened her, and her boldness has been passed down through the generations.[143] Her descendants continue to make this mistake to this very day, assuming that apparent success in numbers, in violence, in hatred of Israel and in arrogance indicates that they are blessed by G-d.

There were to be three generations of patriarchs and matriarchs: Abraham and Sarah; Isaac and Rebecca; Jacob, Rachel and Leah. In each of these generations, besides adding their own heroic values, our progenitors worked to remove impurities from our collective national personality in order to prepare us to become a nation of G-d. Theirs was an awesome responsibility.

In the first generation, Abraham had already made his choice. He separated himself from idolatry and responded to the call of G-d: *"Go from your land, from your relatives and from your father's house to the land that I will show you. And I will make of you a great nation; I will bless you and make your name great, and you shall be a blessing."*[144]

In the second generation, the corruption found in Ishmael was removed from the national personality because Ishmael was bypassed and G-d told Abraham, *"I will maintain My covenant through Isaac whom Sarah will bear to you at this appointed time next year."*[145]

In the third generation, the corruption found in Esau was removed because Jacob became the recipient of the covenant. Furthermore, Esau spurned his birthright[146] and Isaac later blessed Jacob.[147]

The children of the following generation, the progenitors of the Twelve Tribes of Israel, were – as a result – purged of these character flaws from the inception of their lives, and refined and dedicated as a priestly kingdom.[148]

There is, however, a crucial difference between Ishmael and Esau. Ishmael had a different mother than Isaac; they were half brothers. But Esau and Jacob had the same mother; they were twins. In Torah Law, the mother's nationality determines the child's nationality. Ishmael inherited the characteristics of his Egyptian mother, but Esau, the son of Isaac and Rebecca, had the potential of being part of the lineage of the servants of G-d. He did not make it, but he could have.

Ishmael embodied a totally foreign ingredient that was antithetical to the service of G-d. His mother, after all, came from Egypt, the home of black magic and sorcery. Now, as I write this book, the contention between Ishmael and Isaac (the Moslems and the Jews), which began at the very inception of the history of Israel, is reasserting itself at the culmination of our history. The chapters that were opened then are being closed now. The troubles that started at the beginning of our history are now coming to a final resolution. It seems that the last trouble is the first trouble, and that is the trouble between Isaac and Ishmael.

Where did it start? Why did it start?

Abraham's father Terach, although a descendant of Shem and a bearer of the tradition of Adam, himself had impurities, which had to be filtered out of the children of Abraham. Terach was a practitioner of idol worship.

Ishmael clearly had alien traits "built in" to his psyche through his mother, who came from Egypt, the hotbed of materialistic excess and perverse worship.[149]

Ishmael is described as "pe-re adam,"[150] a "wild ass of a man," a combination of animal and man. According to our sages, what sets man apart from all other creatures is the ability to speak. Man is called a "speaking soul"[151]; no other creation is capable of speaking. Because of Ishmael's nature, his articulateness is impaired.[152] He tends to act without explanation and his actions are often beyond description. The attack upon the World Trade Center was an act that defies words.*

The ability to speak articulately affects a person's behavior.

Imagine a child having a tantrum; he did not get what he wanted. He will cry hysterically and act irrational, perhaps hurting himself. Imagine an adult so angry that he becomes inarticulate. He will smash his fist on a table, or break a window. Inability to express oneself clearly can lead to anger, which often results in violence. On the other hand, when man uses his power of speech to come closer to G-d, he eliminates anger from

---

* Significantly, one television anchorman's words at the moment the first tower collapsed were, "there are no words."

the world and increases peace. True power in the world comes through speech. That is why King David said, *"some [fight] with chariots and some with horses, but we [call out] in the Name of our G-d."*[153] Our power comes from holy and pure speech.

Some said, after the events of September 11, 2001, that if the great Torah sage Rabbi Avraham Pam – who had passed away in New York several weeks before the attack – had still been alive, his presence might have prevented the tragedy. How could that be? Torah sages protect the world. Words of purity flow from their mouths, bringing peace into the world.[154]

It is our job to try to emulate our Torah sages. The Jews are called "people of the Book." Our prophets have bequeathed a written legacy that is the source of the entire world's knowledge of G-d. We are the children of men who spoke and wrote G-d's words. Words are the most powerful force in the world; after all, G-d created the world with words!

Pure words protect and elevate the world; impure words endanger the world. Our destiny depends on words. Words emanating from G-d, like the Bible and the Oral Law upon which Jewish life has been based since Mount Sinai, increase blessing and bring light into the world. Words emanating from men who are rebelling against G-d bring darkness into the world.

"Sarah saw [Ishmael], the son of Hagar, the Egyptian…mocking."[155]

Our Sages tell us that "mocking" means violence and bloodshed. *"Ishmael said to Isaac, 'Let us go and see our portions in the field.' Then Ishmael would take a bow and arrow and shoot them in Isaac's direction, while pretending to be playing.'"* Ishmael pretended to play, but his game was murder!

Ishmael's murderous desires go back to his very earliest origin, and that is why our Mother Sarah told our Father Abraham, *"Drive out this slave-woman with her son, for the son of that slave-woman shall not inherit with my son, with Isaac."*[156] Thirty six hundred years ago, Sarah perceived Ishmael's nature and expelled him from her home. Immediately after this, G-d told Abraham, *"Whatever Sarah tells you, heed her voice, since through Isaac will offspring be considered yours."*[157]

This is the passage in which the Torah states that the legacy of Abraham goes through Isaac and not Ishmael, and that legacy of course includes the deed to the Land of Israel for his descendants for all time.

Why did Ishmael want to kill Isaac? The question is timely, because Ishmael's descendants, the Arab nations, are living the obsession that began thousands of years ago when Ishmael and Isaac were young. His jealousy against Isaac caused Sarah to expel him and Hagar from their home in order to save the life of Isaac, as we described above. Ishmael has never forgotten that, but he brought it upon himself. As the Torah describes him, *"his hand [shall be] against everyone, and everyone's hand against him."*[158]

His grievance has been carried through the centuries. To this day Arab children from their earliest years are trained to hate their half-brothers and sisters, the children of Abraham, Isaac and Jacob.

Our society teaches us that facts influence thought. In other words, if you read the newspaper every day, you will supposedly be able to form opinions based on the "facts" and then act accordingly. But human beings do not really act like that. The Biblical Pharaoh, always a classic example, saw the facts (that his country was being destroyed by the Ten Plagues) with his own eyes, but his hatred of the children of Israel distorted his perception of reality, and so he refused to acknowledge the facts.

The Bible warns, do not *"follow after your heart ... after which you stray."*[159] In other words, do not let your desires distort your perception of reality.

The children of Ishmael have invented a scenario to justify the fantasy that they are the recipients of the spiritual heritage of our Father Abraham. Let us examine, for example, their claim that the child brought to the *"binding of Isaac"*[160] was not Isaac at all, but Ishmael.

This is clearly impossible. How do we know? The same Bible that tells us there was a *"binding"* in the first place goes to great lengths to state explicitly that Isaac was the one who was bound.[161] Secondly, the Bible also explicitly says (as we stated above), *"through Isaac will offspring be considered yours,"* Isaac and not Ishmael!

Even if the Moslems were correct in saying that Abraham brought Ishmael and not Isaac up to the *"binding of Isaac,"* why did it take them twenty three hundred years to say so?

The binding of Isaac occurred in the year 2085 from Creation. The founding of Islam occurred approximately 2297 years later! If the children of Ishmael are correct about this, then why did no one say anything for twenty-three centuries? This is what is called "re-writing history." It is like telling someone who lived through Auschwitz that there was no Holocaust.

There is clearly no way to believe that Ishmael is Abraham's spiritual or legal heir. If you want to try to rewrite your uncle's will so you will inherit his estate, you had better be sure no one else has an authentic copy of the original. But in this case, the entire world had read "the will" since the time thousands of years earlier when it had been promulgated at Mount Sinai.

Is it not amazing that Mount Moriah, the site at which Isaac was bound, is the subject of the original dispute between the children of Ishmael and the children of Isaac? It is amazing because the center of our contemporary conflict between the children of Ishmael the children of Isaac is that very same mountain (which is today called the Temple Mount, the site of our Holy Temple)![162] From this we can readily understand that the origin of the present conflict can only be understood with reference to the earliest origins of the conflict between Ishmael and Isaac.

The Temple Mount, Mount Moriah: the same place.

The children of Isaac and the children of Ishmael: the same players.

Who is the legitimate heir of Abraham? The same question!

It is clear when you see this behavior why Mother Sarah was so anxious to have Ishmael removed from her household, a household in which Isaac was to be raised in purity with the aim of ending mankind's rebellion against G-d and restoring tranquility to the world.

As we said above, the Torah clearly states that the lineage of the servants of G-d goes through Isaac and not through Ishmael. The Arab peoples have a legacy, but it should not be confused with our legacy. Their claim to the spiritual heritage of Abraham and the geographical heritage of the Land of Israel is based on falsehood.

We say to the children of Ishmael: by all means, live out your heritage! You are our cousins, the children of Abraham.

But you are NOT the children of Isaac and Jacob, nor are you the children of Sarah, Rebecca, Rachel and Leah.

You are NOT the Nation to whom G-d spoke directly at Mount Sinai.

You were NOT given the Deed to the Land of Israel!

The children of Israel do not attempt to deny to any nation the right to their heritage. It is rather they who try to deny us the right to our heritage!

This has been our struggle for over two thousand years!

THE SECOND GENERATION:
THE CHALLENGE OF ESAU

And what of Esau? What about the next generation (i.e. Esau and Jacob)? From Esau, whose name is also Edom,* came Rome. Rome destroyed the Second Temple and sent us into the exile that has lasted almost two thousand years to this day. Rome, in the name of the religion that grew up in that city, claims that its adherents are the "new Jews," and that the covenant G-d made with the children of Israel has been transferred to them. In other words, the heirs of Esau (who rejected his "birth-right" when he sold it[163] to Jacob for those red lentils) have for two thousand years been trying to claim what their ancestor rejected. The children of Israel have been struggling for millennia with the children of Esau. The children of Esau have perpetrated against us the greatest crimes of any nation in history, with the Holocaust of the Twentieth Century as its culmination. *May G-d spare us from any more troubles!*

We have already seen that Ishmael did not receive the spiritual heritage of Abraham, but what about Esau?

Esau as the twin of Jacob obviously descends from the same parents. As we said above, that already distinguishes him from Ishmael, who had a different mother than Isaac. You might think that because Esau and Jacob are twins, they would be close friends, but everyone knows how terrible fights can be within the family. It is a historical truism that *"Esau hates Jacob."*[164]

What is bothering Esau?

Esau is angry at himself and he is taking it out on us. As we have noted, he rejected the blessings that could have accompa-

---

* The name Edom is derived from Esau's desire for the "red, red" lentils. The word "red" in Hebrew is "adom," from which "edom" is derived. The Bible states, "he therefore called his name Edom." (Gen. 25:30). From Edom later came the civilization of Rome and what we call the Western world.

nied the birthright. He rejected the spiritual greatness he could have inherited as the son of Isaac and Rebecca. He was different from his brother; nevertheless a blessing was awaiting him. But literally from their conception, Jacob and Esau fought. Jacob's entire personality was focused on achieving closeness to G-d. Esau desired the things of this world, not the G-d Who created it.

Esau knew he had made one of the great mistakes in history. *"When Esau heard his father's words [that he had already blessed Jacob], he cried out an exceedingly great and bitter cry, and said to his father, 'Bless me too, Father!'"*[165]

Esau is still crying out, *"Bless me too, Father!"* But he himself had given those blessings away through his desire for the material world. His desires had overcome him. And now Esau wants his brother Jacob to pay for his own mistake!

The Talmud tells us that in the day when G-d will destroy the evil inclination in the presence of the righteous and the presence of the wicked, the righteous will weep and the wicked will weep. *"To the righteous the evil inclination will appear like a high mountain and to the wicked it will appear like a strand of hair…. The righteous will weep [with gratitude and happiness] and say, 'How were we able to overcome such a high mountain?' and the wicked will weep and say, 'How were we not able to overcome this strand of hair?'"*[166]

Esau looks at his life and he sees what he gave away. He sees how empty and fleeting was the reward he received, how immeasurable the eternal benefits lost by him and received by Jacob. *"Why was I such a fool?"* Now that he sees his fatal error, he wants to undo what can never be undone, so he tries to rewrite history, to pretend that he never gave it away. He is forever angry that Jacob never lost sight of the Truth. Since Esau has rejected G-d, he is not too bothered by scruples, so he can pretend that he never gave away his spiritual inheritance; he can pretend that Jacob stole it.

When you think about it, the scenario is amazing.

Jacob, who was conceived first,[167] buys his birthright (which was already his by order of conception) in a legal transaction from Esau for the lentils.[168] Then, he is forced to resort to sub-terfuge so that his father Isaac will give him the blessing that is already his by conception and by purchase! And later he has to fight the angel of Esau!

What is going on here? This is the strangest thing in the world. Jacob is forced to fight for something that already belongs to him several times over! Why does he have to fight and then resort to what seems like trickery to possess what is already his? And Jacob is the quintessential man of truth!

Ma'ase avos siman l'banim; the actions of the forefathers are signs for the children.[169] This is the paradigm[170] for the future of the children of Israel; this explains the rest of history.

Why did Jacob have to fight for something that already belonged to him?

Already in the womb the characters of Jacob and Esau were formed and evident. *"The children agitated within her.... And G-d said to her, 'Two nations are in your womb... two regimes from your insides shall be separated.'"*[171] On this verse Rashi comments, *"One [shall be separated] to ... wickedness and one to... flawless-ness."*[172]

Jacob was drawn to G-d; Esau was drawn to the material world and idol worship. Jacob was by destiny and by choice the bearer of the tradition of holiness that began with Adam. Esau was not, but – since he was a trickster – he pretended that he was.

The implications are profound. Jacob, the man of truth, was forced against his will to acquire a reputation as a trickster, a deceiver, one who had to resort to deceit for his status in life!

To this day the children of Israel are characterized as thieves and devious characters. The world says to us, "you are thieves"[173] when we claim our spiritual or geographical birthright. Even in the so-called "civilized" nations we are characterized as Fagins and Shylocks! Over the centuries the rationalization for trying to destroy us has been based on this vicious characterization of the Jew as the evil deviant and mercenary trickster. We, the holy nation,[174] a nation of kings, prophets, and priests, have been portrayed as vermin.

This is the legacy of Esau!

This false characterization of the children of Israel as thieves originated in the very beginning of our history and is the very basis of our relationship with Esau, who became Edom, which is Rome, which became the source for the religious movement that has dominated the Western World for the past two thousand years. The history of those two thousand years – the pogroms, tortures, expulsions and brutality leading up to and including the Holocaust – all originated in that relationship between Jacob and Esau. Because of Esau's subterfuge, Jacob is portrayed as the thief, the deceiver, the Fagin of history, who operates in darkness and steals his blessings from his "innocent, naïve brother."

What is going on here?

The conception and birth of Jacob and Esau is compared to two peas in a tube.[175] The one who entered first comes out last; Jacob entered first and came out second. But who went in first? Jacob went in first; Esau went in second.

What does this mean?

In the hidden world, the world of the spiritual and eternal, the world that we don't see clearly here, Jacob is first.

But in the material world, the world in which you are reading these words, Jacob appears to have been second. His hand was grasping Esau's heel, and so, in this world, Jacob appears attached to the heel. Jacob appears lowly, the one you step on! The world regards us Jews as the bottom in this world.[176]

This episode teaches us the future history of the relationship between the children of Jacob and the children of Esau. The entire Exile through which we have suffered for the past two thousand years is based on Esau's anger at Jacob. The only way Esau can claim his desired – if not deserved – place in the world is to denigrate Jacob and his descendants, to claim that we have no legitimate place or rank in their world. In their eyes, any preeminence, let alone predominance we have in this world is stolen, any rank is undeserved. We are the heel, the thief, the "grasshoppers"! We "deserve" to be pushed down and pushed back ... forever!

The relationship between Jacob and Esau is prophecy.

They say that we lost the covenant and they are the new Jews. Why? Because to them we are the deceivers; whatever we have, we stole. We are like Abel was to Cain after their "bargain"; nothing Abel could do gave him any legitimacy.

Of course Esau is very upset at himself, because he would have had a blessing from Isaac, regardless of the fact that his spiritual status was below that of Jacob. But even that secondary status he relinquished. He relinquished his claim to the world to come and in the end he lost even his claim to this world. Of course he didn't want the spiritual world. But he pretended that he did, because he does not want to cede anything to Jacob.[177]

Then what does he want? He wants to be able to claim in this world that "I believe in the world to come." He is not interested in the world to come, but he wants to pretend that he is interested in the world to come! He wants to able to say "I am number one in the spiritual world and number one in the material world." He has released his claim to the eternal world, but in this world he wants to say that he did not release it! His entire claim is a fabrication.

What did Jacob really receive when he bought back his own birthright and received the blessing from Isaac? The blessing from Isaac is for this world and not the next world! Jacob had the world to come to begin with. The only question concerns this world. Who has this world? That is what the fight is about. All that he was purchasing and the whole blessing he received from his father Isaac concerns this world.

Why did Jacob care about this world? Why should a man who dwells constantly in the tents of Torah care about this world?[178]

I think that this profound question goes to the very heart of what it means to be a child of Israel and to adhere to the tradition that begins with the creation of Adam in the Garden of Eden. This is the difference between the Jew and the rest of the world. There is no way of life that resembles the Torah way of life.

How is Jacob unique?

While Jacob's eyes are on the World to Come, his feet are on the material ground of this world.* He understands that there is only one way to gain entry into the next world, and that is by his actions in this world. That is why G-d gave us rules, Torah, for this world. That is why Abraham, Isaac and Jacob had to find the Torah, because the Torah contains the guidelines for the path from this world to the Next World.[179] Once we discover G-d, we need the Torah to get to Him.

Esau's ceaseless effort is to try to block Jacob's access to the World to Come by attempting to block his path in this world. If Jacob cannot walk along the path to the World to Come, which

---

* Jacob's bridging of two worlds is symbolized by the ladder in his dream (Genesis 28:12), the feet of which were on the ground and the top in the heavens.

passes through this world, then his entry into that world is threatened.

And so, when Esau's appetite overcomes his reason, and he sells to Jacob his claim to priority in this world, he has reason to hate himself and curse his own weakness, which caused him to lose sight of his quest to destroy his brother. His own desire for material satisfaction has caused him to lose his mastery of this material world. But although he had sold his birthright and his mastery of this world, Esau is not content to abide by the bargain he himself had made. Esau, who will later accuse Jacob of being a deceiver, in his anger at himself, pretends that he had not in fact made the bargain. He wants Jacob's blessings, even though he had already sold his right to those blessings. It may seem that Jacob is a deceiver, and Jacob resists the role, but Esau has forced him into the role by rejecting the bargain he himself had freely agreed to.

Esau goes for Jacob's blessings[180] and Jacob is forced to defend what he already possesses. That is the pattern for two thousand years of history: Esau attacks the children of Jacob and then blames us for defending ourselves! Esau denies that he sold his birthright and forces Jacob to resort to subterfuge to claim what is already his!

And Isaac? What part does their father play in this? When the Torah says that Isaac was blind[181], it would seem to indicate that he did not see the deceit in Esau because he desired to see him as better than he was, he closed his eyes to Esau's true nature. Isaac wanted Esau to sanctify G-d by using the things of this world to glorify Him. Jacob, on the other hand, was focused entirely on spiritual matters; his attention was focused on the Next World. Between them could have arisen a symbiosis of brotherly accomplishment similar to that of Issachar and Zevulun[182] in the next generation. But this plan was spoiled by Esau's hatred. If Esau had followed his father's plan, then the truism

"Esau hates Jacob"[183] would never have materialized; the two brothers would have lived in an eternal relationship of mutual harmony. World history would have been totally different.

But Rebecca knew Esau's nature; she had borne the pain of his personality in her womb before anyone else understood who he was.[184] She saw his passion for idolatry and his earthy selfishness. He did not want anything left over for anyone else; he wanted that "red, red food" for himself alone.

So Rebecca, with her intuitive wisdom, caused her son Jacob to respond to the threat from Esau in the only way he could, by resorting to Esau's own treacherous tactics. I am reminded of the saying: "There may come a day when we can forgive the Arabs for killing us, but we can never forgive them for forcing us to kill them." Can we ever forgive Esau for forcing us to become like him, forcing us to kill, even in self-defense?

Maase avos siman l'banim: the actions of the forefathers foreshadow the destiny of their children.

When the angel of Esau attacks Jacob,[185] the conflict foreshadows the exile that has engulfed the children of Israel for the past two thousand years. When does the angel attack? At night, which represents the material world, the world in which we cannot see reality. The fight ends only at dawn.

THE NEXT GENERATION: THE TWELVE TRIBES

How do we distinguish the generation of the twelve sons of Jacob from the two preceding generations? In the preceding generations brother tried to kill brother: Ishmael tried to kill Isaac and Esau tried to kill Jacob.* Joseph's brothers tried to kill

---

* Please note the remarkable fact that Isaac never tried to kill Ishmael and Jacob never tried to kill Esau. This is also a model for history. In every succeeding generation, as our enemies have tried to kill us, we have never been guilty of trying to kill them except against our will in the process of defending ourselves.

Joseph, and yet the Torah regards this generation – all twelve brothers – as the legitimate bearers of the holy tradition beginning with Adam. How are they different from Ishmael and Esau? If Ishmael and Esau are disqualified from carrying on the thread of holiness throughout the generations, how could it be that the brothers who tried to kill Joseph are qualified?

There is a passage in the Book of Joshua that is so lucid in its clarity on this point that it has been incorporated into the Passover *Haggadah*, where we read it every year. Joshua is reviewing with the children of Israel their entire history

"Thus said... the G-d of Israel: 'Your forefathers – Terach, the father of Abraham and the father of Nahor – always dwelt beyond the [Euphrates] River and they served other gods. But I took your forefather Abraham from beyond the River and led him throughout all the land of Canaan; I increased his offspring and I gave him Isaac. To Isaac I gave Jacob and Esau. To Esau I gave Mount Seir to inherit, and Jacob and his sons went down to Egypt.'"[186]

Then G-d makes it clear that "Jacob and his sons" are the recipients of His special destiny to carry forward the knowledge of His existence and represent Him in this world. Esau has been given "Mount Seir." Jacob, by contrast, has been given the Spiritual Tradition, the responsibility to represent G-d in this world, which he had inherited by conception and by nature and which was then ratified by "purchase" of the birthright from Esau (that did not belong to Esau in the first place) and for which Jacob later fought against the angel of Esau.

The Maharal of Prague[187] makes the following comment on the passage from the Book of Joshua quoted above, which puts the entire process in perspective: *"By taking this narrative through three generations, [the Torah wanted to show through] Joshua ... that G-d winnowed Israel, as it were, until it was completely worthy to be His chosen people. He chose Abraham over*

Terach and Nachor; he chose Isaac over Ishmael; he chose Jacob over Esau. Having made these three choices to arrive at the designation of Jacob, G-d's process of selection was complete, and all of Jacob's offspring were holy and worthy."[188]

Now we will be able to understand how the passage from Joshua could go on to describe Israel's continuing history under the leadership of Moses and Joshua, culminating with its entry into the Land of Israel. It will be clear from this that the Twelve Tribes, the children of Israel, are in G-d's eyes the intended recipients of the Spiritual Tradition, the ones to whom the Torah is directly addressed and the recipients of the right to dwell in the Land of Israel.

"I sent Moses and Aaron, and I plagued Egypt with all that I did in their midst, and afterwards I brought you out. I brought your forefathers out of Egypt and you arrived at the sea. The Egyptians pursued your forefathers with chariot and horsemen to the Sea of Reeds. They cried out to G-d and He placed darkness between you and the Egyptians and brought the sea upon them and covered them – your own eyes saw what I did with the Egyptians – and then you dwelled in the Wilderness for many years. I brought you to the land of the Amorite, who dwelled across the Jordan, and they battled with you, but I delivered them into your hand and you inherited their land; I destroyed them from before you. Then Balak the son of Zippor, king of Moab, arose and battled against Israel. He sent and summoned Balaam son of Beor to curse you, but I refused to listen to Balaam, and he pronounced a blessing upon you; thus I rescued you from this power. Then you crossed the Jordan and came to Jericho. The inhabitants of Jericho battled against you – and Amorite and the Perizzite and Canaanite and Hittite and the Girgashite, the Hivvite and the Jebusite – and I delivered them into your hand. I sent the hornet-swarm ahead of you, and it drove them out before you – the two kings of the Amorite – not by your sword and not by

your bow. I gave you a land... vineyards and olive groves...."[189]

Although the brothers fought and were punished by the resulting division among the family and the descent into Egyptian Exile, (and although we are still being punished because we are still fighting), it is vital to keep in mind that we are still one family. All the children of Israel are bearers of the thread of spirituality. The proof is that all of us, in the persons of our ancestors, the Tribal Patriarchs, gathered around our Father Jacob as he was about to leave this world.[190]

We all received his blessing, each different, according to our particular abilities, but all together forming a unified whole. Despite our disunity and dispersion over the centuries, we twelve tribes are one, and each of us has a particular attribute to contribute to the unity of Israel. G-d signified our unity and our common destiny by sending us spiritual leaders (Moses and Joshua), Priests and High Priests (Aaron and his sons) and kings (David and his sons) and by bringing us as one nation into the Land of Israel.

Despite our stumblings on the long road, our task is to carry G-d's banner as One Family through the ages until our final reunion, reconciliation and return to the Land of Israel in the days of the Messiah.

CHAPTER THREE

IN THE LAND:
MOSES TO KING DAVID

"G-d admonishes the one He loves."[191]

When Moses died and Joshua took over, it seemed that the sun had set and the moon had risen.[192] There was a great change in the life of the children of Israel. Not only was the trusted leader gone, so was the direct relationship with G-d that had sustained and guided the people throughout the final years in Egypt and the Desert years. The light that illuminated our way had become reflected light, not the direct light we had enjoyed before we crossed the Jordan River.

This change had been foreshadowed at Mount Sinai when the children of Israel asked G-d to stop speaking directly to them after the first two commandments. They could not tolerate hearing the voice of G-d directly![193] They asked instead that Moses act as an intermediary.

Not only was Moses gone. The Pillar of Fire and the Pillar of Cloud were gone! The manna and Miriam's well were gone! Joshua had become the leader, but of course things would not be the same as they had been before.

The Presence of G-d was removed somewhat more from us.

That has been, generally speaking, the story of every generation since the Garden of Eden, and the story of the children of Israel since Mount Sinai. With each passing generation, the presence of G-d is hidden a little more. At first we stood at Mount Sinai with Moses, and then, as we entered the Land of Israel under the leadership of Joshua, evidence of G-d's presence was not as visible, so we built a Tabernacle and then a Temple where His presence would come to meet us. But even then we began to stray, spiritually and physically. The Temple was destroyed and we went into exile in Babylon. After several decades, G-d allowed us to build a new Temple, but it was not the same as the first, and many Jews remained in Babylon. Then other nations invaded our Land and the Second Temple was destroyed. We were sent into exile around the world, and the presence of G-d became even more distant to us. Would we survive as a nation?

Even in the Desert, the visible presence of G-d and His servant Moses had not been enough to guarantee our loyalty to the Torah. The Covenant is eternal, but Moses had made it clear that the road ahead would not be smooth.[194] *"I know that after my death you will surely act corruptly and you will stray from the path that I have commanded you, and evil will befall you at the end of days, if you do what is evil in the eyes of G-d, to anger Him…"*[195]

There is no other nation in the history of the world whose apparent shortcomings have been documented with such utter clarity and subjected to such universal scrutiny. The Bible does not hold anything back; the prophets do not hold anything back; the rabbis of the Talmud and throughout subsequent Jewish history do not hold anything back. But the Author of the

Bible, the prophets and the rabbis are our friends! When they reveal our shortcomings it is only to correct us with love and keep us on the right path.

When the nations of the world discuss our shortcomings, however, it is from a different point of view altogether. In order to justify their constant, murderous attacks upon us, they try to demonstrate that we are morally decadent. Whether it be the Roman legions, the Crusaders, the Cossacks, the Inquisition, the Nazis, the Communists or the Arabs, there has never been since Mount Sinai a reluctance on the part of others to point out the "corruption" of the children of Israel.

And so, when we entered the Land of Israel under Joshua, when the "sun" of Moses had set for us, and the Clouds of Glory and Clouds of Fire that had accompanied us for forty years were left behind on the other side of the Jordan River, we were suddenly in a radically new situation. Of course there was plenty of food in the Land of Israel, but we were used to manna falling from heaven! How would we eat? How would the Torah work in a "normal" land? How would we survive? Were we up to the challenge?

The tests we faced were of a different nature than we had ever faced before. We had spent forty years in the Desert learning G-d's plan for us; now we were going to put it into practice in the Land of our destiny.

THE JUDGED NATION

Throughout the Book of Judges we hear the refrain, *"the children of Israel did what was evil in the eyes of G-d and they forgot G-d."*[196]

Nations of the world, do you weigh us in the balance? Do you judge us?

This is a vital question, because for the last two thousand years the nations of the world have acted as our prosecutors, judges and executioners. To this very day they are zealous to carry out "strict justice" when it comes to the remnants of the children of Israel. The entire belief system that emerged in Rome two thousand years ago is based on the assumption that "because of our sins" we have been removed from our special relationship with G-d and replaced by the Church of Rome.

What in fact does it mean that our sins are spelled out so clearly in the Torah? Are we sinners? Are we guilty?

Please, my friends, open your hearts and think about this question.

Who, in fact, ponders the question whether he is a sinner?

Who asks such a question, an evil person or a good person?

Rebbetzin Esther Jungreis often tells the story of the woman who said, "My only fault is that I am too good!"

How does one determine who is a good Jew?

The person who says, "I am not a good enough Jew" is likely to be a good Jew. Certainly he or she is likely to be trying to be a good Jew. But be careful of the one who says, "I am a good Jew."

G-d's curse upon the snake in the Garden of Eden consists of these remarkable words: *"Because you have done this, you are accursed beyond all the … beasts of the field: upon your belly shall you go and dust shall you eat all the days of your life."*[197]

Why is this a curse?[198] The snake seems so fortunate! He never has to search for food; dust is ubiquitous. We, in contrast, constantly search for food! We seem to be suffering from a curse: *"Through suffering shall you eat… By the sweat of your brow…."*[199]

Who is better off? Shouldn't we envy the snake?

The snake's curse is worst. We humans have to work constantly for food and the money to buy it. If we are smart we also never stop beseeching G-d for His help. And that keeps us in constant touch with G-d. But G-d does not want to hear from the snake ever again! He doesn't want to know the snake!

After eating we say, *"Blessed are you, G-d, Who creates numerous living things with their deficiencies; for all that You have created with which to maintain the life of every being..."*

Why bless G-d for our deficiencies? Unbelievable! What is praiseworthy about deficiencies?

Our deficiencies cause us to realize that in order to be complete in this world we need to attach ourselves to G-d. We ourselves are nothing; recognition of our deficiencies enables us to survive. Those who do not recognize that they have deficiencies are like the snake, who thinks he can live without G-d. He is hopeless, and so are those people who, like the snake, think that they are complete in themselves and that they do not need G-d. The snake has wasted his life in this world, because for him there is no other world. He eats his dust here without gratitude or recognition of the G-d Who provides it. At the end, he will return to the dust, but dust is all he is. There is nothing eternal about him.

Pharaoh believed he was G-d, that he had created himself! [200] That is why his kingdom had to fall. Errors eventually collapse of their own weight.

But we children of Israel are not permitted to believe in illusions. G-d is close to us, so he favors us with constant correction, as a father constantly corrects a beloved son. *"G-d admonishes the one He loves."* [201] Therefore, we are criticized constantly in the Torah!

Fortunate are we! *"Praiseworthy are those who dwell in Your house... Praiseworthy is the man whose [heart focuses] on the path leading upwards."* [202]

The man who recognizes his deficiencies can grow. He is a man of truth. A righteous man is not always right, but he wants to know when he is wrong. Only that way can he keep on trying to be right.

We children of Israel have been given the privilege of being especially close to G-d, of being taught the "upward path." We don't ask to be fooled like the snake or Pharaoh into thinking that we are complete unto ourselves. We want to improve ourselves; for that we need to see reality. Our "lessons" have been conducted in full view of the world so that later generations may be educated by our experiences in learning to follow the upward path.

When the rest of the world reads the Biblical descriptions of the children of Israel, its reaction should be, "I should scrutinize my own behavior; it is certainly no better than that of the children of Israel. If G-d finds fault with them then how can I justify my deeds and thoughts? I must improve myself."

Is there another example like this in history? Is there another nation whose soul has been bared to the world in order to show the upward path to all mankind? Is there another nation who could tolerate that? By our willingness to be corrected in public we have shown the entire world the path of closeness with G-d. What do we get in return? Instead of thanks, which should flow to us in endless streams, we receive streams of condemnation, hatred and scorn, leading to violence.

Nations of the world, wake up! If you continue to hate the children of Israel, your end will be like that of the snake and Pharaoh. You will drown in your arrogance.

If on the other hand you appreciate our role in the world and you honor us for the blessings we have brought to you, you will receive the blessings promised by G-d to Abraham: *"Those who bless you I will bless …"*[203]

ISRAEL'S KING

The Book of Judges ends with the words *"in those days there was no king in Israel; a man would do whatever seemed proper in his eyes."*[204] The idea behind monarchy is that a king should set and enforce an example of proper behavior. In the contemporary world, the concept of monarchy is discredited. There are no real kings. Today's few kings or queens occupy hollow thrones, with at most ceremonial power. Buckingham Palace, for example, is a pageant, an anachronism, a tourist attraction like Colonial Williamsburg. There may be some despots who call themselves king, but no powerful hereditary monarchs.

So we have a great deal of trouble comprehending the idea of majesty. In our world, everyone believes he is king. As a result men do whatever seems proper in their eyes.

I recall reading an article by a famous rabbi on the subject of monarchy in our contemporary world. According to this article, the very concept of monarchy is not welcome in today's world. Our world accepts the concept of democracy, the "wisdom" of the people, as the highest form of government. No matter that "the people" have no inherent wisdom! Certainly there is no guarantee of any greater wisdom among "the people" than in a monarch. But government by a hereditary monarch is not just considered archaic. It is more than that. Acceptance of a monarch is akin to acceptance of G-d. If we accept the concept of absolute rule of a king then we can also accept the concept of absolute rule of G-d over us. Rejection of the idea of a king also implies rejection of the idea of the King of kings!

In today's world we are conditioned to think that we make the rules. Our goals are "life, liberty and the pursuit of happiness." I am my own boss; I make the rules; no king is going to rule over me, and that includes G-d! That is the modern world, and that is why we do not WANT to accept any higher power over us; we are not prepared to accept a higher power. And so, the concept of monarchy is passé in today's world because the concept of submission to G-d is passé in today's world.

This is a background to the subject of monarchy in the Bible. Classically, the children of Israel are not afraid to admit our human weaknesses. We know that to reach the highest possible level of submission to our Father in Heaven, we need help on earth; we need a leader who will elevate us. Therefore, we desire a monarch in order to reach the ideal state of unity among ourselves and submission to the King of kings.

There is a commandment, *"You shall surely set over yourself a king, whom your G-d chooses. From among your brethren you shall set a king over yourself."*[205]

But isn't monarchy inherently cruel and despotic?

As we said above, the contemporary world looks down its nose at the concept of monarchy as passé, anachronistic. The American and French Revolutions marked a turning point in the attitude of the Western World. But in the post 9/11 era, as we are once again being forced to rethink all our assumptions, it would be wise to try to understand the meaning of *"malchus,"* royalty, because that in fact is how the universe is structured. There is a King in the universe, an absolute Ruler.

We have to ask ourselves: Is the concept of monarchy absurd or are we absurdly out of touch with reality?

If there is a King in heaven, why should earth not reflect heaven?

There is an implicit debate in the Torah concerning monarchy.

"It was wrong in Samuel's eyes that [the people] said, 'Give us a king to judge us.'"[206] G-d replies to Samuel's hesitancy, *"Listen to the voice of the people... for it is not you they have rejected, but it is Me*

whom they have rejected from reigning over them."[207] The people
"*refused to listen to the voice of Samuel. They said, 'No! There shall
be a king over us, and we will be like all the other nations; our king
will judge us and go forth before us and fight our wars.*"[208]

But this exactly illustrates my point. Samuel was not wrong.
Here the people of Israel wanted a king "like all the other
nations," and their first king was Saul, whose reign failed
because he listened to the voice of the people and not the voice
of G-d.[209] As Samuel said to him, "*Though you may be small in
your own eyes, you are the head of the tribes of Israel, and G-d has
anointed you to be king over Israel.*"[210] Samuel further states, "*G-d
would have established your kingdom over Israel forever [if you had
observed what G-d commanded you].*"[211]

Here we seem to have the Biblical viewpoint on democracy!
This indicates its inherent weakness. The only means to bring
about a perfect society is to find a leader who will subordinate
himself to G-d and His prophets, not to the voice of the people.
As Samuel says to Saul, "*G-d has sought a man after His own heart
and appointed him as ruler over His people,*"[212] and that of course
was King David, the progenitor of the eternal monarchy of
Israel.

It may be Israel's weakness that we need a king, just as it was
our weakness that we could not bear to hear G-d's voice directly at Mount Sinai. But our strength is that we admit our weaknesses! That is, after all, why we need the Torah. Angels don't
need the Torah because they are already perfect. But we, who
are not perfect, do need the Torah. It is to our credit that we
desire it in order to perfect ourselves. So we need a king to help
us on this path, but the king must be selected in order to achieve
these Torah goals, and we must not try to be "like all the other
nations." The Torah ideal is that the children of Israel should
live in the Land of Israel, with a Temple presided over by a High

Priest, a court system through which Torah law is enforced, and a king over us, to ensure our national unity and adherence to a Torah lifestyle in every detail.

We are suffering because we don't have it.

"In those days there was no king in Israel; a man would do whatever seemed proper in his eyes."[213]

Acceptance of a king and the acceptance of G-d's sovereignty go hand in hand. In contemporary society, where we emphasize freedom to do *"whatever seems proper in our eyes,"* we justify rebellion both against G-d and against the idea of an earthly monarch.

Monarchy is not intrinsically less fair than democracy; there is no guarantee that "the people" will be less despotic, cruel or amoral than a king. Very interesting words on this subject were uttered a century ago by Sir Winston Churchill, then a young member of Parliament: "In former days when wars arose from individual causes, from the policy of a Minister or the passion of a King, when they were fought by small regular armies of professional soldiers, and when their course was retarded by the difficulties of communication and supply, and often suspended by the winter season, it was possible to limit the liabilities of the combatants. But now, when mighty populations are impelled on each other, each individual severally embittered and inflamed – when the resources of science and civilization sweep away everything that might mitigate their fury, a ... war can only end in the ruin of the vanquished and scarcely less fatal dislocation and exhaustion of the conquerors. Democracy is more vindictive than Cabinets. The wars of peoples will be more terrible than those of kings."[214]

The King of Israel must subordinate himself to the Torah. *"It shall be that when he sits on the throne of his kingdom, he shall write for himself two copies of this Torah in a book... It shall be with him, and he shall read from it all the days of his life, so that he will learn to fear his G-d, to observe all the words of this Torah and these decrees, to perform them, so that his heart does not become haughty over his brethren and not turn from the commandment right or left, so that he will prolong years over his kingdom, he and his sons amid Israel."*[215]

The law for all Jews is that we bow four times during the Shemoneh Esrei prayer.[216] But the king must bow during the entire prayer! His temptation to haughtiness is that much greater, so his effort at subordination must be that much stronger.

We could ask why contemporary people resist becoming religious. The answer in general is that we do not want to subordinate ourselves to G-d or limit our freedom in any way. The world now believes that "all men are entitled to life, liberty and the pursuit of happiness." We live in the "land of the brave and the home of the free." The ideal is to live life in whatever way we choose, and the test of correctness is "just as long as you are happy."

That is not the ideal of a religious person. Moses is referred to as a "servant of G-d," and he was the greatest person who ever lived. The highest level is to be a servant! One must, however, be very careful to choose the right master!

Contemporary society has rationalized its rebellion against G-d by postulating a mechanical world in which G-d does not exist. We say that the world started with a "big bang," but we do not want to think about Who set off the bang. We postulate the evolution of species, not because we believe it, but because if it were not true, we would have to acknowledge that G-d created us, and that would necessitate subservience on our part. The Theory of Evolution is an attempt to postulate a world in which G-d cannot exist. If species would indeed have developed by mechanical means from an origin that was entirely mechanical, there would be no place (and no need) for G-d. If there were no place for G-d, then we would be "free." There would be no commandments from Above to bind us; we could do "whatever seems proper" in our eyes.

That is our contemporary world! No wonder that it seems like a mechanical world, a world without a heart. That is the world we have "constructed" out of our desire to escape from G-d.

"In those days there was no king in Israel; a man would do whatever seemed proper in his eyes."[217]

The scenario painted in the Book of Judges[218] foreshadows our modern world. The children of Israel provide a vital lesson for the rest of the world by showing the terrible pitfalls of living without a king who himself is subordinate to the King of kings. Every detail of Biblical narrative is designed with future generations in mind. If we absorb what the Bible reveals to us then we will be able to prevent needless tragedy and live a life full of the blessings that G-d desires to give us.

The period during which the Judges judged Israel was an era of recurring cycles: weakening of faith leading to strengthening of our enemies until finally a Judge brings us back to our senses. This cycle is broken only by the anointing of the king of Israel in the time of Samuel. This recurring cycle foreshadows the entire period of our current Exile, an era that will end only with the anointing of the Messiah.

After the death of Joshua, there was a leadership vacuum on a national level. No one was able to replace Joshua as the leader of the entire nation. So the nation drifted apart. The strong leadership, common family history and Torah loyalty that had bound the people together since Mount Sinai, began to unravel as internecine struggles broke out among and within the Twelve Tribes.

As the nation drifted apart, the depredations of its enemies became alarming. It is remarkable how conditions in the Land of Israel between the reigns of the individual Judges resemble the conditions in the Land of Israel today!

"The wrath of G-d would flare against Israel… and He would deliver them into the hands of their enemies all around, so that they could no longer stand before their enemies."[219] *A man would go to draw water at the well and never return, a sniper's arrow having pierced his body!*[220] *Even in the days of David, "the Philistines would conduct raids while the Israelites were harvesting their crops. They would kill or capture individual farmers and burn their crops, to starve the Israelites into submission."*[221]

The children of Israel at times during the period of the Judges were forced to live in caves and hideouts to protect themselves from their enemies, who were for practical purposes in control of the Land. One never knew if a loved one would return at the end of the day.

Does this sound familiar? The difference is that in our day the weapons are more powerful and are often detonated by remote control, and the enemies are called "Palestinians" rather than "Philistines."

And then a judge would arise, unite the people and cause them to return to G-d. G-d would strengthen the children of Israel to cleanse the land of the enemy. But after the death of the judge, the people would once again lapse into disunity and rebellion against G-d, opening the way for the next subjugation. Only the emergence of another judge would rescue them and initiate the next cycle in the seemingly endless pattern.

Such has also been the pattern in the thousands of years of our current exile. Periods of darkness and subjugation, caused by rebellion against G-d, have been interspersed with periods of relative peace, as a result of our repentance, in a seemingly endless cycle.

The books of Joshua, Judges and Samuel make it clear that the solution to this apparently endless cycle in Biblical times was the appearance of King David, who founded the eternal monarchy of the Jewish People.

And today, as we dwell in the darkness of another age in which men do whatever seems proper in their eyes, what will allow us to break the cycle? Also a king from the House of Judah, a descendant of King David, who will unite us as a nation and cause us to return to our G-d and His laws and give us permanent relief from our enemies.

The books of Joshua, Judges and Samuel as well as the Prophets who follow are quite clear in their depiction of this scenario. The ancient maxim *"ma-ase avos siman l'banim,"*[222] the actions of the fathers are portents for the children, is demonstrated here. The Torah comes to guide us through life. How are we to know what to do except through the medium of the Torah, that was given to us to indicate what would happen in the future days and how to react to the tests to which we would be subjected?

MA'ASE AVOS SIMAN L'BANIM

The concept of *"ma'ase avos siman l'banim"* enables us to gain insight into our own times. Everything we see in the Bible is going to be played out in history. All events of our day are foreshadowed in the Torah; therefore we can learn how to deal with them by seeing how great people dealt with corresponding events in Biblical times. We can also perhaps know what to expect. The Bible is a massive prophecy of all future history, and we are living that history! If we can understand what the Torah is telling us, then we are in a position to understand the events of the past, present and perhaps even the future.

Let's examine the outlines of the history of Israel with this concept in mind.

There was no "Israel" until our Father Abraham and our Mother Sarah appeared. G-d told Abraham, *"Know with certainty that your offspring shall be aliens in a land not their own and they will serve them, and they will oppress them four hundred years."*[223] Abraham and Sarah gave birth to Isaac. Isaac and Rebecca gave birth to Jacob, whose name was changed to Israel, and from Jacob and his wives descended the children of Israel. After his brothers sold Joseph, he descended into Egypt, where he became the ruler. From that position he saved his family, not just physically, but also spiritually, by reuniting them. After this salvation, however, they lapsed into slavery in the country to which they had been drawn, in fulfillment of G-d's prophecy to Abraham.

The children of Israel were released from slavery 210 years after they had descended to Egypt, when Moses freed them so that they could achieve the spiritual lifestyle for which the Patriarchs and Matriarchs had prepared them.

Then followed forty years in the Desert, a movable yeshiva in which our fathers studied Torah day and night, and absorbed it into their system so that it would remain with their children forever. The Five Books of Moses end at the moment in which the children of Israel are about to cross over the Jordan River into the Land of our Destiny. Just over four hundred years later, David was anointed king over Israel. After his death, the Temple was completed, but David's kingdom was divided, ten tribes were lost, the First Temple was destroyed and Israel went into the Babylonian Exile. Following this, the books of the Bible were completed and the era of prophecy came to a close.

With the completion of the era of prophecy it would seem that the era of *"ma'ase avos siman l'banim"* has come to an end.

In other words, as the Biblical Era is closed and completed, the era of prediction ends, and the era that has been predicted begins. We should then begin to see the events of the Bible replicated in the course of history.

Let's look at the history of Israel from the point of view of its king, because that is what we want to understand right now. We want to understand the meaning of monarchy in Israel. This will have tremendous implications for us in the contemporary world, because we are waiting for the Messiah, and we will only be able to understand the Messiah in terms of the kings of Israel, because the Messiah is a spiritual and physical descendant of the kings of Israel.

TWO LINES OF KINGS, TWO MESSIAHS

Why does Israel need a king?
Who is the king of Israel?

Well, Israel really has two kings. One king is a descendant of the Tribe of Joseph and one from the Tribe of Judah.

Joseph himself was a "king," really the first king of Israel, who reigned as viceroy in Egypt but in effect was the king who saved Egypt as well as his own family. His descendant, Saul, was Israel's first anointed king, and in the end of history the first Messiah will be the Messiah, the son of Joseph.

Judah himself also acted as a king; he led his brothers in the confrontation with Joseph (before Joseph revealed his identity). Judah's descendant, David, became the second anointed king of Israel and is the head of the eternal royal family of Israel, culminating in the Messiah, the son of David, who will reign until the end of time. Jacob blessed Judah as the king of Israel when he said, *"the scepter shall not depart from Judah."*[224]

There is also a third leader of Israel, Moses, from the Tribe of

Levi, although he is known more as the father of all prophets than as a king. But Moses led his people.

What are the differences among Joseph, Moses and David? In what ways do their royalty differ?

Joseph's monarchy arose in direct response to disunity among the brothers. From disunity arose bitterness and from bitterness arose the decision to exile Joseph by selling him into slavery, although the brothers came close to killing him. Joseph became the ruler of a culture that was totally at odds with the culture of the family in which he had been raised. But it was not only miraculous occurrences that propelled Joseph upward; it was self-control to a degree that is almost impossible to comprehend.[225] Joseph, completely alone in a corrupt culture, was able to resist the temptations of Potiphar's wife, and that moral greatness elevated him to a stature that enabled him to rise above Egypt in every way. He rose so high that he alone saw and was able to overcome the impending catastrophe. Like someone standing on the summit of a high mountain, he looked into the distance and saw what nobody else could see. His vision saved his family and it saved Egypt.

Joseph became the prototype leader in exile. One of the great challenges in exile is not assimilating into the surrounding culture. Every other exiled nation has disappeared into the surrounding host culture, but not Israel. We exist today as a discrete people, a minority in every nation. We have survived for that reason.

But although Joseph maintained his spiritual integrity, he was also invisible in Egypt. His brothers sat at his table and did not know him, even though he seated them in age order and obviously had intimate knowledge of them. Joseph had to be invisible to his brothers, because otherwise he would not have been able to guide them toward repentance by seeming to be their adversary. All these details are symbolic revelations of the future of our people: *"ma'ase avos siman l'banim."*

After the death of Joseph, the children of Israel endured slavery until Moses arose to lead them to freedom and Torah. So we see that Joseph was a king in exile. He taught us how to survive in exile, but the precise method of release from exile was taught to us by Moses, from whom we learned to submit ourselves to G-d's laws. Moses brought us out of Egypt to become G-d's nation at Mount Sinai. Finally, when we entered the Land of Israel, we were provided with a monarchy designed to lead us forever in our eternal adherence to a Biblical lifestyle.

OUT OF THE PROPHECY STAGE

Between the eras of the First and Second Temples we left the Prophecy stage and entered the age of the Realization of Prophecy. In other words, if the Bible predicted everything and Biblical era was ending, then we were now entering that predicted future, and in order to understand what was happening to us and how to deal with it, we should look backward into the events depicted in the Bible to understand the times in which we were now living. *"Ma'ase avos siman l'banim,"* what happened to the Fathers would enable us to understand what we, the sons, were experiencing.

We were going into exile. What is our frame of reference? How do we understand exile? What was the first exile, the prototype exile?

IN THE BIBLICAL ACCOUNT, there was jealousy against Joseph. When the brothers sold Joseph, they came to their father Jacob and pretended not to know what had happened to him. When they showed him Joseph's bloodstained royal garment[226] they asked, *"Is this your son's tunic?"*[227]

IN THE POST-BIBLICAL WORLD, our current exile is caused by sinas chinom, unwarranted hatred of brother against brother.[228] In the era before the destruction of the Second Temple, there was terrible conflict of brother against brother. Some of the children of Israel saw the blood of their brothers being shed and would pretend before our Father in Heaven that they did not know what had happened to their brother. *"Is this your son's tunic?"* was said again, tragically to this very day!

IN THE BIBLE, the remaining ten sons lived on in the land for a while after Joseph was sold, but soon a famine forced them to leave the land to go into exile to search for food.

IN THE POST-BIBLICAL WORLD, as the influence of foreign armies and foreign ideas began to increase in the Holy Land, the children remained there for a while, but soon a "famine forced" them to go into exile to search for food. What was the famine? In Israel we lived on Torah and commandments; that was the spiritual sustenance which had enabled us to survive. As foreign armies and ideas entered Israel, our ancestors began to consume more and more a non-kosher spiritual diet, and our source of Torah nourishment began to dry up. Some felt they needed the "food" of other cultures and other countries, so we started to stray, to leave the Land of Israel, either under duress or willingly, to enter other lands for "food."

IN THE BIBLE, the ten brothers left the Land to search for food in Egypt, a culture corrupted by idol worship and necromancy. They entered Egypt through ten separate gates. There they were then looked upon with suspicion and subjected to apparently cruel and bizarre treatment from the Viceroy of Egypt.

IN THE POST-BIBLICAL WORLD[229] ten tribes are lost. Idol-worship, which we could call "foreign spiritual food," had separated them from their brothers, and weakened them. Foreign nations attacked them. They disappeared, each in its own way, somewhere into the maze of foreign cultures and have not been seen since.

IN THE BIBLE the ruler of Egypt is Joseph, who survived as a loyal servant of G-d by a supreme effort to maintain self-control[230] and not allow himself to be sucked into the immorality of the country in which he lived.

IN THE POST-BIBLICAL WORLD, the spiritual descendants of Joseph, the Jewish People, have survived as adherents of G-d by a supreme effort to maintain self-control and not allow ourselves to be sucked into the immorality of the countries in which we live. It is only those who clung to the commandments by that supreme effort who have survived as Jews. All who did not, have disappeared into the surrounding cultures.

IN THE BIBLE, Joseph was not the king but the viceroy, who saved the Egyptian culture but was separate from it. He was not the head of the country. And after Joseph's death "a new king arose over Egypt, who did not know of Joseph."[231]

IN THE POST-BIBLICAL WORLD, the Jews have been the driving force and trusted advisors in many countries, a spiritual and material inspiration although always a tiny minority. But we are not the heads, and when times change we – along with our spiritual and material contributions — are quickly forgotten; the "new king" does not know us.

IN THE BIBLE, the ten brothers did not recognize Joseph.

IN THE POST-BIBLICAL WORLD, somewhere out there are ten tribes of Israel, who regard the Jews of today with suspicion and distrust and believe that we act very strangely. Yet they are our brothers.

IN THE BIBLE, Joseph revealed his identity when he felt that his brothers had repented for their jealousy.

IN THE POST-BIBLICAL WORLD, it appears that there will

come a time when we, the Jewish People, will reveal our identity as the children of Israel. At that time our brothers will recognize us and all the children of Israel will once again be reunited. This will apparently be what is called the time of Messiah
the son of Joseph.

But, you will ask, have we not already revealed our identity?
No, we have not.

The moment when we will reveal our identity is when every
Jew acknowledges that we are the children of Israel, that we all
are equally responsible to adhere to the commandments given to
those children and when we love each other as brothers and sisters and cease to be jealous of each other. That is when we will
reveal ourselves and be reunited with our brethren.

There is one place in the annual Torah cycle at which I cry
uncontrollably every year.

*"Now Joseph could not restrain himself in the presence of all who
stood before him, so he called out, 'Remove everyone from before
me!' Thus no one remained with him when Joseph made himself
known to his brothers. He cried in a loud voice. Egypt heard and
Pharaoh's household heard. And Joseph said to his brothers, 'I am
Joseph. Is my father still alive?'"*[232]

Why do I cry here? Because this is the prophecy of the day
when all the brothers will be united under Messiah the son of
Joseph.

That is the moment I picture to myself every year when we
come to the Torah portion in which Joseph reveals himself to his
brethren. It is the emotion of the moment when we will suddenly understand not only that we are all brethren but we will
all see how G-d has been operating the world. We will understand all the seemingly incomprehensible events, the events
that seemed to make no sense whatsoever. We will see that
every event in the world made sense and that nothing was ran-

dom. We will understand that all our apparent troubles were messages from G-d reminding us to act as one family and return to Him in repentance.[233]

What has enabled the Jewish People to endure almost two thousand years of exile since the destruction of the Second Temple? The legacy of Joseph, who endured and rose to become the leader of his family in exile.

Joseph was subjected to tremendous temptation in Egypt. The wife of Potiphar was attempting to seduce him. From where could he derive the strength to resist? Our rabbis tell us[234] that at the moment of greatest temptation, the image of his father appeared to him. That image brought him back to reality.

Just as it was for Joseph in Egypt, so has it been for us in exile. When temptation seemed too strong for us, the image of Joseph has saved us… Joseph, who withstood so much temptation; Joseph, who remained true to his father and his G-d even in the utter loneliness of Egypt. The image of Joseph has stayed with us and reminded us who we are.

That is why, when Jewish parents bless their sons, they say, *"May G-d make you like Ephraim and Menashe,"* the two sons of Joseph.[235] Joseph is the leader of Israel whose unique ability was to rise to the highest level even in an environment that is steeped in corruption. Just as he bequeathed this ability to his two sons in Egypt, so has he become for us the leader who has taught us how to survive and maintain our spiritual dignity and even royalty throughout the devastating years of exile.

You would think that once Joseph had revealed himself, our problems should have been over. Clearly that was not the case, because once Joseph died, the following generations descended into a cruel slavery. What is the lesson for us?

After Joseph died… if the lesson of Joseph dies, if the attitude of Joseph dies, if the dignity and the commitment and the spiritual strength dies, then we descend into slavery.

And that is also *"ma'ase avos siman l'banim."* In other words Joseph's death is also a "portent for the children." We children of Israel should know that during our long exile, there will be bright periods and dark periods. There will be times when our unity is great and "Joseph is alive." And then there will be times when our unity falls apart and "Joseph is dead." We should be prepared.

When "Joseph dies" – in other words, when the unity among the children of Israel is weak – then a king will arise who "does not know Joseph," who hates us, who will enslave us, just as the children of Israel were enslaved in Egypt after Joseph died.

What is the solution for this terrible enslavement? Of course it is once again clear from the Biblical account: the solution to Israel's slavery and near extermination is the appearance of Moses, leading to the monumental moment when we stand together at Mount Sinai and receive the Torah. In order to bind the brothers together eternally, we need to live in a structured existence according to the eternal laws of G-d. I am not inventing this; it is there for everyone to see, in our national history as recounted in the Five Books of Moses.

MOSES

What is the difference between the laws under Moses and the laws under Joseph? Didn't the children of Israel live by the laws of the Torah before Mount Sinai? They did,[236] but it was not until Mount Sinai that the laws of the Torah became binding upon us. At that time we accepted the Torah in its entirety and became liable and responsible for keeping it until the end of time. So Moses brought us to a position that was "further down the road" than Joseph, because at Mount Sinai we entered into a covenant with G-d through which we agreed to abide by his laws eternally and *"meditate [upon them] them day and night."*[237]

Here is how the entire story of our future Exile is foretold in the Five Books of Moses. First, *"sinas chinom,"* causeless hatred among the brothers, drives our family apart and into Egyptian exile. Then Joseph comes to reunite all the brothers and to bind them once again to their father. But when Joseph dies and his influence is weakened, an evil king appears to enslave us. Then we require Moses to lead us out of slavery to meet G-d, and there at Mount Sinai we take upon ourselves as a permanent and binding way of life the laws that our Fathers discovered.

But wait! This is also not enough, because even under Moses we rebel, and after Moses' death, when we enter the Land of Israel, we endure hundreds of years of trouble before we finally coalesce into national unity under our eternal king, David.

Let us try to understand the difference between Joseph and Moses on one hand, and David on the other.

Joseph and Moses are our leaders for exile. Moses was not allowed to enter the Land of Israel! Our national existence in Israel was the goal of our entire existence up to the time we crossed the Jordan as a new nation with Joshua as our leader. So it can be seen that everything up to the point at which we crossed the Jordan forty years after Mount Sinai was really a preparation for our eternal existence in the Land of Israel. The fact that later we were not able to endure in the Land was a result of our sins.[238]

DAVID

King David is the embodiment of the final phase of our leadership. He is the prototype of our eternal monarch, because he reigned over a united people in the Land of our final destiny, the

Land of Israel. Yes, he had to fight for it; he had to lead us to that point, and that in fact is part of the model he has provided for us. Yes, he had to overcome his own human limitations, and that is also part of the model he has provided for us. Yes, he was an unknown shepherd; yes he was ridiculed; yes he was even suspect in his own family; yes he was suspected by King Saul; yes he was even "invisible" briefly to the Prophet Samuel, who came to anoint the next king.... But yes, he also learned through all these terrible trials to trust completely in G-d and attribute all his greatness to G-d. This is all *"ma-ase avos siman l'banim,"* a lesson for us forever on what a king should be (and how we should act). For we all are to learn from David how to rise up from the dust and ashes of our human-ness to a level that is eternal, a level on which we can rule in the wisdom of the Torah and compose eternal songs to our Creator![239]

The man who can sing, *"Oh G-d, how numerous are my tormentors!"*[240] can also sing *"G-d is my light and my salvation. Whom shall I fear?"*[241]

David combines the qualities of Joseph and Moses. He unites the brothers in national autonomy, as Joseph had united us in exile, and he imbues the nation with Torah, making permanent the congregation bound by Moses to the Eternal G-d. If Joseph and Moses are our prototype leaders in exile, then David is our prototype leader in redemption from exile. If Joseph and Moses led us outside the Holy Land, then David leads us within the Holy Land. If Joseph and Moses are is our leaders "during the weekdays" of our national existence, then David is our leader for the "Sabbath."

Thus at the end of our history we have two Messiahs, the son of Joseph – who according to the Talmud, may "be killed"[242] – and the son of David, who will never die. Messiah the son of Joseph may be killed, because exile is temporary. When we enter the Land of Israel, as one nation attached to G-d, Joseph's function as our leader in exile will have been completed.

That is apparently one reason why the Talmud includes the possible death of Messiah the son of Joseph in the same discussion with the death of the *"yetzer hara,"* the evil inclination, the inclination of man toward sin and rebellion.[243] After Messiah the son of Joseph has completed his work, we will be entering the Holy Land, the final phase of our long national journey, and the evil inclination will finally have been conquered. We will then enter the Seventh Millennium, the eternal Sabbath, when we will finally be at peace and *"the world will be filled with the knowledge of G-d as the sea fills the ocean bed."*[244] At that time Messiah the son of David will be our eternal leader. On the Sabbath we conquer our evil inclination!

Why is there no Messiah the son of Moses?

Moses is not a king in the ordinary sense of the word, as we will see below.

Joseph's function was to rule in exile and David's function is to rule in the era of redemption, but Moses' function is to lead us forever in Torah. That function is eternal. Joseph's bones were carried into Israel by the children of Israel and buried in Shechem, so Joseph finally has rest in the holy land when David takes over. But Moses waits for us in exile, outside the Land of Israel; he is buried in the desert;[245] he will enter at the time of Final Redemption along with all his children. He is eternally with his people, both outside and inside the Land, because the Torah, which was given to us through Moses, is the one constant in the life of the children of Israel, and it is with us at all times.

The function of Torah is the same at all times; the nature of the king may change when we enter the Holy Land but the nature of the Torah sage, the Prophet who connects us with G-d, never changes. There are not two "stages" in the work of

Moses; his work is forever. Joseph, on the other hand, is our leader for exile and David is our leader for the days of redemption.

Messiah is the one who is "anointed with oil." The king is anointed but the prophet does the anointing. Moses is the prophet.

WHY IS THE KING HIDDEN?

There is one more subject we must discuss at this point, and that is the remarkable fact that our greatest leaders were almost completely hidden from view until the time came for them to be revealed. Joseph, Moses and David were all hidden.

Joseph disappeared for twenty-two years after he was sold by his brothers. His father believed he was dead. His brothers did not know if he was alive, and, if so, where he was. Even when they saw him in Egypt, they did not recognize him. His father could not believe he was alive when he heard the news.[246]

Moses was hidden while still in Egypt, growing up in Pharaoh's palace. Pharaoh, who was attempting to kill the future savior of the children of Israel, was actually raising that savior in his palace without realizing it! Moses was also hidden in the sense that he spent many years away from his people while he lived in Midian.

David was hidden in several ways. First, he descended from a nation that was so degraded morally and so antagonistic to Israel that Torah law prohibits its males[247] from joining the nation of Israel. To think that the future king of Israel could come from such a nation is almost beyond belief. The world would never have thought of looking for a diamond in this rubbish heap, but Ruth, David's great-grandmother, was that diamond. The leaders of Israel were not convinced as to whether David's family were even legitimate Jews, because the law as to whether a female Moabite could convert was at that time unclear.

But David's greatness was hidden even from his father and brothers and from the Prophet Samuel, whom G-d sent to anoint him King over Israel.

"Jesse [the father of David] presented his seven sons before Samuel, but Samuel said to Jesse, 'G-d has not chosen these.' Samuel said, 'Are these all the boys?' And he said, 'the youngest one is still left; he is tending the sheep now.'"[248]

Jesse had not even thought to bring David home when the prophet arrived!

"So Samuel said to Jesse, 'Send and bring him, for we will not sit [to dine] until he arrives here.' He sent and brought him. He was ruddy, with fair eyes and a pleasing appearance. G-d then said, 'Arise and anoint him, for this is he!'"[249]

The phrase in the Psalms, *"the stone the builders despised has become the cornerstone,"*[250] is said to refer to David.[251]

Why is the king hidden?

Before we answer that, let's try to understand an underlying concept. The phrase we use to describe exile is *"hester panim,*[252]*"* which means, *"the face [of G-d] is hidden."* In the Garden of Eden, as we have seen, Adam and Eve tried to hide from G-d after they rebelled against Him by disobeying His commandment and eating from the fruit of the Tree of the Knowledge of Good and Evil. They became aware of their guilt* and as a result they tried to flee from G-d's presence. They knew they could not hide their guilt from G-d. So they covered their bodies with clothes, and then *"hid from G-d among the trees of the garden."*[253]

---

* "Guilt" has a bad connotation today because our society is geared toward pleasure. The psychiatrist will tell you not to feel guilty, because guilt is depriving you of pleasure. But the pleasure principle does not guide the life of a Jew. Guilt is the voice of G-d communicating with us. Our guilt enables us to say *"chattasi... I have sinned!"* on Yom Kippur. Without guilt, we would not have remorse over our sins. Without remorse, how could we repent? Without repentance, how could we ever come back to G-d?

But one cannot hide from G-d; He sees everything in this world that He created.

Here again is a matter of *"ma'ase avos siman l'banim… the actions of the fathers are a portent for the children."*

Throughout history, whenever we rebelled against G-d, we have followed this pattern. We have become aware of our own guilt (no matter how we tried to deny or repress it) and we have tried to hide from G-d. We describe it as *"hester panim,"* *"the face of G-d is hidden."*

Some people say, "Where was G-d in the Holocaust?" Some people try to ridicule the very idea that G-d could exist. And some people who believe in Him beg Him to reveal His face and save us. In the end, the truth – which can be seen clearly from what happened in the Garden of Eden – is that we are all guilty of rebellion.

We are the ones who are hiding from Him, not He from us!

If we would come back to Him with honesty, a willingness to obey His laws in every detail, and an intense desire to be close to Him, we could see Him as Adam and Eve once saw Him before the sin.

And we will! May it be soon, in our own days!

THE STONE THE BUILDERS DESPISED

Why does the king of Israel have to be hidden?

Let's examine in turn each of the "prototype" kings.

JOSEPH was hidden from his father and his brothers.

MOSES was hidden from Pharaoh, the leader of the "outside" world.

DAVID was hidden from both the outside world (by his origin among the debased nation of Moab) AND from his brothers!

Is this not amazing! This is the pattern for the rest of history.

Why was Joseph hidden from his brothers? Because they wanted to kill him!

Why was Moses hidden from Pharaoh? Because, if he had realized who Moses was, he would have killed him! And when he did find out who he was (after Moses had killed the Egyptian who was beating an Israelite)[254] Moses indeed had to flee for his life.

Why was David hidden from both the world and from his brothers?

If the nation of Moab had known that the future leader of Israel – the nation whom they abhorred[255] – was to come from within their own people, they of course would have killed Ruth! And in his own family, David was the subject of jealousy and suspicion, as Joseph had been among his brothers. *"I became a stranger to my brothers, an alien to my mother's sons."*[256] David's brothers *"drove him away and held him in contempt."*[257]

So why in the case of Joseph, Moses and David was each leader hidden until the very moment when he was revealed?

IN ORDER TO SAVE HIM!

This is why Messiah must be hidden until the very moment of his revelation! If he were to be revealed one microsecond before G-d is ready to reveal him, then he would be killed and the world could not be saved!

Is this not truly amazing? Here we can see that every event in history is planned by G-d! It is part of G-d's mercy and kindness to us that, until the very moment they are revealed, the identity of our redeemers is not just hidden but hidden in utter darkness, in the very last place we would ever have thought to look for them!

Moab is the LAST nation on earth we would ever suspect that the future exemplar of purity and holiness would be found. Moab, the nation whose very origin occurred in the darkness of a mountain cave in which a drunken father (Lot) impregnated his own daughter![258] Moab, the nation that staked its very existence on a plot to curse and corrupt us![259] Moab, the nation whose males are prohibited forever from joining the children of Israel!

And David's family? Once Samuel the Prophet was told to anoint a king from among the sons of Yishai, it never occurred to either the father or the brothers that David could be the anointed one!

I would like to quote here some remarkable passages from *The Book of Our Heritage*, by Rabbi Eliahu Kitov.

"All that we have seen regarding David ... is a linked chain of events that the Creator wondrously formed to bring the light of Messiah to the world. In His profound wisdom, He saw fit to veil this light within a curtain of darkness that will only part when the time arrives for it to be revealed. The strength of the revealed light will be directly proportionate to the depth in which it was concealed.

"Why was it necessary to conceal this light so deeply? It is the Divine will that when the light of Messiah appears, all darkness will be dispelled and all that had previously been hidden in the darkness will be revealed. Darkness will no longer be dark and the night shall be as light as day...

"When G-d chooses to invest mortal man with His honor, to make him master over all creation, to crown him with sovereignty that is an example of His own and to give him eternal dominion, he first makes him master over himself so that he might not become haughty. G-d places a guard over him to ensure that he does not become subject to the evil designs of others nor to his own foibles. He who is perfect in three traits —- whose eye sees the good in all, who is humble, and who has a generous soul – is worthy of sovereignty."[260]

In this world, G-d is hidden and His servants are hidden.

Where was Joseph tested and formed if not as a result of the rejection by his brothers and then his exile in the debased and corrupt kingdom of Egypt? Where was Moses tested and formed if not in the debased and corrupt court of Pharaoh and then alone with his sheep in the desert of Midian? Where was David tested and formed if not before his birth in the morass of Moab, and then as the result of his rejection by his brothers, who drove him away to the wilderness to be alone with his sheep?

Where for that matter were the children of Israel tested and formed, if not in the desert of rejection by the entire world, alone with G-d?

"How many are the obstacles and stumbling blocks in the way of a person who seeks to cleave to G-d when he is in the company of his fellow man! Distractions stand in one's way and the eyes of others watching are damaging to he who seeks to draw close to G-d. Man is constantly distracted – either by the love of those who are fond of him or by the enmity of those who hate him. When does he have the time to study the statutes of G-d and know His laws so that he might cleave to Him? David, however, spent all of his days in the wilderness, free from the love of his fellow man and their longing for him and free from their enmity. Without the distraction they bring and the eyes with which they observe, he was able to devote his body and soul to G-d alone. G-d was both his father and his brother. All of the pleasures with which society occupies itself were meaningless to him."[261]

Just as the world failed to see the destined greatness of Joseph, Moses and David, so the "seers" among the nations of the world have consistently failed to discern the holiness of the children of Israel. Like our holy ancestors, the children of Israel have been rejected, scorned, abused, banished to the wilderness, whispered against and accused of being the world's "illegitimate child."

Other nations possess their own destinies, but Israel was chosen by G-d to be His spiritual emissary. Different nations have different functions, just as different people have different talents. *"And G-d has distinguished you today to be for Him a treasured people ... and to make you supreme over all the nations ... for renown and for splendor and so that you will be a holy people to your G-d."*[262] These are not my words, but the words of G-d as stated in the Torah.

If the nations of the world respect the rule of G-d they will have a positive role in the world. But G-d anoints whom he anoints, and it is usually the one rejected by the mass of men. The world thinks "the bigger the better." The world believes there is no question but that Goliath will defeat David, and that the enemies of Israel will eventually prevail.

But power does not reside in physicality. David was smaller than Goliath. Moses was the *"most humble of men."*[263] The Torah was given on *"the smallest"* of mountains.[264] Israel is the smallest of nations.[265]

We do not know the ways of G-d. *"Many designs are in a man's heart, but the counsel of G-d ... only it will prevail."*[266] Judah, the tribal progenitor of King David, was publicly shamed in the incident of Tamar.[267] How could he show his face in public again? At that point he appeared to be eternally rejected among his brothers. But in fact, Judah became the eternal father of kings precisely because of his conduct at that incident!

Why? Judah publicly accepted his guilt, just as all his descendants do every Yom Kippur. By taking responsibility for the sin, Judah rose to the heights of greatness. In the way he responded to his deficiency he became a model for all mankind, just as Israel – by taking public responsibility in the eternal pages of the Torah for all our weaknesses – has become a model for mankind in how to elevate oneself in this world!

Yes, I take responsibility for my failings and my sins! My trouble is caused by my shortcomings. Please G-d; help me to rise above myself. Save me from my weaknesses! I know that salvation comes only from closeness to You.

Please observe the actions of King David, the descendant of Judah, when Nathan the Prophet said to him, *"You have scorned [G-d] and taken the wife of Uriah the Hittite."*[268] Instead of arguing, making excuses, or having Nathan executed (which was within his power if not his prerogative as king) he said, *"I have sinned to G-d!"*[269]

Such is the character of G-d's anointed.

And each Yom Kippur, instead of making excuses, we say, *"Chatassi, I have sinned."*

Such is the character of G-d's anointed.

The nations of the world should not take Israel's willingness to acknowledge our failings as a sign of weakness or disfavor in the eyes of G-d. Rather, the world should recognize in the behavior of the children of Israel the signs of G-d's anointment.

We are the perennial recipients of the whiplashes of the entire world, but the nations are making a terrible mistake. Just as Joseph and Moses and David were hidden and the Messiah is hidden and G-d is hidden, so is the true nature of the children of Israel hidden from the eyes of the world. Those who have scorned Israel for millennia should be aware that they are castigating the nation that G-d appointed to be His representatives upon earth, not only for our sake but for the welfare of all mankind and for the eternal promulgation of His life-giving Torah.

No nation or individual is above the law. Israel submits itself to the Torah, but the nations must also submit to it. If the nations reject Israel, they are rejecting G-d.

Now it is clear why the identity and the timing of Messiah must be hidden! It is no accident; rather, it is part of his essence. Just as Joseph, Moses and David were hidden, just as the soul is hidden and the body is obvious, just as the Next World is hidden and this world is obvious, so must the Messiah be hidden until it is time for him to be revealed, because his essence is tied to the Eternal World of Truth, which is hidden in this world. And of course, the ultimate in the category of "hidden" is G-d Himself, Who is "visible" in this world only through hints, as a shadow or reflection, so to speak.

The Talmud discusses these things quite openly, in the following passage: *"Rabbi Isaac further said, 'Blessing is only possible in things hidden from sight... Blessing is only possible in things not under the direct control of the eye.... Blessing is not to be found in anything that has been already weighed or measure or numbered, but only in a thing hidden from sight."*[270]

In the contemporary world everything is counted, numbered and weighed, which is why in general we do not perceive the spiritual. Comfort is measured by counting money. The value of men and ideas is determined by public opinion polls. Political leaders are chosen by counting votes. Wall Street is obsessed with quantifying the value of companies. Corporations are obsessed with counting everything from paper clips to how many pennies per share they will earn four quarters from now. Sports fans are obsessed with counting home runs or baskets, and how much each player is paid. Health is measured in calories and cholesterol. China enforces a population quota, but a Jewish mother will not tell you the number of her children nor will her husband count men for the *minyan*.[271]

One of most unforgettable scenes in the Bible is the epic struggle between Jacob and the angel of Esau,[272] which our rabbis have understood to be a prophetic revelation of the fate of the children of Jacob during the coming centuries of exile.[273] Why does the struggle take place at night? Because in the current state of the world, Israel's exile is a long, dark night filled with constant struggle. Our life is in constant danger from a nameless enemy fighting with us for no apparent reason.

Why do they hate us? Why do they fight with us? Why are we always beneath their contempt? Why are we accused of everything? Why do the fascists call us communists and the communists call us fascists?

But we are G-d's chosen nation, *a nation of priests, a holy people!*[274] Everything is backwards! The world is dark! The holy is hidden and corruption rules!

"Jacob [Israel] was left alone and a man wrestled with him until the break of dawn."[275]

Very soon, when we cease to fight among ourselves and return to the light of Torah,[276] the sun of Truth will appear on the eastern horizon and the hidden will be revealed.

THE DESTINY TO INHERIT ISRAEL AND JERUSALEM

It is appropriate here to discuss the right of the children of Israel to live in the Land of Israel and Jerusalem. In the period after the death of Moses, we entered the Land under Divine decree and the leadership of Joshua. We began to conquer the Land that had been given to us by the Ruler of the Universe. It is clear that the entire purpose of the wanderings of the children of Israel through the desert had been to come to the Land of Israel. That is the destination and that is the commandment.

"If the nations of the world will say to Israel, 'You are bandits, for you conquered the land of the seven nations [who inhabited the Land of Canaan], [Israel] will say to them, 'The whole earth belongs to the Holy One, Blessed is He, He created it and He gave it to the one found proper in His eyes. By His wish He gave it to them, and by His wish He took it from them and gave it to us.'"[277]

The Book of Joshua begins, *"It happened after the death of Moses, servant of G-d, that G-d said to Joshua son of Nun, Moses' attendant, saying, 'Moses My servant has died. Now arise, cross this Jordan, you and this entire people, to the land that I give to them, to the children of Israel. Every place upon which the sole of your foot will tread I have given to you, as I spoke to Moses. From the desert and this Lebanon until the great river, the Euphrates River, all the land of the Hittites until the Great Sea toward the setting of the sun will be your boundary."*[278]

The entire aim and purpose of traversing the desert for forty years from the time the children of Israel left Egypt was to enter the Holy Land. The boundaries of the Land to be given to the children of Israel are spelled out explicitly and frequently in the Bible. Many commandments, like those associated with the cities of refuge and the Holy Temple as well as agricultural laws, concern obligations that specifically relate to the Land of Israel. The Torah makes it clear that when the children of Israel *"observe this entire commandment to perform it... to love G-d... and to walk in His ways..."* then He will *"broaden your boundary"* to include the East Bank as well as the West Bank of the Jordan River.[278a]

The entire destiny of the children of Israel is to enter and inherit the Land of Israel, to conquer it, to drive out the inhabitants and clear it of idol worship in order that it should become the land in which we dwell in accordance with G-d's commands. Nobody who even glances at the Bible could dispute that. In fact, the Bible tells us that, if we allow the nations to remain, they will be *"pins in your eyes and... thorns in your side."*[279]

That being the case, then what is the question? Why should anyone dispute the destiny and the right of the children of Israel to inherit the Land of Canaan? The only one who could question that is someone who questions the legitimacy and authenticity of the entire Torah and the existence of G-d.

What about Jerusalem?

Which location will G-d choose for His Temple?

The exact boundaries of the Land of Israel are spelled out clearly but the location of its capital, *"the place where I choose to rest My Name,"*[280] is a mystery until King David makes Jerusalem his capital and begins to construct the Temple there. Look at this sentence, for example: *"They direct their prayers to G-d by way of the city that You have chosen and Temple that I have built for Your Name."*[281] Why is the name of Jerusalem not mentioned? Why does G-d refer to Jerusalem indirectly? Why is the identity of Jerusalem a mystery while the boundaries of the Land of Israel are openly spelled out? What is the difference?

I will ask you another question.

Why are Jacob's sons known as the bearers of the holy tradition but their leader is not revealed until it is necessary, in the court of Joseph? No one knew who their leader was until Judah revealed himself. Perhaps Judah himself did not know until then!

In the same way, the Land of Israel is known as the location of the greatest holiness, but the "king," the holiest place in Israel is hidden and unknown. Like Judah and Moses and David and Mount Sinai itself and ultimately Messiah, it was only revealed at the last moment, because G-d keeps the ultimate source of holiness secret until the very end!

When I realized this, I was amazed! Here again, in the case of Jerusalem, what is most holy is most hidden! The seat of sanctity is a secret! Just as the identity of the Messiah is a secret and the date of Messiah's arrival is a secret, so is the place from which the King of Israel will rule a secret, not to be revealed until the identity of the King from the tribe of Judah is known.

CHAPTER FOUR

THE KINGDOM: KING DAVID TO THE DESTRUCTION OF THE SECOND TEMPLE

"Akiva, you have comforted us."[282]

The period from King David's reign to the fall of the Second Temple witnessed the descent of the children of Israel from our period of greatest national glory to our lowest moment of despair and degradation. How did we survive the destruction of our First Temple? How did we survive the destruction of our Second Temple?

Looking back now, thousands of years later, it is clear that we did survive, so we tend to take it for granted. But at the time, we had had no prior experience of such catastrophe unless we go all the way back to the Garden of Eden. There also, a glorious and beautiful world was taken from us, and we were cast away into a cruel, dark and unknown future.

The Torah had warned us – *"Beware lest your heart be seduced and you turn astray and serve other gods and bow to them. Then the wrath of G-d will blaze against you.*"[283] But who can believe such things until after they happen? Frequently, we don't believe such things even after they happen!

As our beautiful world was being brutally smashed, how could we know that we would survive, let alone endure? In fact, we could learn from the Garden of Eden. Adam and Eve survived, their story endured, and we were their descendants!

We are a unique people. That we exist is in itself miraculous. In the days of glory, when our Temple stood in Jerusalem and King Solomon reigned, there was no other nation like us in the world. In fact there has been no other nation like us before or since! We flourished because we served G-d. We were pure and righteous, existing through obvious miracles in a Land that would support no other peoples than its own children. We had survived and endured through open miracles. Our leaders were warriors of the soul rather than warriors of the sword (although when called upon they could handle the sword better than our adversaries). We were attached to G-d, and the world came to imbibe wisdom from us in our Holy City. It was an ideal time, a perfect world, or so it seemed.

"Solomon ruled over all the kingdoms, from the [Euphrates] River [to] the land of the Philistines, until the border of Egypt... and he was at peace [with the lands] on all sides, roundabout. Judah and Israel dwelt in security, each man under his grapevine and under his fig tree, from Dan to Beer-sheba, all the days of Solomon... They came from all the nations to hear the wisdom of Solomon."[284]

"The Queen of Sheba heard of Solomon's fame, that it was for the Name of G-d, and she came to test him with riddles. She arrived in Jerusalem with a very large entourage, with camels bearing very large amounts of spices and gold, and precious stones. She came before Solomon and she spoke to him about all that was in her heart. Solomon told her [the solutions to] all her questions; there was not a

thing hidden from the king that he could not tell her. *The Queen of Sheba saw all the wisdom of Solomon; the palace that he had erected; the food [served] at his table and seating of his servants; the station of the attendants and their uniforms; his cupbearers; and his passageway by which he ascended to the Temple of G-d – and she was overwhelmed.*"[285]

Please hear the description of the inauguration of the Temple.

"*Solomon gathered together the elders of Israel and all the heads of the tribes, the leaders of the ancestral families of the children of Israel, to … Jerusalem, to bring up the Ark of the Covenant of G-d from the City of David, which is Zion. They gathered before King Solomon – every man of Israel – for the festival of [Sukkos] in the … seventh month. All the elders of Israel came, and the Kohanim bore the Ark. They brought up the Ark of G-d, and the Tent of Meeting, and all the sacred vessels that were in that Tent; the Kohanim and the Levites brought them up. King Solomon and the entire assembly of Israel that had assembled with him were with him before the Ark, offering sheep and cattle, too abundant to be numbered or counted.*"[286]

Please listen to the description of the High Priest returning from the Temple after the Yom Kippur services.

"*How majestic was the High Priest as he left the Holy of Holies in peace… Like the heavenly canopy stretched out over those who dwell above… was the appearance of the High Priest. Like lightning bolts emanating from the radiance of the [angels]… Like the image of the rainbow amidst the cloud. Like the majesty in which the Creator clothed [Adam and Eve… in light]. Like a rose that is placed amid a precious garden. . Like a crown that is placed on a king's forehead. Like the graciousness granted to a bridegroom's face. …Like the morning star on the eastern border. …All this occurred when the Temple was on its foundation and the Holy Sanctuary was on its site, and the High Priest stood and ministered – his generation watched and rejoiced. Fortunate is the eye that saw all these…*"[287]

Can you imagine such splendor? Can you imagine such magnificence? An eternal kingdom, built on the service of the Eternal G-d!

And yet it was not to last. Almost as soon as it was built, the first ominous cracks began to appear in the facade. Do you remember the Garden of Eden? A perfect garden, with nothing lacking, and yet the heart of man desired more. And here is the Kingdom of Solomon. Nothing is lacking, and yet the heart of man desires more.

Think of it! The scenario is truly amazing! Here are the books of the Prophets – Joshua, Judges, Samuel, Kings, Isaiah, Jeremiah, Ezekiel to Malachi —- and here is the period of the Holy Temple, the glorious days of King David and King Solomon, the culmination of all that we had been working towards from the time G-d spoke to us at Mount Sinai, no ... since G-d spoke to Abraham!

And what follows? An eternally perfect world?

No! A plunge into disaster!

And now it begins.

"It happened at that time, while Jeroboam was leaving Jerusalem, the prophet Ahijah the Shilonite found him on the way; he was clothed in a new garment, and the two of them were alone in the field. Ahijah grabbed hold of the new garment that was upon him, and he tore it into twelve pieces. He said to Jeroboam, 'Take for yourself ten pieces, for so said ... the G-d of Israel, 'I am tearing the kingdom away from the hand of Solomon and I shall give the ten tribes to you. But the one tribe shall remain for him, for the sake of My servant David and for the sake of Jerusalem, the city which I have chosen of all the tribes of Israel. [This is] because they have forsaken Me, and bowed down to Ashtoreth, the god of the Siddonians...."[288]

How can it be? The garment is rent! We tear garments at a funeral.

This is the funeral for the entire nation.

"Rehoboam [the son of Solomon] … gathered together the entire House of Judah and the tribe of Benjamin… to fight against the House of Israel."[289]

Oh G-d! Don't we ever learn? Are we condemned to fight each other for eternity? The nation is split and already we begin to hear the tragic refrain, *"he did what was evil in the eyes of G-d."*[290]

Two kings, often fighting each other, and idol worship, rebellion against G-d.

It gets worse.

"And so it was that the children of Israel sinned to … their G-d, Who had taken them up out of the land of Egypt from under the oppression of Pharaoh king of Egypt, and they feared the gods of others. They walked in the decrees of the nations whom G-d had driven out from before the children of Israel …. The children of Israel imputed things that were not so to … their G-d and built themselves high places in all their cities, from the [solitary] watchtower to the fortified city. They erected for themselves pillars and Asherah-trees upon every tall hill and under every leafy tree. They burned incense there at all their high places, like the nations whom G-d had exiled before them; and they did wicked things, to anger G-d.

" They worshiped the execrable idols, concerning which G-d had told them, 'Do not do this thing.' G-d has issued warning in Israel and in Judah through the hand of all prophets of any vision, saying, 'Repent from your evil ways, and observe My commandments and My decrees in accordance with the entire Torah that I commanded your forefathers, and that I have sent you through My servants the prophets.' But they did not listen, and they stiffened their neck like the neck of their forefathers, who did not believe in … G-d. They rejected His decrees and His covenant that He had sealed with their forefathers, and His warnings that He had warned about them; and

they went after the worthless, and became worthless; and after [the ways of] the nations that surrounded them, concerning whom G-d has commanded them not to do like them.

"They forsook all the commandments of … their G-d, and made a molten image for themselves – two calves; and they made Asherah-trees and prostrated themselves to all the hosts of the heavens and worshiped the Baal. They passed their sons and their daughters through fire and practiced divinations and sorcery; and they dedicated themselves to do that which was evil in the eyes of G-d, to anger Him.

"Then G-d became very angry with Israel and removed them from His Presence; none remained except the tribe of Judah alone. (And even Judah did not observe the commandments of their G-d....) So G-d rejected the entire offspring of Israel and oppressed them; He delivered them into the hand of plunderers, until He had cast them away from His presence. For Israel had torn [itself] away from the house of David, crowning Jeroboam son of Nebat [over themselves], and Jeroboam pushed Israel away from following G-d and caused them to commit a grave sin. The children of Israel went in the [the way of] all the sins of Jeroboam, which he committed, and they did not turn away from them, until G-d removed Israel from His Presence, as He had spoken through the hand of all His servants the prophets. So Israel went into exile from their land to Assyria, to this day."[291]

"To this day." Even until today!

Samaria, northern Israel, is captured.[292]

"It was in the fourth year of King Hezekiah, it was the seventh year of Hoshea son of Elah king of Israel: Shalmaneser king of Assyria invaded Samaria and besieged it. They captured it after three years – in the sixth year of Hezekiah, it was the ninth year of Hoshea king of Israel – Samaria was captured. The King of Assyria exiled Israel to Assyria, placing them in Halah, in Habor, by the

Gozan River and in the cities of Media. [This was] because they did not heed the voice of...their G-d, and they transgressed His covenant – all that Moses, the servant of G-d, had commanded, they did not heed and they did not fulfill."[293]

And the final destruction.

"It happened in the ninth year of [Zedekiah's] reign, in the tenth month, on the tenth of the month, that Nebuchadnezzar king of Babylonia, he and his entire army, came [to wage war] against Jerusalem and encamped near it, and built a siege tower around it. The city came under siege until the eleventh year of King Zedekiah. On the ninth [day] of the [fourth] month the famine in the city became critical; there was no food for the people of the land. The city was breached, and all the men of war [fled] during the night, by way of the gate between the walls, which was near the king's garden.... The Chaldean army pursued the king and overtook him at the plains of Jericho, and his entire army dispersed from him. They seized the king and brought him up to the king of Babylonia at Riblah, and they spoke [words of] judgment to him. They slaughtered Zedekiah's sons before his eyes; [Nebuchadnezzar] blinded Zedekiah's eyes, then he bound him in leg-irons and brought him to Babylonia.

"In the fifth month, on the seventh of the month, which was the nineteenth year of Nebuchadnezzar king of Babylonia, Nebuzaradan, the chief executioner, servant of the king of Babylonia, came to Jerusalem. He burned the Temple of G-d, the king's palace and all the buildings of Jerusalem, and every great house he burned in fire. And the walls of Jerusalem all around, the entire Chaldean army that was with the chief executioner smashed. The remainder of the people who were left in the city and the defectors who had surrendered to the king of Babylonia, and the rest of the masses, Nebuzaradan the chief executioner sent into exile.

"The copper pillar of the Temple of G-d and the laver–stands and the copper sea that were in the Temple of G-d, the Chaldeans shattered *and carried off their copper to Babylonia. The pots, the shovels, the musical instruments, the spoons and all the copper utensils with which [the Kohanim] served, they took away. The pans and the bowls, whether of gold or of silver, the chief executioner took away.*

"The chief executioner took Seraiah the chief Kohain and Zephania, the deputy Kohain and the three gatekeepers.... Nebuzaradan, the chief executioner, took them and brought them to the king of Babylonia at Riblah and the king of Babylonia struck them down and killed them at Riblah, in the land of Hamath. And Judah was exiled from its land."[294]

Oh G-d! What had we done!

We had achieved the ultimate, the culmination of centuries of effort and suffering, the hope of the world, a kingdom glorifying G-d and living by His covenant, a kingdom from which blessings emanated to the entire world. We had our eternal King David. We had King Solomon. We had peace, each man under his vine. The Temple was built, a home for G-d, the wonder of the world. Everything for which we had struggled for hundreds of years had been achieved.

And as soon as we got there — AS SOON AS WE GOT THERE – it began to fall apart!

What are we to make of the descent of our People into chaos?

THE END OF PROPHECY

A dramatic transition takes place in the period between the First and Second Temples: at the beginning of the period of the Second Temple, the era of prophecy comes to an end and with it the era of the Books of the Bible.

Abraham, Isaac and Jacob's children had always been identified closely with G-d, Whom we represented in the world. G-d's presence was visible and palpable among the children of

Israel. Prophets dwelt among us, people out of whose mouths came speech of such great purity and strength that it was clearly from beyond this world. The prophets predicted the future, and those predictions were seen to have been accurate. But in a broader sense, the prophets anchored our Nation to G-d, and kept us anchored, no matter how rough the sea.

We didn't make it up. The world had seen what had happened to Egypt. The world saw what had happened at the Red Sea. The world saw what had happened at Mount Sinai, when G-d spoke to us. The world saw that a nation of millions had spent forty years in the barren, scorching desert, a moonscape inhabited only by snakes, scorpions, and beasts that slithered by night. How did we survive? We were fed from heaven, and drank water that flowed from a rock, protected and guided by clouds of glory during the day and pillars of fire that illuminated the darkness!

Even within the Land of Israel, where we lived a "normal" life, our victories were miraculous. We consulted the "*urim v'thumim*"[295] on the breastplate of the High Priest for direct guidance from G-d. Prophets lived among us; the voice of G-d was in our midst. The world knew this.

This was the unique gift to the children of Israel.

But as our alienation from G-d and each other grew, our ability to speak with G-d diminished, until prophecy disappeared from among the children of Israel. In the Garden of Eden, after Adam and Eve sinned, they hid from G-d. They covered their eyes, as it were, so they would not see Him. This is what happens at each instance of rebellion. G-d is still there, but we shut our eyes and pretend that He isn't.

At the same time as prophecy ended, the period of the Written Bible ended, which is no surprise, since the criterion for inclusion in the Bible is that the words have issued from the "mouth" of G-d. Once men stop speaking words that emanate from G-d, there is no more possibility that their words can become books of the Written Bible. It was during this period, after the building of the Second Temple, that our last prophets spoke. The dramatic reduction of G-d's obvious presence among the children of Israel was one of the major differences between the First and Second Temples.[296] We were preparing to go into exile, and the hallmark of exile is "*hester panim*," the hiding of G-d's "face."

This was the period of the Book of Esther, the story of Purim, which took place during the Babylonian Exile after the destruction of the First Temple. "*Esther*" is related to "*hester*" ("hidden") and please recall that the name of G-d is not mentioned in the Book of Esther. We were now entering a period in our history when G-d's presence would become hidden as a matter of course and the direction of our destiny would be indicated only by hints visible to the wise, who see behind the material veil.

From the prophets, the leadership of our Nation shifted to the scholars of the Torah. A new phenomenon arose, which was part of the transition to the hidden. Our Torah is two, Written and Oral. The Written Torah, known as the Bible, which was completed and sealed in this period, is known to the entire world, to such an extent that two major belief systems claim it as their own, although it is not their own. It was dictated to our prophets by G-d. We are the "light to the nations,"[297] and our Bible has guided the world since Mount Sinai.

But G-d gave us two Torahs, the Written Torah,[298] (the "Bible") dictated to Moses on Mount Sinai during the day, and the Oral Torah, consisting of the explanation of those books given to Moses at night,[299] and passed down orally through every generation since then, to this very moment. Night means Exile, and the Oral Torah has sustained us — it is really the only thing that has sustained us – in Exile.

Malachi, the final prophet, indicates the transition from prophecy in the very end of his writings: *"Remember the teaching of Moses, My servant, which I commanded him at [Sinai] for all Israel, decrees and ordinances."*[300] This is the point at which the prophets cease to guide the children of Israel and the rabbis of the Mishna and the Talmud take over as the leaders of our people until the time of the Messiah.[301]

What is the Talmud that fathers have passed down to sons, *rebbes* to their students in every generation to this very day, but that Oral Torah revealed to Moses at Mount Sinai and then passed down through the generations? What has sustained the children of Israel? What has guided our lives and enabled us to survive and maintain our holy tradition, indeed our very existence, through all our trials and the wanderings of our exile? Only this invisible thread, this spiritual chain, the Torah of words passed down from father to son, *rebbe* to *talmid*.

The fact that this invisible chain of words became our only means of sustenance is an indication of the nature of our lives during our long exile. What do we have that is uniquely ours but the Oral Torah? You can say that the Children of Israel possess an eternal link to the Land of Israel and to each other as a result of our common ancestry, but how would we even know that if it were not for our Oral Torah?

But where is it? You cannot find it, because it is invisible! Yes, its outline may have been "captured" in books, but essentially the Oral Torah is invisible, because it is words, and only words. Words are invisible.

Words are the most powerful force in the world; G-d created the universe with words. To say, "the pen is mightier than the sword" is not even to begin to understand the power of words. It's not that the pen is mightier than the sword; it is that the pen IS the sword!

You might say that because the Oral Torah is not visible it is not real, but quite the contrary. The truth is that because it is invisible it is also invincible! Our enemies cannot find it and therefore they can never destroy it. Although it is in this world, it is not a part of this world, and thus it is eternal and indestructible.

Only we who live it know what it is and where it is!

This is what is responsible for the unique blessing bestowed upon the Nation of Israel. *"Rabbi Yitzhak said, there is blessing only in things hidden from the eye... In the School of Rabbi Yishmael it was taught, 'Blessing is only possible in things not under the direct control of the eye... Blessing is not to be found in anything that has been already weighed or measured or numbered, but only in a thing hidden from sight.'"*[302]

DEPENDANCE UPON THE INVISIBLE

Let's trace the cycle of Biblical holidays through the year. We begin with Passover, with matzah and our release from slavery in Egypt. Very tangible.

We continue with *Shavuos* and the receiving of the Torah at Mount Sinai. That was an eminently visible event, but we received something spiritual, so the visible and the invisible have begun to merge.

Where do we end the holiday cycle?

First there is *Rosh Hashanah*, on which we somehow associate our survival and the complete cleansing of our souls with listening to the sound of a ram's horn.

Then, on the holiest day of the year, we pray in bare feet.

Finally, we end the season in a flimsy hut, waving plants in the air, with branches over our heads, surrounded by invisible guests![303]

Are we crazy?

If we are, it is certainly effective, because we are still here after thousands of years of ceaseless attacks and the unwavering hatred of the entire world.

The *sukkah*, a hut with no roof, has protected us since we marched in the desert under Moses. While steel skyscrapers buckle and fall, our flimsy *sukkahs* stand eternally! What holds them up? What sustains us?

Who visits us in the sukkah? Invisible guests: Abraham, Isaac, Jacob, Joseph, Moses, Aaron and David. Where are they? You can't see them? You say they are not real? OK, but when every other nation, no matter how strong, has fallen and we are still here, doesn't it make you wonder just who is real and who isn't?

What is our protection during exile? What enables us to survive the dark winter until Passover returns in the spring? A bundle of fruit and branches and leaves! That is a sword? That is protection? Other nations have "real" weapons and we have a toy sword!

"Some [fight] with chariots, and some with horses, but we … in the name of G-d. They slumped and fell, but we arose and were invigorated."[304]

We are the heirs of King David. You may say his weapon was a stone, which was nothing compared to the power of Goliath, but when you examine David's words, you will see that his weapon was not even the stone. Please listen to David's words: *"You come to me with a sword, a spear and a javelin – but I come to you with the Name of G-d, Master of Legions, the G-d of the battalions of Israel that you have ridiculed."** David's weapon was words, words of Torah, words of reliance on G-d!

---

* I Samuel 17:45. The incredible fact is that David and Goliath were cousins, and one sees from this that all of history can hang on a few words! David's great grandmother Ruth told Naomi, "where you go, I will go.…your G-d is my G-d" (Ruth 1:16). But Ruth's sister Orpah returned to her native Moab with its corruption and idolatry. Orpah became the great grandmother of Goliath!

When we take a pill or go into surgery, is it the pill that saves us? Is it the surgeon who saves us? If G-d wants the pill to work it will work. If G-d guides the surgeon's hands they will heal.

Our friend had to have open-heart surgery in the early days of that procedure.[305] It was a long trip to the surgeon, but there was no choice. When he and his wife arrived at the hospital, unable even to meet the great doctor, they were overwhelmed and frightened. On the morning of the surgery, after her husband was wheeled into the operating room, our friend's wife found the hospital chapel and broke down in tears. Soon she heard a man's voice.

"What is wrong? Why are you crying?"

She looked up to see a stranger.

"My husband has just now gone into surgery. I don't know if I will ever see him again. We haven't even met Dr. Jarvis."[306]

"My dear lady, I am Dr. Jarvis. Before every operation, I come here to ask G-d to guide my hands. Please be assured, your husband will be fine and he will resume a healthy life. Don't be afraid."

Our friend recovered.

What sustains Israel? Is it material or is it spiritual? Is it visible or is it invisible? Is it buildings of steel or is it the seemingly flimsy *sukkah* in which we dwell by Divine command? Are we bound by time and space or do we transcend the limits of this world?

These are the teachings of *Sukkos*, and, revealingly, *Sukkos* is the last holiday before the darkness of winter. *Sukkos* is the holiday that sends us into the winter with the proper orientation and armament. In the darkness of exile the face of G-d is hidden, but ironically in the darkness the reality of G-d is affirmed.

In the period between the two Temples the Nation of Israel became completely dependant upon the invisible. The Oral Law became our only means of support, the staff upon which we leaned as we walked – and sometimes limped — through history. It has supported us! How do we know? The proof is clear: we are still here! Of course the nations of the world mock us, just as Goliath mocked David. But we are here, *"they slumped and fell, but we arose and were invigorated."*[307] The Nation of Israel lives, *"Am Yisroel chai!"*

CAUSELESS HATRED BETWEEN JEW AND JEW

As we became dependant upon the invisible, we also became prey to an "invisible" sin, which more than any other is identified with the destruction of the Second Temple and the exile which continues to this day.

"Why was the First Temple destroyed? Because of three things that prevailed there: idol worship, immorality, and bloodshed… Why was the Second Temple destroyed…? Because of groundless hatred [between Jew and Jew]."[308]

What is so serious about groundless hatred between Jew and Jew? I understand that it is serious, but is it serious enough to cause the destruction of the Second Temple and the seemingly endless exile that followed its destruction?

The origins of this devastating problem go back to Joseph and his brothers. After idolatry was strained out of the Jewish family during the generations of the Patriarchs and Matriarchs, we were twelve tribes, wholly dedicated to the service of G-d. But as soon as this generation appeared, its own particular problem became visible, and that problem was internal disunity. The children of Israel simply cannot exist as one family without that unity, and the problems began at once.

"Joseph dreamt a dream which he told to his brothers, and they hated him."[309]

How serious was the hatred?   Look what happens when brother hates brother. First, the brothers wanted to kill Joseph. They almost did, except for the protestations of Reuben and the fact that Judah caused him to be sold rather than killed.[310] But they did sell him, into slavery in Egypt. After a while, all the brothers and their father were also taken into Egypt. At first they were treated with honor, but after Jacob died they themselves became slaves, in the classic pattern that their descendants have followed so often during our many exiles. This was prophetic, a harbinger of the future; *"ma'ase avos siman l'banim."*

Hatred among the brothers leads to exile, slavery to our enemies, from which we are saved only by the mercies of G-d when we cry out to Him. Our history has been one exile after another, and the genesis of them all is this tragedy of brother against brother.

Tragically, when our enemies try to destroy us, they are only imitating our actions![311] What did Joseph's brothers say? *"Let us kill him, and throw him into one of the pits."*[312] It was only because Reuben said, *"shed no blood"*[313] that Joseph was sold into slavery instead. But how many children of Israel were to die later in Egypt as a result of that slavery!

The actions of our fathers are a sign to us, the children. The archetypal slavery in Egypt was the pattern of all future slaveries. When the brothers fight, when we allow jealousy to motivate our behavior, when we as individuals became enslaved by our own jealousies, then we all go down into slavery at the hands of our enemies among the surrounding nations. This is the tragedy that enveloped us during the period of the Second Temple.

Our salvation is based on unity, unity among the brothers

and unity of the brothers with G-d. Division among the brothers results in division between us and G-d. And since the Jewish People were created to guide the world to G-d, when we become divorced from G-d, the entire world becomes divorced from G-d.

G-d created all mankind from one set of parents. When Eve put her personal desires above the will of G-d, the result was tragedy in her own family and separation from G-d. So it seems that it is in our interests to sublimate personal desire in favor of unity. That does not mean we should eliminate natural differences and become homogenous, not at all.[314]

Each of the twelve tribes is different, each has its unique characteristics, but all are expected to act in such a way as to enhance the life of the community and to act for the sake of the others. In a marriage, husband and wife are different; "opposites attract." It may be better that a very creative person be married to a very practical person; the two may make a perfect couple because each completes the personality of the other. Two halves make a whole, as long as they act as a unit, each living for the welfare of the other.

It seems this is how the children of Israel are expected to act. People of different personalities, different temperaments, different talents, living in harmony as one family, an orchestra whose different instruments create a beautiful song. If we do not live in peace with each other the harmony will not be heard, either on earth or in the spiritual realms.

Here is what the Code of Jewish Law says about what our state of mind should be before we start to pray: *"You must determine to love every Jew as yourself, because if there is… dissension within Israel in this world, there is no harmony in the world above. However, unity in this world promotes spiritual unity in the worlds above, and as a result, our prayers also become unified, and when our prayers are unit-*

ed into one, they are accepted favorably before G-d."[315]   It is very
interesting that unity among us enables us to communicate with
G-d.

Judah became the hereditary king because Judah was willing
to humble himself, willing to admit his faults in order to preserve truth and the honor of another person.[316]   King David
ruled because he was willing to humble himself to preserve truth
and the honor of another person and to let the will of G-d
rule.[317]   These are the character traits that enable the children
of Israel to exist eternally.   The opposite character traits –
enhancement of one's own interests at the expense of others –
are what destroy our unity and threaten the existence of Israel
as a nation.   When hatred and bitterness reign among us, that is
when our nation becomes subject to the bitter hatred of our enemies and slides into exile and destruction.

The differences between the eras of the First and Second
Temples are frightening.   It isn't just that in the Second Temple
obvious miracles were lacking and the presence of G-d receded.
Israel was a different land entirely in the time of the Second Tem-
ple.   While the First Temple stood, especially during the reigns of
David and Solomon, Israel was independant, beholden only to
G-d and blessed by Him.   Not only were we militarily secure, but
kings and princes came to marvel and to learn from us.

During the glory of the First Temple, we were a living sancti-
fication of G-d's Name; our national existence brought honor to
Him.   But the Second Temple was built only because the ruler of
Persia permitted it!

The Second Temple itself and the State of Israel that existed while it stood, endured only because foreign governments
permitted them to endure.   We were no longer an independant
nation, beholden only to G-d.   The sanctification of G-d's
Name that had occurred during the existence of the First Tem-

ple was not possible during the period of the Second Temple, because our attachment to G-d was no longer as visible. Our very ability to live by the precepts of the Torah was granted only by the whim of the ruler whose empire was currently in control... and sometimes it was <u>not</u> granted! Along with foreign rulers came foreign influence. During the times of foreign influence certain Jews began to believe that their welfare depended on alliance with foreign foes, rather than alliance with their brethren and devotion to the Torah.[318]

No iron tools were used in the construction of the Temple. Iron symbolizes war and the Temple is the antidote to war, the symbol of world unity and peace under the Law of the Creator.[319] There was no sound of cutting. But now the sound of war was heard in the Holy Land. The most frightening sound was the sound of Jew fighting Jew.

LOSHON HA'RA

An outgrowth of groundless hatred, indeed its most dangerous manifestation, is "*loshon hara*," evil talk.

When I have a criticism of someone, do I speak <u>to</u> the person or <u>about</u> the person? That is the essential question concerning *loshon hara.*

If I speak <u>to</u> the person, with humility and without anger — not easy! — I am acting out of love.[320]

But if I speak <u>about</u> the person, my words will cause others to see that person negatively, creating a gulf between them. Then I am not acting out of love, but out of revenge, anger or jealousy. I am creating a division among my brethren, destroying my family!

If I have spoken negatively about someone, or have listened to negative comments about someone, I know that I cannot look at that person in the same way any more. The accusations or innuendoes I have heard are always between us. If we brothers and sisters cannot look at each other with love, but are separated by suspicion, anger or feelings of superiority, the fabric of our family has been destroyed, like a garment that has become moldy and rotten and can no longer clothe us with dignity.

Division among the members of our family has resulted in the destruction of the Second Temple and the death and exile of millions of our brethren, from the time of the Romans through the European Holocaust and up to our very day.

We are selling Joseph again and again. Whenever we exile Joseph we are exiling ourselves.

COMPETITION

In the Desert we were attached to G-d by an umbilical cord. He fed us and led us; His prophet Moses was our shepherd. In the time of the First Commonwealth, His Temple stood in our midst, His anointed Kings ruled over us and His miracles were seen clearly in the Land. We were on a high level. We were very close to Him. Even in times of rebellion our closeness was obvious. For example, during our years in the Desert, if we had distanced ourselves from G-d by some act, our portion of *manna* was immediately placed at a more distant location from our tent. The result of speaking *loshon hara* was the immediately visible sign of "*tzaraas,*" a skin disease, upon our bodies, our clothing or our homes.

In the time of the First Temple, if we ran into trouble, it was because we worshipped an idol, a non-god, a stick or a stone or a statue built with our own hands. Those who came to correct us and lead us on the right path had a direct relationship with G-d; they spoke in His Name, with His words.

But in the time of the Second Commonwealth, G-d's presence was no longer as clear and near to us. Even in our periods of relative obedience to G-d we were not as close as in our periods of rebellion in the Desert.

In the generation before Abraham, men had built a tower from which to fight directly with G-d. In the time of the First Temple, men fought against G-d by worshipping something that He created (like a heavenly body or a stick or stone), not G-d Himself. But in the time of the Second Temple, men turned their attention downward; instead of fighting G-d they fought each other; G-d was receding further and further from our perception of reality. The distance was becoming greater, the barrier thicker and reality fuzzier.

I will give you an analogy from our personal experience. Several years ago, our family took a summer trip to Glacier National Park. On the last morning, we awoke at 4 a.m. and drove to one of the highest points in the park, from which we hiked along mountain trails. There, in a bracing wind, with no other people in sight, we saw the sun rise over a wilderness of shining peaks, glistening with snow as far as the eye could see.

By noon we were on our way back, and by that night we were once more in the gritty, smoggy air of New York, among honking taxis and pushing pedestrians. Had we really been in the pure light of that glistening wilderness only a few hours earlier? Was it possible that such a place even existed? Had we been dreaming?

In perhaps the same way, the memory of our pure, shining days with G-d receded from our national memory in the days of the Second Temple.* G-d says to Israel, *"I remember for your sake the kindness of your youth, the love of your bridal days, your*

---

* It should be emphasized, however, that the Second Temple, although not on the level of the First Temple, was an extremely important instituation. In our present exile, we are in a much lower condition than we were in at the time of the Second Temple

following after Me in the wilderness, in a land not sown."[321] Was it real? Had it happened? Were we dreaming? G-d seemed so far away!

This is the era from which we descended into our present exile, an exile in which G-d is so hidden that men, when they desire to fight Him, fight among themselves because their eyes are not accustomed to looking upward. Remember the legend about the man who worshipped G-d by a fire in the forest? His son could not find the spot where his father had made the fire, and in each succeeding generation the memory became blurrier until the son's son's son could not even remember <u>the story</u> of how his ancestors had worshipped G-d at a fire in a clearing in the forest.

Today, we live in a world in which G-d is not real to us, and that world began in the era of the Second Temple. In that era, man descended to the level of jungle warfare, a world in which man competes and fights against man. We had come so far down that we were, for all practical purposes, in a G-d-less world.

This is the world of *sinas chinom*, groundless hatred. This is the world of *loshon hara*, evil talk, in which slander and gossip are accepted materials for conversation and entertainment. Certainly in our own days this is accepted and expected in radio and television and the print media as well as social life. Once slander and gossip become acceptable, then the idea of competition among men becomes acceptable. Character assassination becomes a sought-after weapon in the war.

As I wrote these words,[322] an unknown gunman was killing people day after day near Washington, D.C. Why would a man shoot people he doesn't know? When Cain killed Abel, he ostensibly had a purpose. Every evil has its rationalization. Later on, one hopefully realizes that one is wrong, and repents (hopefully it is not too late). Cain was wrong, and later he admitted it.[323] At least he could have argued at the time that he had a rationale for his killing. But why would someone want to destroy the life of someone whom he doesn't even know?

The Western World, the world of our current exile, has been trained to believe that competition is our lifeblood. Wall Street, the focus of so much of our attention in America, is based on competition among businesses. In business, it is considered normal for one business to destroy another. Giant chains of stores routinely destroy individual, unaffiliated businesses by reason of superior size and power.

Sports are the glory of the Western World. Even small towns have teams in which young children compete against each other, with parents so involved in the competition that there have been cases of violence and even murder committed at neighborhood athletic events. The passion to defeat, even destroy the other team is so overwhelming that in Europe it is not unusual for riots among sports fans to result in deaths.

Advertising is the glue that holds our media, almost our entire society together. Sixty seconds on certain television shows cost tens of millions of dollars, in order to try to prove that one product is better than another. Politicians and manufacturers openly denounce their competitors, informing listeners that their competitors or products are worthless or even dangerous.

The concept behind advertising is the idea that we are lacking something.[324] In other words, my life is empty unless I take a vacation in Bermuda this winter. My life would be good if I could drive that particular car. Or perhaps I have a computer, but it is not the latest model; it is not good enough. My happiness will not be complete, my needs will not be fulfilled until I buy a better computer or a better car or go to a better restaurant.

But what happens if I am satisfied with my life? That is no good! You cannot be satisfied with your life, because then you will never buy anything!

But the Torah says, *"Who is rich? He who is happy with his lot."*[325]

This is anathema to the advertising world. Advertisers want us to be unhappy with our lot!

This was exactly the sin of the snake in the Garden of Eden.

The snake said to Eve, in effect, *"G-d wants you to think you are complete, but you are not complete; you should not be happy with your lot. Have you ever wondered why G-d wanted you to keep away from the Tree of the Knowledge of Good and Evil? Think about it. Isn't something lacking in your life? Why should you not be like G-d?"*

This is the song of the advertising age, the song of competition, the song of unrest. This is why there is no tranquility in our world. We have led ourselves to believe that only by constant competition, only by focusing on how deprived and unhappy we are, can we live in this world.

This is the catastrophic legacy of *sinas chinom*, hatred between one man and another, which leads to evil talk and competition. Through competition, man becomes no better than beast against beast.

The Second Temple era saw unspeakably cruel wars, both of Jew against Jew, and of the surrounding nations against us. How could we possibly survive in our Holy Land and remain close to G-d when we were fighting each other? Measure for measure, just as we turned on ourselves in violent and bitter confrontation, so the world turned upon us, and the bitter legacy of self-hatred fueled the fires of anti-Semitism, fires that continue to burn and pollute our world today.

When the Sabbath falls on the day before the New Moon, we read in the synagogue a portion from the First Book of

Samuel that describes events that took place on the day before the New Moon. King Saul is sitting at his table in the palace and he is asking, *"Where is David, the Son of Jesse?"*[326]

This is prophetic, for in reality it is the question we have been asking for thousands of years. *"Where is David?"* means, *"Where is the Messiah (who is the Son of David)?"*

What is the answer? Where is David?

The answer is amazing! David is not at King Saul's table because King Saul has driven him away! Because of causeless hatred on the part of King Saul, David is not there!

And because of causeless hatred on our part, David is not here!

Because the children of Israel are fighting the Messiah does not come![327]

Alas, we are so deep in bitter competition that it is extremely difficult to comprehend how we will ever escape. The whole world is on fire, and even if we have the will to put out the flames, we do not know where to start.

THE FOUR EXILES

The Torah tells us there will be Four Exiles in the course of our history, the Exiles of Babylonia, Medea-Persia, Greece, and Rome.[328] At the very dawn of our history, G-d informed our Father Abraham that his children would be taken into Egyptian exile. *"Your offspring shall be aliens in a land not their own... But also the nation they will serve I will judge."* His words implied all the future exiles until this very day.[329]

The exiles of Persia and Greece take place and the Exile of Rome begins during the time we were are still living in the Land of Israel.

How can we be in exile while living in our land?

Well, how can we be in exile today? Aren't millions of Jews living in the Land of Israel right now?

Of course, the answer is the same. Exile is not simply physical dislocation; exile is spiritual dislocation. If we are not serving G-d as a united People, if we are subservient to foreign enemies who allow us to live in our land at their whim, or if we are subject to the control of our own people who reject G-d's laws, then we are very much in servitude and very much in exile.

This is why our Sages tell us that the exile was in force even during the period of the Second Temple.

"Throughout the Talmud and Midrash, and based on the Book of Daniel[330] *Israel's long series of exiles and persecutions are always treated as four main periods of subjection to foreign oppressors – either in the Land of Israel or in the Diaspora. These periods are known collectively as "the Four Kingdoms"*[331] *and each is called by the name of the empire dominant in the world at that particular time... Paradoxically [during the Greek Exile] Israel lived on its Land and the Temple stood. Nevertheless, it was a very turbulent era marked with civil strife, foreign domination, vicious anti-religious campaigns, and the rejection of Torah values by a large number of Jews who adopted Greek culture with all its abominations."*[332]

Let us remember that the prototype exile in the Bible is the Egyptian Exile. And what precipitated that exile? The enmity of Joseph and his brothers! *Sinas chinom*, causeless hatred between brother and brother!

All this is a lesson for today. We are clearly not free from exile until our one and only Master is neither a foreign concept, an idol, nor a foreign nation that dominates us, but rather our Creator.

Our sins during the First Temple era were idol worship, bloodshed and immorality; our counterbalance was the prophets who spoke with the voice of G-d.

Our sin in the Second Temple era was causeless hatred. What was the counterbalance? The voice of the rabbis. The rabbis carry on for the prophets.

Rabban Gamliel, Rabbi Elazar ben Azariah, Rabbi Yehoshua and Rabbi Akiva...were coming up to Jerusalem. When they reached Mount Scopus (and were able to see the City of Jerusalem in its destruction) they rent their garments. When they came to the Temple Mount, they saw a fox emerging from the Holy of Holies, and they started to weep. But Rabbi Akiva smiled. They said to him, "For what reason are you smiling?" He replied to them, "For what reason are you weeping?" They said to him, "A place about which it is written: 'the non-Kohain who comes close shall be put to death'[333] and now foxes are walking about there! Should we not weep?"

He said to them, "For this very reason I am smiling, for it is written: 'I will summon trustworthy witnesses to testify for Me, Uriah the Kohain and Zechariahu ben Yeverechiahu'.[334] Now what connection does Uriah have with Zechariah? Uriah [prophesied] during the [era of] the First Temple, whereas Zechariah [prophesied] during [the era of] the Second Temple. [Why are they mentioned together?] Rather, Scripture made the prophecy of Zechariah dependant upon the prophecy of Uriah. In the prophecy of Uriah it is written, 'Therefore, because of you, Zion will be plowed like a field...'[335] In the prophecy of Zechariah it is written: 'Old men and old women will yet sit in the streets of Jerusalem.'[336] As long as the prophecy of Uriah had not been fulfilled, I had feared that the prophecy of Zechariah would not be fulfilled. Now that the prophecy of Uriah has been fulfilled [and Jerusalem and the Temple Mount are totally desolate] it is obvious that the prophecy of Zechariah will be fulfilled."

[Rabbi Akiva's colleagues] said to him... "Akiva you have comforted us; Akiva you have comforted us."[337]

Rabbi Akiva is still comforting us.

Rabbi Akiva and other shining luminaries like him have enabled the Jewish People to survive to this day, through the most terrible anguish and hardships that any people on earth have experienced.

Do not let any nation tell you, "We have endured more than you." There are nations that have endured hardship and suffering, but all else pales besides the suffering of the children of Israel. We are the prototype and the epitome, precisely because we are carrying in our hands the thread of destiny. The world – which is filled with jealousy – wants to rip that thread from our hand. They attempt not only to rip the thread from us, but to destroy us forever, G-d forbid, so that we should never again be able to bother them with our tales of G-d and morality, our unceasing efforts to elevate ourselves to the service of G-d.

We are different precisely because consistently, from the time of Abraham our Father, the world has consistently and unceasingly attempted to kill us – "*In every generation they rise up against us to destroy us*"[338] — in a never-ending campaign. There is no other nation that has been the victim of such consistent and universal jealousy and hatred. And ironically, there has never been a nation so consistently concerned with the welfare of other nations as well as the elevation of our own conduct and the spiritual level of the world.

We must explore precisely how we were able to survive the destruction of our beautiful civilization, our holy City, our shining Temple. Because if we understand that, we will be able to understand not only how we survived the ensuing two thousand years of bitter exile, but how we will continue to survive whatever comes next and how we will endure as we enter the era of Messiah the son of David.

HOW RABBI AKIVA COMFORTS US

Perhaps the greatest danger in our period of Exile is the danger of depression. Succumbing to it renders one helpless and paralyzed.

Over the past two thousand years and up to this day, the array of internal and external threats against the Jewish people has been so overpowering that one could easily give up. We are a tiny minority in the world, a nation that relies upon belief in what the rest of the world cannot see. Unless our attachment to the invisible Source of our sustenance is constant and unyielding, we cannot possibly survive.

Please consider what Rabbi Akiva was saying; it constitutes the basis of our survival in the face of potential disaster.

Rabbi Akiva was staring at the ruins of our civilization, the rubble of our greatness. This was not even from our First Temple, but the lesser, Second Temple, ruin on top of ruin! Those ruins were the harbinger of countless catastrophes to come, and the rabbis knew it! Any person who relied only upon the "logic" of what his eyes perceived would have given up long ago!

How do we survive in spite of such clear reason for despair? Our Torah tells us, *"Do not follow after your heart and after your eyes, after which you stray."*[339]

Recently, a study was published showing that the population of the Jewish People is dwindling in the United States. Those who commissioned the study declared that this bodes ill for our survival. For thousands of years, the secular minds of the world have been predicting the demise of the children of Israel.

But we are still here!

Think of it!

We were entering a period in which we would be scattered to the four corners of the earth, a tiny minority in each country, and there is hardly a country in the world without Jews. In most countries we were deprived of the rights of citizens, often deprived of the right to own land or enter respectable professions, and almost always prevented from bearing arms to defend ourselves against the nearly universal and constant hatred, abuse and violence that was to be directed toward us. All this after we had been the glory of the world, the object of wonder!   The Queen of Sheba had come to gaze in awe at the Temple of G-d … and now the children of Israel were being sold as slaves, tossed to the winds, at the mercy of the cruelest of the cruel.

Here is Rabbi Akiva, eyeing the destruction of all that is holy and – knowing what is to come – he is laughing! How can it be?

The root of the name Isaac means "laughter." At the end of history, the children of Isaac will be laughing. *"When G-d will return the captivity of Zion, we will be like dreamers. Then our mouth will be filled with laughter and our tongue with glad song."*[340]

But how can Rabbi Akiva laugh? He was standing at the <u>beginning</u> of the Exile, not after G-d had returned the captivity of Zion! Is he a prophet? Is he living in the present? Does he know what he is seeing?

Oh yes! Rabbi Akiva knew. We should only know what he knew!

He is giving us the secret of our survival through the long, dark night of exile.

It's not that he is a prophet, for the age of prophecy was over. But he <u>believed</u> the prophets. Listen to his words. The prophet stated that, *"Zion would be plowed like a field."* Do you think that prophecy is depressing?

The fact that Zion was plowed like a field is tragic. But the fact that the prophet told us so in advance is <u>liberating</u>! It is our <u>freedom</u>! It is our <u>hope</u>! It is our <u>sustenance</u>!

Why?

It shows that we are above all that happens to us. The very fact that we are warned in advance by G-d indicates that our destiny is eternal, and that we will prevail over time.

There are two passages in the Bible called "*tochecha,*" admonition.[341] They are so terrifying that they are read in a low voice. Traditionally the Torah reader himself makes the blessings over these passages because no one else wishes to be called up to this passage as if it should apply to him. They are the prophecies relating to the destruction of the future First and Second Temples[342] and all later tragedies, and the details related in those two prophecies are such that one can hardly bear to hear them.

The unbelievable fact is that those two passages, like the prophecy of "Zion will be plowed like a field," are in one sense the most liberating passages in the Torah.

Again, why?

Because when we get to that terrible moment, when we see the destruction all around us, the unfathomable depth of horror confronting us on every side, the cruelty, the viciousness of man, the unspeakable destruction which spares neither grandfather, grandmother, father or mother, or innocent child, which aims for the holiest of the holies, the nation of G-d and the people of G-d, when we see the un-seeable and hear the un-hearable and bear the unbearable, <u>there is only one thing that can sustain us: that it was all predicted</u>!

Do you understand what I am saying?

If these things would have come upon us without having been predicted, then there would be no consolation. If the Temple had been destroyed and G-d had not told us it would be destroyed, if He had not warned us exactly what was going to happen, then there would have been no hope for us, there would be no way ever to overcome our grief, no future but the grave.

But G-d told us this would happen! The entire scenario had been spelled out in advance. We had been told in very blunt terms that, if we rebelled against Him, the consequence would be exile and the agonies that accompany it. We were given every detail of that exile. After that, if we do rebel and then we are exiled and every detail occurs just as it was foretold, are we not receiving precise confirmation that all G-d has told us in the Torah is true, down to the tiniest dot on the smallest letter!

Those, for example, who say "G-d is dead" after the recent Holocaust, are reading Torah and history upside down and backwards.[343] If anything, the events of the Holocaust era are stark and unassailable confirmation of the truth of the Torah and the omnipresence of G-d. The events of those terrible times had been preceded by ominous changes in the European Jewish Community. Never before had there been such a wholesale abandonment of our ancient heritage by so many of our brothers and sisters. The winds of assimilation were blowing strongly all over Europe, but nowhere more than in Germany, the birthplace of the vicious darkness that spread out like poison gas to destroy almost the entire European Jewish community.

And people ask, "where was G-d?"

G-d was where He always is, keeping His promises, according to the Torah that spells out the rewards of keeping close to Him and the consequences of rebelling against Him. Two times a day we say, *"beware lest your heart be seduced and you turn astray and serve gods of others and bow to them. Then the wrath of G-d will blaze against you. He will restrain the heaven so there will be no rain and the ground will not yield its produce. And you will swiftly be banished from the goodly land which G-d gives you. Place these words of Mine upon your heart and upon your soul..."*[344]

Are these words empty? Why does G-d say we should place

them "upon your heart and your soul?" Because if we are to survive, these words had better be placed upon our heart and upon our soul! What was Rabbi Akiva focused on if not the words of prophecy that predicted the destruction he saw before him? It is those words that permitted him to smile, those words that confirmed "in his heart" and "in his soul" the eternal conviction that G-d's prophecy of comfort would also come to pass.

THE AGE OF ANGER

Why is the period from the Second Temple to the present designated as the period in which "causeless hatred between Jew and Jew" ruined our national life? Why is causeless hatred the hallmark of our times and the cause of our troubles? Why not something else?

When the Presence of G-d departed from our midst with the destruction of the First Temple, we lost something comparable to what was lost when Adam and Eve were expelled from the Garden or when the Flood destroyed the once-pristine earth.

During the era of the First Temple, the world had been a different place. G-d had come down to earth! *Would G-d truly dwell on earth?* Yes, He did dwell on earth; His Presence had been seen and felt in the Temple. As long as He was in our midst, the world was different. Our evil inclination was subdued; our ability to stray was limited, because G-d was being "welcomed" to earth by the presence of the Holy Temple. Atonement for sin was possible because of the Temple sacrifices. Spiritual defilement could be nullified by the ashes of the red heifer. Even when we sinned – and the means of purification were given to us precisely because G-d knows how human we are! – we were able to purify ourselves and the world in those holy times through the presence of the Temple in our midst.[345]

But when the First Temple was destroyed and the Presence of G-d was removed somewhat from us, we were "alone in the world," so to speak. The barriers against raising ourselves above our earthly tendencies became that much more powerful. If Mount Everest becomes our highest goal, then we are limited to the material, like the generation of the Tower of Babel, who thought they could find G-d by climbing higher materially.[346]

See how King David viewed the world: *"I raise my eyes to the mountains; whence will come my help?"*[347] But no, the mountains are not enough. David sees he has to go above the earth for help. He doesn't stop at the mountains. *"My help is from G-d, Maker of heaven and earth."*[348]

For us Jews, the only escape from the world of exile has been through the door to Eternity offered us by the Written and Oral Law, the allegiance to which has reestablished our living relationship with G-d.

Why do you think that our enemies over the centuries wanted more than anything to eliminate – G-d forbid! – the "Talmud Jew"? Because the Jew who lives by the Talmud, the Oral Law, is the Jew who will bring the presence of G-d back into the world. Our enemies do not want G-d back in the world. They don't want G-d to look at them. Evil people do not want to know that everything they do is seen and recorded. They don't want to know that *"above you [there is] a watchful Eye, an attentive Ear and [that] all your deeds are recorded in a Book."*[349]

Since the disappearance of the First Temple, the traits of anger and competition among men have increased in the world. Why? Since we live in a world of materialism, we blame other men – rather than our own spiritual shortcomings – if we cannot achieve what we want. We feel that other people stand between us and the fulfillment of our desires. We cannot see beyond men. The pursuit of happiness becomes our goal rather than the satisfaction of G-d's will. If we are denied happiness, then whom do we blame? There is no one to blame but all those other people who are putting their happiness before my happiness! I am entitled to happiness! I am entitled to picket, demonstrate, push other people out of my way, even to shoot and kill.

This is the world after the Presence of G-d has departed, a world in which we no longer look "above the mountains." This is the world of bitterness and competition. This is the world we have created and inherited. This is the catastrophe of the destruction of our Temples and the exile of the *Shechina*. This is the disastrous world that confronted our fathers as they surveyed the smoking ruins of the holiest civilization that ever existed upon the earth. This is our boundless grief.

The only way out was the way of Rabbi Akiva, to look back upon the prophecy and realize that <u>even this</u> is within the purview of G-d, <u>even this</u> was predicted. If the very emptiness of this post-Temple world drives us closer toward G-d, then we will find what Rabbi Akiva found. If this prophecy of destruction has come to pass, so will the all the other prophecies of redemption, hope and fulfillment.

"Even though I walk through the valley of death, I will fear no evil, for You are with me."[350]

As we walked through the Valley of Death for the next 2000 years, we knew G-d was still with us. As we walked we kept the Talmud, the Oral Law, in front of our eyes. It was our guide, our <u>only</u> guide. With it, we were to survive and prepare for the day when we would return to Zion and rebuild the Temple and the ancient cities, and live together in peace in the Garden *"flowing with milk and honey."*

"Ki mitzion taitzay Torah u d'var Hashem M'Yerushalayim."

"From Zion goes forth Torah and the Word of G-d from Jerusalem."[351]

"Thus said G-d: 'There will again be heard in this place about which you say 'It is destroyed, without man and without animal,' in the cities of Judah and in the streets of Jerusalem that are desolate... the sound of joy and the sound of gladness, the sound of groom and the sound of bride the sound of people saying, 'Praise G-d, Master of Legions, for He is good, for His mercy is forever,' bringing thanks-giving offerings to the Temple of G-d; for I will return the captivity of the land as at first, said G-d."[352]

"Behold, days are coming – the word of G-d – when I will fulfill the favorable matter that I spoke concerning the House of Israel and the house of Judah. In those days, at that time, I will cause a sprout of righteousness to sprout forth for David and he will administer justice and righteousness in the land. In those days Judah will be saved and Jerusalem will dwell in security."[353]

"[G-d] raises the needy from the dust, from the trash heaps He lifts the destitute... to seat them with nobles...."[354]

Rabbi Akiva will be smiling.

CHAPTER FIVE

THE EXILE OF ROME: DESTRUCTION OF THE SECOND TEMPLE TO SEPTEMBER 11, 2001

"Let him put his mouth to the dust - there may yet be hope."[355]

The dominating occurrence of this period is the destruction of our national existence in the Land of our heritage and our dispersion into alien cultures.

The Bible refers, as we noted earlier, to Four Exiles that will envelope the children of Israel: Babylonia, Persia and Medea, Greece, and Rome (or Edom, who are the descendants of Esau).[356] Our rabbis[357] tell us that at the end of the Roman Exile will be a final Exile in which we will confront the children of Ishmael. This final Exile appears to be the era in which we are now living.[358]

Why are Rome and Edom equated?

When Esau was born he *"emerged red,"*[359] *"admoni"* in Hebrew. From this root, the name *"Edom"* was applied to Esau. The Bible tells us that, *"Esau ... is Edom."*[360] *"Edom ... evolved into Rome, the perpetual enemy of Israel.*"[361]

Esau never forgot his ancient enmity toward his brother Jacob. Esau and Jacob could have worked harmoniously as brothers, Esau to elevate the material world to its highest level and Jacob to prepare us for the eternal spiritual world.[362] But Esau had become infected by the "disease" that first broke out in the Garden of Eden. He was not satisfied with his destiny, and as a result the seemingly endless battle of brother against brother began, the battle that has resulted in so much tragedy and so many tears over the thousands of years since it began.

The two most consistent antagonists of the children of Israel over the centuries have been the children of Esau and the children of Ishmael. It was to these two nations that we were exiled after the tragic destruction of the Second Temple. Besides their seemingly eternal war against us, the children of Esau and the children of Ishmael have also conducted a seemingly endless war against each other. Especially since the founding of Islam in the year 622, the two nations have engaged in a seesaw battle for control of the western world.

The children of Ishmael have generally resided to the south and east of the Mediterranean Sea, and the children of Esau to the north and west. In general, the children of Esau have prevailed as the leading and more powerful culture of the Western World. Starting, however, with the discovery of oil-fueled engines, the power of the oil-rich world of Islam has begun to grow, until now the children of Ishmael have assumed enormous economic, political and demographic influence.

Now this conflict is coming to a climax. In our generation we have witnessed the cataclysmic attack of the children of Ishmael against the children of Esau on September 11, 2001, and the counter-attack, in which the children of Esau invaded Afghanistan and Iraq.

All this is coming to pass as we enter the final period in history before the coming of Messiah the son of David. But we are
getting ahead of ourselves, and before we come up to the Exile
of Ishmael, let us try to build a foundation for our understanding by discussing these two cultures in greater depth.

As we said, the children of Ishmael and the children of
Esau/Rome have existed – albeit in tension – side by side in the
Western Hemisphere since the time of their progenitors. For
some fourteen hundred years, since the rise of Islam, the tension
has increased. There is a key that gives deep insight into the
nature of these two cultures and shows vividly their contrast not
only to each other, but also how both of them are in stark contrast to the culture of the children of Israel. That key is to be
found in our respective calendars. I would like now to delve
into the remarkable differences among these three calendars.

THE WORLD OF THE SUN, THE WORLD OF THE MOON

The Roman calendar is based on the sun. The children of Esau
are people of the sun. Their achievements – constructing
great monuments, palaces, skyscrapers, fortresses, aqueducts,
bridges, roadways and railways — take place under the sun.
Their ethic is work; they are builders. They have raised an
empire of stone, brick, and steel, countless inventions designed
to make agriculture, business and all material aspects of life easi-
er and more efficient. They desire to exploit nature to man's
advantage. Later came factories, engines, new weapons and new
means of locomotion. The civilization of Esau, what we refer to
in general as European culture, also enjoys the products it creates
under the sun: the great cuisines of the world include the French,

the Italian, the Viennese. France in particular is obsessed with eating and drinking. Materialism, exploitation of the earth: these are the goals of the people of the sun. Like the sun, they are a dependable, steady people, whose course of life, while varied, is predictable.

The Islamic calendar is based on the moon.

The children of Ishmael are people of the moon. In fact, the symbol of Islam is the crescent moon! While the children of Edom toil dependably every day under the sun, the children of Ishmael move with the shifting sands of the desert, here one day and there the next. They shift and change in their personality as well as their physical location. As a result, they are mysterious and elusive, like a desert wind, moving in semi-darkness from place to place. Because the light and heat of the desert preclude daytime travel, their movements must often be at night.

The children of Ishmael became a spiritual people, emphasizing philosophy and attempting to reach G-d under the light of the moon. Since the nature of their environment precludes them from concentrating on material achievements, they have concentrated rather on the world of the spiritual, a pursuit associated with night, when the earth is still. Like the moon, they seem to wax and wane; sometimes they are strong and sometimes their influence seems almost to disappear. Their holidays and months revolve around the seasons in a fluid dance, whereas the holidays and months of Edom/Rome are firmly stuck to a fixed spot in the solar calendar, the calendar of the seasons.

The children of Esau are material to a fault; the children of Ishmael are spiritual to a fault.

THE CHILDREN OF ISRAEL, SEPARATED FROM BOTH

Separated from both[363] are the children of Israel. Our calendar is based upon both the sun and the moon!

Please listen, my friends, to something remarkable. The first commandment given to the children of Israel under the leadership of Moses and Aaron was the commandment to establish a calendar.[364] Upon this calendar our entire national life is based, with its yearly cycle of holy days and a system of agricultural and communal laws tied to Biblically-ordained months.

Our calendar is unique.

Our months are based on the moon; our years are based on the sun.

Each month begins upon the appearance of the new moon. Yet, we know that the total of lunar months does not add up to a solar year. If we depended entirely upon the lunar months, as the Moslems do, our months would "migrate" around the calendar; eventually the month of Nissan, for example, in which Passover takes place, would wind up in the summer or autumn or winter.

But there is a Biblical commandment that Passover must be in the spring, which is a season defined by the position of the sun.[365] How then do we reconcile months based on the cycles of the moon with a year based on the cycle of the sun?

We adjust our years periodically to include an extra month, in order to keep the holidays at their Biblically-ordained times in the solar year. Seven times in each nineteen-year cycle we add an additional, thirteenth month in order to keep our lunar months and our solar years in proper adjustment. This unique calendar system has guided us through hundreds of years of exile and torturous dislocation, with our national life and laws intact. Like the

Pillars of Cloud by day and Pillars of Fire by night that accompanied our ancestors in the Desert, this unique system has shepherded and guided us through history!

Other nations have tried to copy us. They take one part of our system or another part of our system but the synthesis of moon and sun, spiritual and material that is uniquely ours they cannot understand nor can they live by.

That is how we are able to exist both in the material and the spiritual world. Like Jacob's ladder, our feet are on the ground but our head is in heaven. Those who dwell to an excessive degree in the material world or the spiritual world live an extreme and unbalanced existence, but we combine, incorporate and harmonize both the material and the spiritual, the temporal and the eternal. We are high but we are also deep. In the material world of history we wax and wane like the moon, but in the spiritual world our flame burns steadily like the light of the sun.

We have a balance that is shared by no other nation. Our calendar tells the story.

THE MOON VERSUS THE SUN

The Torah contains a remarkable discussion concerning the sun and the moon. G-d created these two heavenly bodies of equal size, but the moon complained to G-d, *"it is impossible for two kings to use the same crown."* G-d "punished" the moon for its contentiousness and jealousy by reducing its size.[366]

What a charming fairy tale!

This is no fairy tale.

This "fairy tale" perhaps explains the history of the past fourteen hundred years!

We have just said that the sun is associated with Esau/Rome, and the moon with Ishmael/Islam.

I was trying to understand why Islam constantly attacks the descendants of Esau. What is the origin of the events of September 11, 2001? Why have the two cultures been fighting ever since Islam was born some fourteen hundred years ago? We know that Islam demands that the entire world adhere to its belief; one who refuses is deserving of death. That is the origin of "Jihad," so-called holy war. Islam has always tried – sometimes with greater and sometimes with lesser success – to take over the world. Islam and the Roman world have been jockeying back and forth for centuries.

How do we explain it? What do they have against each other? If you go back to their origins, isn't Ishmael really fighting Isaac and Esau fighting Jacob? Yes, that is true, but why are they fighting each other?

This made no sense to me until I remembered how these two nations are compared to the sun and the moon. And then I remembered that the moon attacked the sun in the beginning of time. And why are they fighting? Here again is what Rashi says: *"The [two] great lights ... were created equal and the moon was reduced because it complained and said, 'It is impossible for two kings to use the same crown.'"*[367] The moon wanted to rule the world and so it attacked the sun. On September 11, the moon attacked the sun.[368]

Israel is concentrating on the Eternal World. We are not competing with anyone. The Eternal World, the World of Truth, is there for anyone, Jew or non-Jew,[369] who cleaves to G-d. But Ishmael and Esau do not desire the World of Truth; they are busy fighting each other, as the moon fought the sun.

Israel is not competing against them, but they cannot tolerate Israel. By attaching ourselves to the eternal World of Truth, the children of Israel have declared that we are independent of their world, beyond its control and beyond the control of Ishmael and Esau.[370] The children of Ishmael and Esau hate us because they desire to control everything in this world and they know they cannot control us as long as we cleave to G-d. They therefore try to separate us from G-d in order to remove our protection and make us vulnerable to them.

In the mastery of the Western world, Esau has generally prevailed over the past two thousand years, but our rabbis tell us that the children of Ishmael will prevail in the very end of history, until they both fall. Then Messiah, son of David, will usher in the era in which G-d's laws will govern the earth. Little Israel, who <u>never</u> fought for control of this world, will then become the *"head and not the tail."*[371]

ABOVE THE MOON AND SUN

Edom/Rome's domination of the Western World for the past two thousand years corresponds to the fact that the sun is the dominant body in the heavens. The light of the sun is self-generated; the light of the moon is a reflection of the light of the sun. When the sun is up, the moon is invisible. Only in periods of darkness does the moon appear. Edom/Rome has been the driving force behind "progress," which is considered in the Western World the *raison d'etre* of civilization. Ishmael/Islam has taken a back seat to Rome in contributing to the development of what we call the "modern world."

But Islam is not happy with that designation, just as the moon was not happy with sharing rulership of the world with the sun. In the material world, no one likes to be second best. The jealousy of the moon against the sun is a fact of life, and that apparently is why the Torah discusses it. The Torah does not tell us about things that are inapplicable to us; it describes what we need to know in order to live. The rivalry of the moon with the sun is a key to our world.

The Roman and Moslem calendars are completely sub-servient to the heavenly bodies. Is there any choice about the way the months fall in the Roman calendar? January, February …all the way to December. Is there any choice about their order? When they begin and end? Is there any choice about Ramadan? When the month comes, the month comes; no one can change it.

Is there any choice about the beginning of a Jewish month?

Yes, there certainly is!

The month does not begin because a new moon appears; the month begins because two witnesses <u>see</u> the new moon and then go to the Sanhedrin and declare that they have seen it. The Sanhedrin, if it is satisfied with the witnesses, declares that a new month has begun. Once the Sanhedrin declares a new month, the month begins. Even if the witnesses' information later proves to be incorrect, the new month begins only when the Sanhedrin declares it, because G-d has given this power to the children of Israel. The language in the Bible is, *"this month shall be <u>for you</u> the beginning of months."*[372] Perhaps "for you" because G-d has given this power to us.[373]

Joshua commanded the sun and the moon to stand still. *"Then Joshua spoke to G-d… and he said before the eyes of Israel, 'Sun, stand still at Gibeon, and moon, in the Valley of Ayalon."*[374] The Children of Israel are above the sun and the moon, above nature.[375]

The children of Israel are not bound by astrological signs and the change of seasons. We are above the influences of the zodiac that bind other nations. According to logic we should not survive, but we are above logic.

In the Roman year 1999, the Western world was shuddering

with something called "Millennium Madness," a fear of the technological consequences that might occur when the next "millennium" began in their calendar. In that year, during the week when the Jewish world was reading the Torah portion *"Chaya Sarah"* in the Book of Genesis, I received a copy of an English scholarly journal containing an article entitled "Not Everyone's Millennium." That article described certain cultures whose calendar system was unique. Chief among those were the Jewish culture and the cultures of certain tribes in India. Their calendars share certain traits, among which are lunar months but solar years! Their days begin at sundown, and they have a recurring nineteen-year cycle in which seven leap years – consisting of one additional month – occur in every cycle.

At the end of the portion of *Chaya Sarah* we learn that Abraham, after the death of our mother Sarah, married a second wife named Keturah, with whom he had additional children. He *"gave [them] gifts; then he sent them away ... to the land of the east."*[376] Rashi tells us that those "gifts" were spiritual powers, to give them certain powers over nature.[377]

Could these tribes in India using the Jewish calendar be descendants of the children of Abraham and Keturah? In any case, our calendar distinguishes us from all other peoples and cultures (with the exception of the tribes we have just mentioned) and identifies our unique spiritual qualities.

"GODS" OF WOOD AND STONE

The Bible tells us that, if our sins cause us to be driven out of our Land, *"G-d will scatter you among the peoples, and you will be left few in number among the nations where G-d will lead you. There you will serve gods, the handiwork of man, of wood and stone, which do not see, and do not hear and do not eat and do not smell.*"[378]

What are "gods of wood and stone"?

This is a startling prophesy of the Exile that was to befall us. What is the god of wood but the symbol of the religion of Rome? What is the god of stone but the symbol of the religion of Mecca?[379]

Wood and stone also relate to the sun and the moon.

Wood is organic; it grows under the light of the sun. Without sunlight, trees do not grow. Moonlight does not stimulate growth; sunlight does. The fact that wood is associated with the belief system of Rome also conforms to the Roman concept of progress, because wood grows.

Stone is related to the belief system of Islam. Stone is cold; it is related to the moon because the moon (remember, please, that the crescent moon is the symbol of Islam[380]) is also cold. Stone does not grow; it is related to the night, because objects that do not grow do not need sunlight. Stone is also related to weapons, and Ishmael is associated with violence. Arab children throw stones.[381]

The special day of the Roman calendar is Sunday, the first day of the Biblical week. (Revealingly, "Sunday" is named after the sun, the heavenly body associated with Rome.[382])

The special day of the Islamic belief system is Friday, the last day of the Biblical week.

This seems to conform to the prophecy that the beginning of this Exile belonged to Rome, but the end of the Exile will belong to Islam, and their "day" will come right before the Sabbath, the coming of the Messiah. Exile is identified with the weekdays; Sabbath is identified with redemption from Exile, the coming of Messiah.

In addition, the Biblical wording implies the same thing; wood comes first, then stone.

Two cultures vying for control of this world, two heavenly bodies vying for control of the heavens, one culture associated with the sun and one with the moon! Look what our Torah tells us! Look what our calendar tells us! The entire course of history is revealed through a study of our calendar.

Is it any wonder that our prophetic tradition explains that in the days of the Messiah the moon will be restored to equal size with the sun?[383] Of course not, because that will finally be an era of peace. Israel's preeminence at that time will usher in an era in which *"swords will be beaten into plowshares"*[384] and the nations will cease to fight just as the heavenly bodies will cease to envy one another. Men who worship material creations become like what they worship, subject to the laws of nature and devoid of spiritual substance. They imagine that they have power of their own – indeed fighting with each other for mastery – when in fact they are slaves to the laws by which G-d governs the world. They have no power.

Little Israel, who has no desire to rule* but only to serve G-d, is the only nation to operate above nature, because Israel allies itself to no heavenly body, to no created object; we ally ourselves only to the Creator of objects! Therefore we are not subject to the laws of nature. We establish our seasons by reference to both the sun and the moon, attaching ourselves to neither.

In the following chapter we will learn more about how in our own days the forces of the moon are attacking the forces of the sun, preparing for the final act in the long drama. In the meantime, we will attempt to understand more about the dominant cultures in the western world of the past two thousand years.

---

* How ironic that our enemies create and circulate libelous fiction such as The Protocols of the Elders of Zion, purporting to show our desire for world mastery when in truth they are the only ones who desire world mastery. As usual, our enemies are looking in the mirror when they accuse us!

HOW WE SURVIVED

The era since the destruction of the Second Temple is a continuous chronicle of jealousy: those who are subservient to wood and stone against those who are subservient to the Creator. Just as they have become like wood and stone, they want us to become like wood and stone. They both try to convert us at the point of the sword.

The entire world is shaking its fist at tiny Israel.

"We have had enough of you! We don't want you to exist any more! Not only do you have no right to live in Israel, you have no right to live at all! Disappear!"

And so, for thousands of years, we have been forced to defend ourselves. It is not just recently, in Israel, that we Jews have had to defend ourselves. For millennia we have been surrounded by those who sought to destroy us. Jacob fought against the angel of Esau *"until the break of dawn"*![385] This is prophecy. It has become our burden to fight for our lives until the dawn of the Great Day when Messiah the son of David will appear and the angel of Esau leaves us forever, may it be soon!

How do we defend ourselves? By strengthening our "dveikus," our bond with G-d, because it is only He Who fights for us. *"You who cling to …your G-d… are all alive today."*[386] There is no other possible explanation of our survival.

"If only My people would heed Me, if Israel would walk in My ways. In an instant I would subdue their foes and turn My hand against their tormentors."[387]

There is a remarkable theory about how we Jews managed to survive in this threatening environment.[388] I want to make it clear that this is a theory. It may or may not be true but it presents an amazing scenario that illustrates the life-and-death environment in which we Jews have been struggling for so long.

In the era of the beginning of the Roman religion, the Jews faced a hidden threat. The initial practice of the new religion was initially almost identical to the Torah lifestyle. Its first adherents were Jews. You could be praying in the synagogue or studying in yeshiva and sitting next to someone who looked and acted like you, but who was completely opposite from you because he believed that a man was G-d.

This subtle plague could have undermined both our unity and our adherence to Torah law. The rabbis had to formulate a plan to save us from this insidious threat. They thought of a daring plan. One of them, a holy Jew, brilliant in Torah law, would infiltrate the church, pretending he was one of them. Through his brilliance he would work his way up through the ranks until he was in a position to influence the church from the top.

The plan succeeded more than they could have imagined, and this great rabbi, who was sacrificing himself for the survival of his people, rose through the ranks of the church.

Everybody knows that Peter was a Jew; the world believes that he was a renegade Jew. Are you ready to believe that he was not a renegade at all? Are you ready to believe that he was such a loyal Jew and devoted servant of G-d that he dedicated his entire life to saving his people from destruction?

What actually, according to this scenario, did he do? He formulated the Roman Church's belief system as it has existed for two thousand years! He separated the new belief system from the Torah by stating that it is not obligatory for members of the church to adhere to the Commandments of the Torah, thus distinguishing once and forever the Jewish way of life from the new belief system. According to the Encyclopedia Judaica, *"by abrogation of the Jewish [law as it applied to adherents of the new church, he] paved the way for the separation of [the Church of Rome] from Judaism....*"[389]

Through personal sacrifice he saved the children of Israel from the danger of being swallowed alive!

Do you understand this!

He sacrificed his entire life to save his people. Hated by his own people and even by many non-Jews, unbeknownst to them he was saving all future Jewish generations!

He created a new belief system, complete with books accepted by the Roman Church. *"He strongly opposed the observance of all Jewish practices in gentile … communities."*[390] Essentially, he created the new religion!

In reality, he not only saved the lives of his People but he enabled our adversaries to save their lives as well, because if our Torah and the role of the Jew in the world had been confused with their philosophies, the world would not have been able to survive! Since the blessing for the entire world comes from the children of Israel, in reality he was saving the entire world.

It is not for nothing that we are called the *"light for the nations."*[391] All morality was taught to the world by and through us! All ethics comes from our Torah. All blessing comes through us. As G-d says to our Father Abraham, *"all the families of the earth shall bless themselves by you."*[392] There is no civilizing principle that does not come from Mount Sinai, and it is only jealousy that prevents the nations from acknowledging their debt to us.

Instead of vilifying us, they should thank us for giving them light and life.

THE CHILDREN OF ISHMAEL

What about the worshippers of stone? From where did their rituals emanate? Five times a day they kneel on a mat, all facing in one direction, praying silently together with their shoes removed. Sometimes they bow all the way down to the ground.

Have you seen that anywhere else?

Jews on Yom Kippur pray five times. We kneel and then bow down on a mat, all facing in one direction, and we pray silently together with our shoes removed.

The origin of these prayers is our Torah. The origin of all the rituals of the worshippers of wood and stone are to be found in our ancient way of life, taught to us by G-d and His servant Moses, who learned them at Mount Sinai in view of the entire nation and in turn of the entire world.

Esau accuses Jacob of theft, the world accuses Israel, but in reality the reverse is true.

We are not unwilling to teach the world. On the contrary, it is our calling and our honor. But if the world pretends that what is ours is theirs, then they are living a lie. They are guilty not only of theft but also of ingratitude. And if, instead of thanking us and acknowledging their debt, they excoriate us and attempt to annihilate us, then they are not only ungrateful and untruthful, but – in addition to their guilt – they are throwing stones into the well from which they drink.

The Tenth Commandment is *do not covet*," do not desire what belongs to someone else. G-d gives us what we need; we will not gain by taking what has not been given to us. "*Do not covet*" stands at the end of the Ten Commandments perhaps because, at the very end, that is the basic sin which poisons our lives and the world. That is what poisoned our life in the Garden of Eden; Eve desired the very thing that G-d had told her is not hers! Since then, death, sickness and conflict have torn the world apart. If we and the nations of the world desire to heal ourselves, we should go right there, to "*do not covet*," and stop desiring what is not ours.

DIVORCE FROM THE LAND, TOTAL ISOLATION

Following the destruction of the Second Temple, there was still a Jewish remnant in the Land, although under Roman domination, but it gradually diminished until the great Torah centers shifted to the Tigris/Euphrates basin and then afterwards to Europe, other parts of the Middle East and lately to America. During these long centuries, the Jews split off into two distinct cultures, the Ashkenazi or European Jews, who were mostly north and west of the Mediterranean Sea, and the Sephardim, who were mostly south and east of the Mediterranean.

In practice, that meant that the Ashkenazim were mostly among those who worshipped wood, and the Sephardim were mostly among those who worshiped stone.

In the last few hundred years, Jewish presence started to increase once again in the Land of Israel. But until that point, our experience had been unique among the nations, a culture scattered among many nations, always identifiable and discrete from other cultures, but tied together only through our attachment to a G-d-given set of laws, a common family history and a shared attachment to a Land in which we did not live. A nation bound to a land that does not live in the land! A weak nation surrounded by strong enemies. Yet the strong enemies disappear and the weak nation survives!

How do we survive? Indeed, our existence defies logic, although the Torah had told us that we would be exiled in the land of our enemies.[393] We should not be surprised when events happen according to prophecy.

Please contemplate this for a moment. For the past two thousand years, we have been a minority in the lands of our enemies, reviled by our hosts and often brutally tortured, killed and

always the subject of frequently forced attempts at conversion.
We have been accused of every possible crime, not simply against
individuals, but against civilization. We have been labeled the
enemy of mankind, a pariah. We have been prevented from living in many areas and often forced to reside in closed communities, away from others, as if we carried a communicable disease.
We have been excluded from many professions and often from
owning land. We have been prevented from defending ourselves
against the inhabitants of the lands in which we lived, although
those same inhabitants were constantly beating us. Our holy
books, our holy buildings, our homes and we ourselves were
burned thousands of times, in country after country, over the
entire world. In many generations, the most powerful nations or
institutions would single us out for destruction. There were occa-
sional respites — the Golden Age in Spain or parts of Europe
after the "Enlightenment"– but those special cases came to an
abrupt end with the fall of an evil hammer that shattered the
short vacation in our otherwise dark fortunes. The United
States, until now, has been a place of respite for us, and, although
it ignored our agony during the European Holocaust, the U. S.
eventually became a refuge for many of the survivors.

Alone, defenseless, outnumbered, subject to unceasing
attack by the most vicious and powerful forces in every generation, our survival is clearly miraculous. Not only that, but what
is just as surprising is that our adversaries did not survive!
Where are the ancient Egyptians, the ancient Babylonians, the
Persians and Medes, the ancient Greeks and Romans, the Crusaders, the Inquisitors, the Turks, the Nazis, the Soviet Communists? Where have they gone? They are just names on the pages
of history books, and so too will be Arafat, Qaddafi, Saddam
Hussein, bin Laden – all of them and all the unnamed haters
along with them – in the not-too-distant future. They are or

will be gone, but how did we survive?

I once again[394] refer my readers to the classic statement by Mark Twain, a non-Jew: *"If the statistics are right, the Jews constitute but one percent of the human race. It suggests a nebulous dim puff of stardust lost in the blaze of the Milky Way. Properly the Jew ought hardly to be heard of; but he is heard of, has always been heard of. He is as prominent on the planet as any other people. He has made a marvelous fight in this world, in all the ages; and he has done it with hands tied behind him…The Egyptian, the Babylonian and the Persian rose, filled the planet with sound and splendor, then faded to dreamstuff and passed away; the Greek and the Roman followed, and made a vast noise, and they are gone; other peoples have sprung up and held their torch high for a time, but it burned out, and they sit in twilight now, or have vanished. The Jew saw them all, beat them all, and is now what he always was, exhibiting no decadence, no infirmities of age, no weakening of his parts, no slowing of his energies, no dulling of his alert and aggressive mind. All things are mortal but the Jew; all other forces pass, but he remains. What is the secret of his immortality?"*[395]

When you contemplate it, it is incredible. Here is a nation that was exiled from its Land and dispersed among practically every nation in the world, a tiny and almost universally despised minority among countless majorities. In every other such case in history, when a nation is exiled, that nation eventually is assimilated into the host nation and disappears. Not the Jews!

In our case, there were always some who assimilated, but the amazing fact is that in every country of our exile, a discrete Jewish culture endured whose members adhered tenaciously to our ancient lifestyle. In our era, despite the tragic disappearance of many into the surrounding cultures, the numbers of Jews returning to our ancient Torah lifestyle is increasing constantly![396]

We took our Torah into exile with us. We brought G-d

along with us. Indeed the Talmud tells us that G-d went into exile along with His children.[397]

What does it all mean? What is exile really? Here in the contemporary Western world, especially in America, we tend to forget that we are in exile. When I was a little boy, growing up in an almost completely assimilated environment, I felt the pain of exile only as a personal spiritual vacuum. I knew something was not right, but I thought it was a problem peculiar only to myself. I thought of myself as an American. But in general, even many religiously observant Jews in America have had a hard time thinking of themselves as out of place here. Why should we in America feel that we are in exile?

I have plenty to eat. I am even free to live as a Jew! This is exile?

Well, we are beginning to feel it now. Our enemies around the world are becoming more brazen and open in their hatred.

Our Father Jacob said, at the first hint of Exile, *"Rescue me, please, from the hand of my brother, from the hand of Esau, for I fear him lest he come and strike me down, mother and children."*[398]

What really is exile?

Let's return to the place where it is most lucidly depicted, the unforgettably graphic scene in which Jacob – all alone – battles the angel of Esau through the long night.

"Jacob was left alone and a man wrestled with him until the break of dawn. When he perceived that he could not overcome him, he struck the socket of his hip; so Jacob's hip-socket was dislocated as he wrestled with him. Then he said, 'Let me go, for dawn has broken.'

"And he said 'I will not let you go unless you bless me.'

"He said to him, 'What is your name?'

"He replied, 'Jacob.'

"He said, 'No longer will it be said that your name is Jacob, but Israel. For you have striven with the Divine and with man and have overcome.'

"Then Jacob inquired, and he said, 'Divulge, if you please, your name.'

"And he said, 'Why then do you inquire of my name?' And he blessed him there.

"So Jacob called the of the place Penie-l – 'For I have seen the Divine face to face, yet my life was spared.' The sun rose for him as he passed Penie-l and he was limping on his hip."[399]

This is prophecy. The long night is our exile and we are Jacob, whose name was changed to Israel. The "man" with whom Jacob wrestles is the representative of Esau, Jacob's brother.[400] They are fighting throughout the long and dark night. It is a known fact that Esau hates Jacob.[401] Esau will tell you that he loves his brother, but Esau is by nature a liar and the Torah tells you that it is actually the reverse.

What is this all about?

What does it mean that Jacob saw "the face of G-d"?

Why was Jacob's name changed? Why then?

What does it mean that the sun rose "for him"?

What does all this have to do with us?

WHAT IS EXILE?

Let us try to comprehend what is going on between Jacob and the angel, because that will tell us the story of our time and our world, the story of the past two thousand years.

The Bible says, "A man wrestled with him."

Why are they fighting? How did it start?

Did Jacob start the fight?

No, a man wrestled with him.

Who is this man?

The respective personalities of Jacob and Esau are revealed in a passage a little further on in the book of Genesis. When they meet and Jacob sends Esau presents, Esau says to Jacob, *"I have a lot."* He protests, but he accepts the presents. Jacob persuades Esau to accept by saying, *"I have everything."* In other words, *"I don't need anything."*

These two phrases, *"I have a lot,"* and *"I have everything,"* tell the entire story of the difference between Jacob and Esau, between the world of Rome and the world of Israel.

"I have a lot," means that, although I have many possessions, I want more possessions. My desire is never complete. A man who focuses on this world never has enough. He looks with his eyes and touches with his hands and tastes with his mouth and smells the beautiful aromas and he wants more and more and more. He never has enough money and possessions and pleasures. And he can never have his way to a sufficient degree. He has an "inalienable right to life, liberty and the pursuit of happiness," and he spends his entire life making sure that he gets that which he has a "right" to obtain.

This is the Western world, the prevailing philosophy, the foundation of competition, of business. It is the basis on which people justify trying to smash and overpower each other and gobble each other up. This is why sports are such an obsession in the Western World, going all the way back to its roots in Greece and Rome. What are two boxers or two wrestlers or two football teams trying to do? One will win and one will lose. To win is best. To lose is to be humiliated. Winning is the purpose of life. Whether you are in business or sports or in your personal life, you must be a winner. In your car, you must be first; the other driver cannot be allowed to go ahead of you.

A spiritual person is totally different. When you light another person's candle, your candle is not diminished; you simply create more light.[402]

In the spiritual world there is no loser; everyone wins. My

winning does not diminish you. Actually, if I lose it does diminish you, so it is in my interest that you win also!

When you become close to G-d, you don't push someone else further from G-d; there is no dimension of space in relation to G-d; there is room for everyone. The Talmud tells us [403] that in the Temple, there was always room for whoever came. When everyone was standing together and there was no more room and it came time for everyone to bow down on the ground, miraculously there was still room. No one was ever unable to find accommodations in Jerusalem. People who worry about such things say, "There will never be enough room for all the Jews in Israel." But when the Messiah comes — may it be soon, in our days! — there will be room for all of Israel in the Holy Land.[404]

The spiritual man does not desire to destroy anyone; he wants to elevate others, not push them down. In Jewish law (in total contrast to practice in the contemporary business world), it is not permitted to open a business if it will deprive another businessman of his customers.[405]

The world of Edom is a world of "I want more." When Esau ran in from the field, he was hungry, and he wanted the red porridge.[406] He couldn't wait; he just had to eat. We saw this also in Cain, who refused to allow Abel to have dominion over that which grew from the ground. He had to possess everything.

Why did Esau's angel attack Jacob?

Jacob had something he wanted.

He wanted the birthright and the blessings that came with it.

We are not talking about the World to Come here, because the World to Come is earned by one's actions in this world. You don't get a free passport to the World to Come; you get what you have earned by your behavior in this world. But property and rights in this world can be dispensed by their owner (to the extent G-d permits), and Isaac had dispensed certain rights, privileges and the blessings associated with them to Jacob. Jacob had bought his birthright from Esau, and now Esau wanted it back.

We children of Israel have been cheated and robbed in this world from our very days in the womb, and it all starts right here. As we discussed in Chapter Two, Jacob was the firstborn of Isaac, but Esau claimed that privilege. Jacob was conceived first,[407] but Esau pushed out ahead of him. [408]

This has been the story of the Nation of Israel since then. The descendants of Esau have constantly pushed ahead of us, attempting to claim and grab for themselves what belongs to us, and that includes not only the land of Israel, not only our Temple and all its vessels and fixtures, including the Holy Ark, but even our religion, our way of life, our Covenant with G-d!

Who taught them to steal from us? Their ancestor Esau.

Esau asserted that our heritage belonged to him, so Jacob said, "I will buy it from you for that red porridge." Esau, ruled by his hunger (his "I have much but I want more" mindset), agreed to the sale. Esau was selling what didn't belong to him, but Jacob went along with it.

This, incidentally, is consistent with a long history of Israel's buying that which is already ours. G-d states repeatedly and openly in the Torah that He is giving the Land of Israel to us, yet we find Abraham buying Sarah's burial place in Hebron,[409] Jacob buying Shechem[410] (where Joseph's bones are buried) and King David buying the Temple Mount in Jerusalem.[411]

Jacob had bought back his own birthright, but Isaac was not yet aware of that. So Isaac himself had to be "tricked" by Jacob into giving Jacob the blessing that was already his. Esau's theft of Jacob's identity[412] forced Jacob to lie in order to recover the blessing that already belonged to him.

What is Jacob supposed to do? He is not going to forfeit his entire existence because Esau wants him to "disappear." Jacob refuses to disappear!

This also is a sign for the coming millennia. The descendants of Esau have been trying to convince us to "disappear" for thousands of years. We are not going to cooperate! If you read very sober newspaper stories, they will tell you that sociological studies "demonstrate" that there will be no more Jews in the world in one hundred years. I believe it was Mark Twain who said, "the reports of my death have been greatly exaggerated."

So Jacob, who has now repossessed the birthright and blessings that were already his, becomes an object of hatred to Esau, because Jacob has out-tricked the master trickster. Esau thought he would rule this world, but Jacob will not die, nor will he relinquish his heritage.

Esau, however, is not finished. He wants the property back that was never his to begin with and that he had voluntarily relinquished in addition. So he sends his "angel" as a surrogate to fight Jacob.

Who is this angel?

Esau acts piously. He pretends that he is very good. He asks Father Isaac how to separate tithes on salt even though he knows that one does not tithe salt.[413] *"When Esau saw that Isaac had blessed Jacob and sent him off to Paddan-aram to take himself a wife from there … and commanded him, saying 'You shall not take a wife from among the daughters of Canaan,"*[414] Esau makes a wedding for himself with a new wife, not from "the daughters of Canaan," even though he continues to maintain many wives from among the daughters of Canaan and has been stealing other men's wives for years.[415] Esau's descendants have been killing our people for thousands of years under the guise of religion. Esau is "pious."

So when Esau tries to kill Jacob he does not do the work

himself. His proxy attacks Jacob when he is alone in the night. Esau is clean; Esau is good; Esau is pious. Who is attacking Jacob? A "man." Esau has "nothing to do with this."

But there is one problem for Esau. Jacob doesn't intend to die. Jacob is attached to Eternity. "The man" cannot kill him!

Notice that neither is killed. Jacob does not kill Esau, nor does Esau kill Jacob. This is also a preview of history.

A fascinating word is used to describe this fight. The Bible uses the Hebrew word "vaya-avaik" for "wrestled." "Vaya-avaik" is derived from "avak," which means "dust."[416] When the angel wrestled with Jacob, a huge cloud of dust was raised. They wrestled on the other side of the "Yabbok" River, which appears to come from the same root as "avak," or dust. And amazingly, the name "Jacob," ("Yaakov" in Hebrew) contains the same basic letters as Yabbok, "yud," "bais" and "kuf." In other words, there is a connection between Jacob and this dust that is raised by the fight between him and the angel. The word "Yaakov" is connected to the word "aikev," which means "heel," as in "heel of the foot."

The heel steps in the dust and Jacob steps in the dust. The angel of Esau comes to us, the children of Jacob, and accuses us: *You are the thief. You are the deceiver. You stole my birthright and you stole my blessings. I am going to throw you in the dust, where you belong; I am going to try to destroy you. I am going to bury you in dust and try not only to take all your physical possessions, but I am going to try to take your spiritual possessions also.*

Esau doesn't want our spiritual possessions; he doesn't believe G-d is real; he doesn't really believe that spiritual possessions exist! He knows only what he sees with his eyes and tastes with his mouth. But he is jealous that we <u>appear</u> to be wise and spiritually connected, and that blessings surround us in this world. So he is going to <u>pretend</u> to be religious. He is going to try to appear in this world to have a connection with another world. He wants to look like a guru, like a person who is spiritually fulfilled, like a teacher of truth. That is part of his desire to possess everything. "I have a lot," (he says) but I want that too; I want to <u>appear</u> spiritual, I want everyone to think that I tithe even salt.

So he tries to steal everything that Jacob has, to destroy Jacob. The dust rises from their fight; the dust fills the atmosphere. Thus, for two thousand years, since the day-beyond-tragedy when Esau's legions overran the Holy Temple in Jerusalem, the sun has been obscured; all truth in the world has been obscured because of this fight against the Jew.

Did you think air pollution is new?

This is the source of all air pollution, smog and confusion in the world. Material pollution mirrors spiritual pollution. The dust from Esau's fight against Jacob has darkened the world. Nothing can be seen clearly. As the Prophet says, *"neither day nor night."*[417]

But what happens at the end of the fight? Oh, listen to this!

Jacob's name is changed!

Jacob is not going down! Jacob is not going to die! He is going to live. The nations of the world cannot believe it, but Jacob is still here, and he is fighting. They thought that when they came to the New World after Columbus that they were finally going to get rid of the Jew, leaving him back in Europe. No more Jews! But look what has happened! Look at America! Yarmulkes all over the place! Jacob is not going to disappear! Never! There is nothing Esau can do! [418]

But Jacob is getting a new name, *"No longer will it be said that your name is Jacob, but Israel, for you have striven with the Divine and with men and you have overcome."*[419]

"Israel" means "prince of G-d."

The angel is going to be forced to concede that the Jews are here forever; they cannot be defeated. What does it mean to be a Jew? To *"strive with the Divine and with men and to overcome."*[420]

What does "to strive with the Divine" mean? Does it mean to fight with G-d?

It means that Jacob is fighting within his own soul concerning his spiritual status. Other men are concerned about fighting to enlarge their business or take over the competition. In the world of commerce they say, *"I will increase my profits by fifteen percent every year for the next five years. I will take over my competitor. I will control the entire silver market (or lumber market or electronics market)."*

A Jew fights for something totally different. A Jew says, *"I am fighting with my self to get closer to G-d. I am fighting my evil inclination. I am fighting to control my anger."*

This is called "striving with the divine."

What does it mean to strive with men?

Other men are concerned with fighting each other. *"I want to be President. I want to win the Academy Award, the Nobel Prize. I want to be the biggest man in the steel business or the television business."*

The Jew does not fight other men; the Jew does not want to amass empires. We do not desire to fight.* We strive with other men only to defend ourselves, so we may live! We fight with Esau only because Esau is trying to kill us!

So we have become "Israel" instead of "Jacob." What does it mean?

"No longer will it be said that the blessings came to you through treachery and deceit, but rather through authority," in other words the authority of G-d. G-d meant that you should have these blessings. *"I concede,"* Esau will say on the day that Messiah

---

* We must, however, defend ourselves against others when we are under attack.

comes, *"that you are the legitimate firstborn of Isaac and that you are entitled to the blessings associated with your birthright."*

"I concede to the reality of hidden things (because our conception was hidden) and I concede that you are not a thief and not a deceiver and that I am the thief and deceiver."

But the angel does not really say that. The angel says only, *"no longer will it be said that your name is Jacob."* He does not say, "Your name is no longer Jacob." That will come later, at the end of history, when our long exile has ended. At the outset, Esau's angel never agrees to it. The angel, who wants to run away because dawn is breaking, is held fast by Jacob and cannot leave. He only says as much as he does because he has no choice; Jacob will not let him go. Along with the reluctant blessing, the angel has struck and injured Jacob in the thighbone, so that Jacob must limp. The sun will cure Jacob when it rises, but during the night Jacob is injured, and the night is long.

We limp through our exile with the injuries inflicted upon us by our enemy.

WHAT IS JACOB'S INJURY?

*J*acob's hip socket was dislocated."[421]

What does that mean? Is this injury so significant that it can be the principal weakness that has plagued Israel during our long exile?

The hip is where the leg is attached to the body. If our hip is out of its socket, we cannot stand up straight. After the fight, Jacob was *"limping on his hip."*[422]

In the Blessing After Meals we ask G-d to allow us to *"guide us erect to our Land."* Every morning we thank G-d, *"who straightens the bent."* What does it mean to limp? To stand erect?

What after all is our weakness? Isn't Jacob's weakness that

he is associated with the heel? The heel is in the dust![423] He has been thrown down. He cannot walk like a prince; he is perceived as a deficient creature, a man whose natural position is lowliness, with his *"mouth to the dust."*[424] Is it not true that in times of mourning, like *Tisha b'Av*,[425] or when we are sitting *shiva*, that we walk with bare feet, in the dust?[426]

But we are supposed to walk upright. We are made in the image of G-d. Our Father Abraham was told by G-d to *"walk before Me and be perfect."*[427] Walking is a metaphor for being in the correct relationship with G-d, and we are supposed to walk upright. When we limp, we are having difficulty walking with G-d.

When the angel strikes Jacob in his hip socket he is trying to prevent him from walking with G-d; he is attempting to inflict the most fundamental damage possible to Jacob, because if a Jew is not walking with G-d then he is denying his most basic nature, his fundamental reason for existing. If you can't walk, you go down in the dust. Do you remember that *"aikev,"* which is "heel," and *"Yaakov,"* which is "Jacob" are the same word? And do you remember that *"avak,"* dust, the dust raised by the fight, has the same letters as *"Yaakov"*?

Jacob's injury signifies the way that Esau characterizes us: he says that we gained our upright, erect position by cheating. Esau says, *"You are not an upright Nation. You are deceivers and swindlers, and you deserve to lie in the dust."*[*]

Don't forget that this is an internal injury. You can't see the injury to the hip because it is inside, but you can see us limping, you can see us covered with the dust of our degradation.

After two thousand years of suffering from Esau's injury, we begin to accept it. A doctor once said to me, "The worst thing

---

* An interesting personal note: the other day I was walking near my home and tripped slightly. A young non-Jewish boy leaned out of a passing car and shouted, "I saw you trip!" Why did it matter to him that I tripped? Why should he care? Obviously he did care, because he carries the "genes" of Esau, who is still trying to trip us.

is when you accept pain as inevitable. Then you will not do anything about it." What happens to us in exile? We forget our identity! We forget that we are royalty who have been addressed directly by G-d at Mount Sinai. We begin to agree with the nations and we say, "Yes, *they are correct. We really did lose the covenant. We really do not deserve the Land of Israel. We are no longer that holy, upright Nation!*"

This is our problem, our internal injury.

We BELIEVE Esau! Fundamentally Esau himself is a man of the dust. His focus is down, upon the earth, the soil, the food that grows in the earth, the animals that walk the earth, the pleasures of the earth. Esau is focused upon the earth. And when we are Jacob, the "heel," we are playing Esau's role.

That is how the angel wounded us: he depressed us; he convinced us that Esau is right! So we say in our depression, "*Yes Esau, I am embarrassed. Yes, I stole your birthright. Yes, I stole your blessings. Yes, I stole the Covenant. Yes, I stole the Land of Israel. Yes, I stole everything. I admit it. I am embarrassed! Forgive me! I have no right to my heritage! I am nothing but dust! I am the heel of history!*"

NO!

NO JACOB!

YOU ARE WRONG!

NO! Your name is not Jacob! Your name is ISRAEL!

You are a Prince of G-d! You are not the heel; you are not a deceiver; you are not a liar and a cheater!

No! You are the son of Abraham, who WALKS with G-d!

You are the son of Isaac, about whom Rebecca said, "Who is that man WALKING in the field toward us?"[428]

You are not Jacob; you are Israel!

"The sun rose for him."

For HIM: so that he would understand that he does NOT

dwell in darkness, that he is not a slave, not a deceiver, not a cheater, not a liar, not an imposter. Jacob may dwell in darkness, but Israel dwells in the sunlight. *"The sun rose for him... to heal his limp."*[429]

"(G-d) raises the needy FROM THE DUST, from the trash heaps He lifts the destitute. To seat them with nobles..."[430]

"He showed me ... the (High Priest) standing before an angel of G-d, and the Satan standing at his right to accuse him.... (The High Priest) was dressed in soiled garments as he stood before the angel. (The angel) spoke up and said to those standing before him, saying 'Remove the soiled garments from upon him.' Then he said to him, ' See I have removed your iniquity from upon you and had you clothed in fresh garments.' Then I said, 'Let them place a pure turban on his head'; and they placed the pure turban on his head ..."[431]

But not yet. Not quite yet.

THE END OF THE EXILE

Please observe the language.

The angel says to Jacob, *"Please let me go, for dawn has broken."*

And Jacob refuses: *"I will not let you go unless you bless me."*

And the angel replies by saying, *"No longer will it be said that your name is Jacob."*

But is Jacob's name changed?

Not yet!

Even when G-d says later to Jacob, *"Your name shall no longer be called Jacob, but Israel shall be your name,"*[432] the Torah still uses the name Jacob at some times and Israel at other times. Even after G-d tells Jacob that He will change his name, he is still at times called Jacob! The name Israel begins to be used, but not exclusively.

What is G-d waiting for?

There is something more that has to happen, and I believe that must allude to the final exile, the exile after Esau, the exile of the children of Ishmael.

For even after Esau's power has waned, the exile is not quite over. Even after dawn begins to break and the fight with Esau's angel is over, even after the actual confrontation with Esau, still he is Jacob. The exile is not over yet.

Even today, after we see the first light of dawn, even after the return of the children of Israel to the Holy Land after almost two thousand years, Jacob is still limping, still wounded, still called a liar, an imposter, a thief; he is still "*aikev*," dust, still the pariah.

Yes, Jacob goes on, limping through history, but going on nevertheless.

His eye is on the promise of G-d. He knows that someday he will be called "*Israel*" by the world, the Prince of G-d. Someday he will be vindicated. Someday he will no longer be accused of stealing his birthright, his blessings, his covenant with G-d and his Land! He knows that day will come, and that is what gives him strength to carry on.

"*A sun of righteousness will shine for you who fear My Name, with healing in its rays, and you will go out and flourish like calves fattened in the stall.*"[433]

"*Is there any doubt that on that day – the words of G-d – I will cause the wise men of Edom to be lost... For your violence to your brother Jacob, shame will cover you, and you will be cut down forever. Because of the day you stood aloof, the day strangers plundered his wealth, foreigners entered his gates and they cast lots on Jerusalem.... You should not have gazed on the day of your brother, the day he was exiled; you should not have rejoiced over the children of Judah on the day of their destruction; you should not have spoken arrogantly on the day of distress!*

"You should not have entered the gate of My people on the day of their disaster; even you should not have gazed upon its misfortune on the day of its disaster; you should not have put your hands on its wealth on the day of its disaster! You should not have stood at the crossroads to cut down its refugees; you should not have imprisoned its survivors on the day of distress. For the day of G-d upon all the nations is near; as you did, so will be done to you, your recompense shall return upon your head.... The House of Jacob will be a fire and the House of Joseph a flame – and the House of Esau like straw."[435]

G-d speaks thus to Esau, but the day has not come, not quite yet.

There is one more test for Jacob, perhaps the most difficult of all, before his name is finally changed forever to Israel. First, he must confront the children of Ishmael.

CHAPTER SIX

THE EXILE OF ISHMAEL: SEPTEMBER 11, 2001 TO THE END OF HISTORY

"I shall provoke them with a non-people."[436]

"Fear not, o worm-weak Jacob, O people of Israel, for I shall be your help — the words of Hashem and your Redeemer, the Holy One of Israel."[437]

On September 11, 2001, the moon struck the sun and a great explosion occurred. Two planes destroyed two towers. The ancient battle of Ishmael against Esau – what has been called "the perpetual struggle between east and west"[438] – exploded into the forefront of world events.

Two planes hit two towers!

The only solution to the terrible battle that erupted on that day was to be found in two tablets, "the mighty twin Torah crowns."[439]

To understand where we are now, let us return to the beginning of time. This is so fascinating that I can hardly contain my excitement, because it appears that we can understand all of history, including the present, by viewing it in the context of the Seven Days of Creation. Please listen carefully, my friends, because from this perspective we can learn exactly what is happening in the world.

In the beginning, there was nothing, utter chaos. The "earth," whatever it was at that point, was *"astonishingly empty, with darkness upon the surface of the deep."*[440] The Divine Presence[441] hovered over the surface of the waters, and then G-d created light. This was called *"good."*

On the Second Day, G-d created a *"firmament,"* which separated between upper water and lower waters.[442] This firmament is the sky, what we, looking up from the earth, perceive as the heavens. These heavens extend for untold light-years outward from our planet.* Apparently, in addition to the waters on earth, there are waters of some type above the heavens. This is the only day of creation that is not called *"good"*; our rabbis tell us that is because G-d did not finish with the waters. Something which is not finished is not called "good."[443]

On the Third Day, G-d gathered the waters together into seas and separated the waters by dry land. So the seas were separated from the land. Now it seems G-d had finished with the waters; this is called *"good."* G-d then, on the same day of creation, said, *"let the earth sprout forth vegetation."* So on the third day there was water and dry land upon the earth, and, in addition, vegetation *"each containing its seed,"*[444] and that was also *"good."* So there are two *"goods"* on the third day.

---

* The very fact that there is life on this infinitesimally small "piece of dust" called earth, which floats in the seemingly endless universe, and that the tiny moving particles called "man" are able to communicate with the Creator of the vast universe, is in itself cause for amazement and would strengthen the belief of anyone who contemplates that. Just as Moses was the humblest of all men, and Mount Sinai was the smallest of all mountains, so the earth itself is totally unnoticeable in the vastness of space. "What is man, that you should remember him?" asks King David (in Psalm 8:5).

On the Fourth Day, G-d created *"luminaries in the firmament of the heaven."* In other words, the firmament that was created on the second day, which separates the upper from the lower waters, now contains "luminaries," the sun, the moon and the stars. Their function is to *"separate between the day and the night; and they shall serve as signs and for festivals and for days and years; and they shall serve as luminaries in the firmament of the heaven to shine upon the earth."*[445] The Torah takes pains to mention that *"the greater luminary [will] dominate the day and the lesser luminary [will] dominate the night."*[446] This was also called "good."

On the Fifth Day, G-d created living creatures to fill the waters and to fly *"over the earth across the expanse of the heavens."*[447] It is noteworthy that G-d created fish and fowl on one day and land creatures on another day. The Fifth Day was also "good."

On the Sixth Day, G-d created living creatures upon the land,[448] *"G-d said, let us make man in Our likeness. They shall rule over the fish of the sea, the birds of the sky, and over the animal, the whole earth and every creeping thing that creeps upon the earth."*[449] G-d said to man, *"subdue [the earth] and rule over the fish of the sea, the bird of the sky and every living thing that moves on the earth."*[450] This was also "good."

On the Seventh Day G-d "abstained" from creating, and "sanctified" the day.[451]

THE MILLENNIA

Now let us look at history. What happened to this perfect world that G-d created? It was all "good." Everything about it was good. G-d had made a perfect Creation. Even if one day (the Second Day) was not "good," the next day was "good" twice; so every aspect of creation was "good." G-d blessed the Sabbath "because on it He abstained from all His work."[452] By the Sabbath G-d had *"completed His work which He had done."*[453] G-d had made a perfect universe; nature had no flaws. In charge of it, He had placed man, and had given man free will.

Here was man, a perfect being in charge of a perfect creation.

What did we do?

WE DESTROYED IT!

Yes, we destroyed it.

That is what happened. From the moment of our creation, we, to whom G-d gave the power to rule and to subdue, have refused to listen to our Creator, have refused to obey Him, and as a result we have made mistake after mistake, and have ruined our perfect world.

How have we ruined it?

This is truly amazing, because you will see that in each thousand years of history we have ruined one day of creation!

Our Sages teach us that one day is compared to a thousand years, *"for even a thousand years in Your eyes are but a ... day."*[454] We will find that in each thousand-year period of history we have ruined the aspect of the world corresponding to each day of creation. It didn't have to happen that way; G-d gave us free will. But if we exercise our free will in the wrong way — if we veer away from allegiance to His commandments – then we unravel the universe; we reverse the process of creation, until we wind up....

Well, let's see where we wind up.

Remember, please, that in each period of history there are different requirements for mankind. Let's review what we have already discussed earlier in this book.

From the beginning of Creation, mankind was given seven

commandments, namely, 1) to believe in Him and to recognize Him as the Creator and Ruler of the universe, 2) not to curse G-d, 3) not to kill, 4) not to steal, 5) not to engage in immoral sexual behavior, 6) and to set up courts of law in order to make this world a civilized place in which people live in harmony with each other and in obedience to G-d. There was also a commandment specific to the Garden of Eden, not to eat the fruit of the Tree of the Knowledge of Good and Evil. Later, after permission was given to mankind to eat meat, an additional commandment was given to the children of Noah (all people who live in the world today), not to eat the flesh of living animals.

Then, at Mount Sinai, the children of Israel were given an additional 606 commandments. In other words, the rest of the world still had seven commandments, but now the children of Israel were obligated in 613 commandments.

If we on earth abide by the commandments that apply to us, then the earth will continue to exist with harmony among all of creation as G-d made it. We will be living in accordance with G-d's intentions.

In other words, if Adam and Eve had not rebelled against G-d's commandment in the Garden of Eden, then we could all be living in that Garden of Eden today. But each time we break a law applicable to us, we break down a part of G-d's creation, we undo G-d's work in creating the world.

The Torah does not require that others should live as we do; we do not try to convert anyone. On the contrary, we discourage conversion. The 613 commandments are applicable to us, but the seven universal commandments are applicable to all mankind.* The rewards of living by them are that blessings will

---

* "Anyone who accepts upon himself the fulfillment of these Seven Commandments and is precise in their observance is considered one of the pious among the nations of the world and will merit a share in the world to come." (Maimonides, Laws of Kings 8:11)

accrue to each individual and to all mankind. Conversely, the consequences of <u>not</u> living by them are disastrous to each individual and to the entire world that G-d created.

How exactly are the consequences of disobedience manifested? Well, we are going to find that out right now, with G-d's help, by going through the millennia and seeing exactly what we have done to G-d's perfect world, how we have destroyed it over the past fifty-seven hundred years.

THE SIXTH DAY; THE FIRST MILLENNIUM

Man, woman, creeping creatures, domestic and wild animals, as well as harmful spirits came into existence on the Sixth Day of Creation.[455] There was a perfect balance among all these creatures, but with the rebellion of Adam and Eve and man's assumption of the Knowledge of Good and Evil, that precise balance was upset, with the result that man, who was created to rule, lost some of his superiority over the animals and harmful spirits.

What is man's superiority over the animals? Animals have no free will and therefore no ability to alter their state of obedience to G-d. They, like the sun, moon and stars, do what they have been programmed to do by their Creator. But man was born with free will, the ability to choose whether to obey his Creator – with all the spiritual elevation that obedience entails – or to disobey his Creator – with all the spiritual degradation that disobedience entails.

When man rebels against His creator, then in a certain sense he descends BELOW the level of the animals, who at least cannot disobey their Creator. Therefore the rebellion in the Garden altered the entire relationship of living creatures created on the Sixth Day.[456] Man's elevated state also had given him power to subdue harmful spirits in the world, but when he lowered himself, that power was suspended and harmful spirits were no longer restrained, with the result that the world now is subject to their influence.[457]

Man had been created in an ideal environment in which he was meant to live forever in a balance of spiritual and material perfection. In addition, all physical creatures were created to live without impinging upon the other's existence. But with the rebellion, all that changed. The perfect relationship that only G-d could bring about was rejected, and man took the direction of the world into his own hands. As a result, that perfect balance between all physical creatures, and even between physical creatures and harmful spirits, was overturned.

As a result of our rebellion, the animals — that G-d had created for our benefit – have became our enemies, attacking us instead of being sources of delight. The entire natural world, that G-d created to be our peaceful and comfortable home, has become a threat because we have acted in such a way as to remove G-d's protection. The skies and waters are polluted; the graceful deer carries Lyme disease; bears attack children in suburban communities. Today we fear the lion and the snake, the spider, the shark and creeping things.

Thus, suffering, sickness and death entered the world and the work of the Sixth Day was overturned as man overturned G-d's plan. The Garden of Eden represented that ideal relationship. Man had been meant to live there forever, without physical or mental pain, sickness, death or strife. A woman was to conceive and give birth immediately and painlessly. No work was to have been required to eat and sustain life. The "sweat of your brow" was not to have been necessary; G-d would have taken care of everything for us. But no, we were "smarter" than

G-d, and we destroyed that paradise for ourselves. Adam and Eve and their descendants, including us, no longer live in that perfect Garden, but rather a very difficult world of our own making. When man overturned that ideal relationship he was forced to leave the Garden of Eden. Thus the work of the Sixth Day was overturned in the First Millennium of time.

THE FIFTH DAY; THE SECOND MILLENNIUM

On the Fifth Day G-d created the birds and the sea creatures. Corresponding to the Fifth Day was the Second Millennium. What happened in the Second Millennium?

Noah was born in the year 1056 after Creation, and the Torah says, just after introducing Noah and his sons, *"the earth had become corrupt before G-d, and the earth had become filled with robbery. And G-d saw the earth and behold it was corrupted, for all flesh had corrupted its way upon the earth."*[458] Here is how Rashi explains these two sentences: *"[The word corrupt is an] expression of sexual immorality and idolatry…Even domestic animals, beasts and birds had relations with those which were not of their species…Wherever you find promiscuity, catastrophe comes to the world and kills [both] good and bad."*[459]

In the Second Millennium, the destruction of G-d's creation continued. Now the creatures created on the Fifth Day, the birds and sea creatures, were destroyed.[460] As we saw above in Rashi's comment, the birds corrupted themselves along with the other animals that had been corrupted in the First Millennium. Although the fish are not mentioned in the list of those animals which corrupted themselves, Rashi does say that, as a result of promiscuity, *"catastrophe…kills both good and bad."* In the mighty

Flood that covered the earth, the birds, which had corrupted themselves, were killed; they had no place to land on the flooded earth. The fish were displaced as the waters covered the earth.

During creation, G-d organized the world by creating boundaries.[461] Those boundaries protect the world. For example, the boundary of the sea is the dry land. If it were not for dry land, the sea would engulf us. That is why, every morning we thank G-d for providing dry land on which to live, when we say, *"blessed are you, our G-d...Who spreads out the earth upon the waters."*[462]

Boundaries are also moral. In the Garden, G-d had said that we may eat of everything except the fruit of the Tree of the Knowledge of Good and Evil. When we broke through that moral boundary, we lost our privilege of remaining in the Garden.

When the Floodwaters covered the earth, the fish were displaced. G-d had placed them within boundaries. Water was not meant to cover the entire earth; parts of it were to be dry land and parts water. But when man destroyed the moral boundaries through robbery and immorality, then G-d removed the boundaries with which the earth had been created, and the water, along with the fish created on the Fifth Day, covered the entire earth instead of being confined to their boundaries.

Thus the work of the Fifth Day was destroyed in the Second Millennium.

THE FOURTH DAY; THE THIRD MILLENNIUM

On the Fourth Day, G-d created the sun, the moon and the stars. In the Third Millennium the world could have been saved from the consequences of rebellion against G-d. (Of course, the world could have been saved in the First Millennium or in the Second Millennium. It could be saved right now, in any moment of history, if we would all return to G-d and obey His commandments!) But the Third Millennium provided a unique opportunity, an opportunity that is still in place. There is a correspondence between the Third Millennium and the Fourth Day of Creation because on the Fourth Day G-d created luminaries in the heavens.

In the Third Millennium of history, luminaries – Abraham, Isaac, Jacob, and their children —- appeared, men who lit up the darkness of the world and whose influence continues to do so. In fact, our Patriarchs and their children are specifically compared to the sun, the moon and the stars: *"[Joseph] dreamt another dream; and related it to his brothers. And he said, 'Look, I dreamt another dream: Behold! The sun, and the moon, and eleven stars were bowing down to me.'"*[463] And Jacob, his father replied, *"Are we to come – I and your mother and your brothers – to bow down to you to the ground?"*[464]

G-d had showed Abraham the stars and told him *"so shall your offspring be."*[465]

In the long nighttime of history, these great men and their children illuminate the darkness with uplifting spiritual guidance. Abraham and his descendants reintroduced the knowledge of G-d into the world. The knowledge of G-d dissipates the darkness that results from ignorance. A life without G-d is limited to the perception of this material world and that kind of life ends in death, since all material things eventually die. That is a life without "luminaries."

So the sun, the moon and the stars that were created on the Fourth Day are compared to Abraham, Isaac, Jacob and their descendants. Our Patriarchs and Matriarchs attempted to rebuild the world, to undo the damage. They attempted to imitate G-d's creative activity and illuminate the world, and this is the legacy they bequeathed to their children.

If G-d built the world by looking in the Torah, then we should be able to REBUILD the world by looking in the Torah!

In other words, the Patriarchs and Matriarchs were attempting to reverse the destruction of G-d's creation that had been occurring since Adam and Eve sinned in the Garden of Eden.

But again, the world rebelled against G-d.

How? Because there were others born in that Third Millennium who tried to destroy the children of Israel and thus prevent the rebuilding of the world.

Who are they? Ishmael and Esau, who both tried to destroy the Children of Israel and are continuing to try to do so to this very day! By trying to destroy the Patriarchs and their children, Ishmael and Esau were trying to prevent the rebuilding of the world.

As we said above, *"Ishmael would take a bow and arrow and shoot them in Isaac's direction while pretending to be playing."*[466] Ishmael pretends to be playing a game, but the game is murder. *"Like someone who wears himself out throwing firebrands, arrows and lethal objects, so is a man who deceives his fellow and says, 'Surely I was joking.'"*[467] Ishmael and his children, the Arabs of today, throw firebrands, arrows and other lethal objects and say, *"Surely I was joking."*

What is a man who blows people up, with explosives spewing forth bolts, nails, rat poison and lethal germs? None other than one who throws *"firebrands, arrows and lethal objects."* And so, since his birth in the Third Millennium, Ishmael has been trying to destroy Isaac and Isaac's children and therefore to destroy what G-d created on the Fourth Day.

Esau's continuing attempts to destroy Jacob are clear for all to see. *"Esau hates Jacob"*[468] is an axiom of history. As we have

said, Esau's descendants, Edom/Rome and the Western civilization that sprung from Rome, have been trying to destroy Jacob's
descendants from the beginning. Who if not Edom destroyed
the Second Temple and drove the children of Israel from our
Land into the exile that has lasted to this day? Who if not Edom
has been responsible for pogrom after pogrom, expulsion after
expulsion, blood libel after blood libel, ghetto after ghetto, murder after murder, culminating in the Holocaust of the mid-
Twentieth Century?

You will recall that in the previous chapter we mentioned
a Talmudic account concerning the moon and the sun, namely that *"G-d created these two heavenly bodies of equal size, but
the moon complained to G-d that the sun was competing with it for
dominion of the earth. G-d therefore 'punished' the moon for its
contentiousness and jealousy by reducing its size."*[469] You will also
recall our discussion about the fact that Ishmael is associated
with the moon and Esau with the sun. But how can that be, if
(in Joseph's dream) the children of Israel are associated with
the sun, the moon and the stars?

This is amazing, my friends, and I call your attention to this
remarkable truth. You will recall that Israel's calendar is founded upon the movements of both the sun and moon, whereas Ishmael's (the Moslem) calendar is connected with the moon alone
and Esau's (the Western calendar) with the sun alone. So
Israel's calendar encompasses both, while Ishmael's and Esau's
respectively encompass only one.

In other words, Ishmael and Esau are splitting up the universe! They are living only according to one aspect of creation,
represented by either the moon or the sun. They exemplify
either spirituality or materialism, moon or sun, but not the totality represented by both the moon <u>and</u> the sun. The children of
Israel, on the other hand, live by a calendar based both on the

sun and the moon. In Joseph's dream, the children of Israel are clearly shown to be a family that encompasses <u>all</u> the luminaries.[470] Thus the children of Israel represent the totality and completeness of creation, while the children of Ishmael and the children of Esau do not.

When "the moon attacks the sun," threatening the world with destruction, it is only a natural consequence of the fact that the "moon" (Ishmael) and the "sun" (Esau) represent traditions that are inherently incomplete, deriving whatever strength they have only from a created, material object (the moon or the sun), objects which are in the end only dust and will return to dust. The children of Israel, on the other hand, derive our strength from the Creator of the moon and the sun, and that is reflected by our calendar, which encompasses the entirety of creation, not just parts of it.

Thus, the healing of the universe, the way out for mankind, is represented by the way of the children of Israel. That is why, in ancient Egypt, it was Joseph who saved not only his family but the entire world[471] from starvation! Joseph — whose family is represented by the entirety of creation, the sun, the moon and the stars – saved the entire world both during the day (the years of plenty[472]) and during the night (the years of famine).

Thus, in the Third Millennium of history, Ishmael and Esau came, like the warring moon and sun, not only to fight Abraham, Isaac, and their children, but also to try to destroy each other. The war of the moon against the sun, which began at the dawn of civilization, is now reaching its apogee. When the two planes hit the two towers on September 11, 2001, we were witnessing the beginning of the end of the battle that had begun with the births of Ishmael and Esau some 3600 years ago, which in turn echoed the competition between the moon and the sun in the dawn of creation.

The moon and the sun are battling. In the end, neither will win. Now, as then, the only solution lies with the children of Israel, who, following the teaching of the Torah as revealed through the Days of Creation, unite the sun, moon and stars and offer the path toward harmony in this world.

THE THIRD DAY;
THE FOURTH MILLENNIUM

On the Third Day, G-d created trees and plant life.[473] Corresponding to the Third Day is the Fourth Millennium, a tragic period for Israel, in which our holy monarchy under King David and King Solomon divided itself, and then crumbled under the power of our enemies. We endured the destruction of two Temples and expulsion from the Land, and we entered the Diaspora in which we find ourselves today.

This millennium corresponds with the Third Day of Creation, the only day about which the Bible uses the word "good" twice, once referring to the separation of the waters from the dry land (in other words, the completion of the previous day's creation) and once referring to the sprouting of vegetation upon the earth.

Do you see what is happening here? In this millennium mankind undid these two great "*goods*" that G-d had created!

The first tragedy undid the creation of plant life and the second tragedy undid the separation of land from water.

How was the creation of plant life undone? Because in it, the Land of Israel ceased to be a "*land of milk and honey.*"[474] From a garden, which it had been when the children of Israel were obedient to G-d, it turned into a desert, from which we were "*vomited out.*"[475]

"Beware lest your heart be seduced and you turn astray and serve gods of others and bow to them. Then the wrath of G-d will blaze against you. He will restrain the heavens and there will be no rain and the ground will not yield its produce. And you will swiftly be banished from the goodly land which G-d gives you…. Place these words of Mine upon your heart and upon your soul… in order to prolong your days and the days of your children upon the ground that G-d has sworn to your ancestors to give them."[476]

Notice what the Torah warns us about here: *"the ground will not yield its produce!"* Exactly that which G-d did on the Third Day – creating vegetation upon the earth — was undone during this tragic millennium in which the children of Israel ceased to merit staying in the Land of Milk and Honey and were expelled to the *"four corners of the earth."*[477] The Talmud tells us also that with the destruction of the Temples and the expulsion of the children of Israel from their Land, not only did Israel become a wasteland, but agriculture throughout the world was negatively affected. Blessing emanates from Zion to the entire world, and if the children of Israel are not flourishing in our Land, the blessing is diminished.[478]

This expulsion undid the second "good" that G-d created on the Third Day. G-d had separated the land from the waters for our good, but we separated ourselves from G-d for our misfortune. As a result of our separation from G-d, our punishment was to become separated from each other when our monarchy was divided and then to become separated from our Land when we were sent into exile.

Today the Children of Israel are so divided that ten of our own tribes have been lost for some 2500 years!

Where are our brothers?

Joseph said, *"I seek my brothers. Please tell me where they are pasturing!"*[479] Joseph is still seeking his brothers!

The separation between land and water that G-d made for our good on the Third Day was undone to our sorrow in the Fourth Millennium, as we were separated from our land and cast upon the waters into exile![480]

THE SECOND DAY;
THE FIFTH MILLENNIUM

On the Second Day of Creation, G-d separated the Upper Waters from the Lower Waters by establishing a firmament between them, which we call the sky. We are familiar with the lower waters; the Upper Waters are spiritual realms, beyond our understanding.

During the Fifth Millennium (which corresponds to the Second Day of Creation and encompasses the years 240 to 1240 in the Roman calendar) the children of Israel were to be found scattered in foreign lands around the Mediterranean Sea. This was the era in which the Jews were forced out of the Land of Israel and into the all-encompassing exile (the "Diaspora") in which we still find ourselves today.

The correspondence between the Second Day of Creation and the events of the Fifth Millennium is positively amazing.

The Jews' purpose is to live a sanctified existence in the Land of Israel, a holy nation in a holy land from which blessings emanate to the entire world. *"Torah will go forth from Zion and the word of G-d from Jerusalem."*[481]

And what happened? The children of Israel were mixed with the other nations. The firmament that had separated Israel and the other nations was abolished; the boundaries were broken; the "upper waters" and the "lower waters" were mixed; the protective barrier that enabled us to exist in sanctity was torn down. As a result, the work of the Second Day of Creation was undone!

THE FIRST DAY; THE SIXTH MILLENNIUM

On the First Day, G-d created heaven, earth and light.[482] And now we come to our own era, the tragic millennium that began some 763 years ago, in the year the Roman calendar calls 1240.

What a millennium! What suffering has there been both for the Jewish and the non-Jewish worlds. Whenever Jews suffer, the rest of the world suffers also. When the recent dictator of Germany let loose his hatred upon the Children of Israel, he unleashed a world war in which 50 million died. When the madman in Afghanistan unleashed his hatred upon the Children of Israel, the World Trade Center was demolished, and that was only the beginning!

Following is a partial list[483] of tragic events that have devastated the Jewish People in this Millennium, beginning with the Jewish year 5000 (1240 in the Roman calendar): the Talmud burned in Paris (5002/1242); Jerusalem sacked by Egyptians and Turks 5004/1244); the Inquisition began (5012/1252); the Jews expelled from England (5050/1290); the Rindfleisch massacres in Germany (5058/1298); the Jews expelled from France (5056/1306); the Jews massacred by the Pastoreaux Crusaders (5080/1320); the Jews of Germany massacred (1596/1336); the Black Death massacres across Europe (5109/1349); the Jews of Spain massacred (5151/1391); final expulsion of the Jews from France (5155/ 1394); Jews of Austria massacred (5181/1421); the Jews expelled from Spain and Sicily (5252/1492); the Jews expelled from Portugal ((5257/1496);

mass burning of Jewish books in Rome (5314/1553); the Jews of
Poland and Lithuania massacred by Chmielnitzki's forces
(5408/1648); more Jews massacred in Poland (5494/1734);
mass burnings of the Talmud in Poland (5518/1757); thousands
of Jews killed and synagogues burned by roving bands in Poland
(5528/1768); anti-Jewish riots in Germany (5579/1819); waves
of unofficial and official pogroms in Russia (5641-5665/1881-
1905); over 60,000 Jews killed during the Russian Revolution
(5678/1918) and uncounted numbers by the brutal, G-d–hating
regime that followed; Kristalnacht (5699/1938), and during the
next seven years six million Jews were killed in the European
Holocaust. As Jews began to return to the Land of Israel, the
Arab nations escalated their attacks, both outside and inside
Israel. Today, in Israel and elsewhere, the brutality and murder
not only continue, but increase in severity and barbarity.

How can we describe the events of our time, our millennium?

*"In the beginning of G-d's creating the heavens and the earth –
when the earth was astonishingly empty, with darkness upon the surface of the deep, and the Divine Presence hovered upon the surface of
the waters – G-d said 'Let there be light,' and there was light. G-d
saw that the light was good, and G-d separated between the light and
the darkness. G-d called the light 'Day' and the darkness He called
'Night.'"*[484]

My dear friends, let us all open our hearts.

Examine, please, the events of our millennium, and you will
see that we are now in the final stages of destroying the beautiful world that G-d created in six days.* It is not too late to draw
back, but we are now standing at the edge of a precipice. We
cannot see the bottom of the abyss that opens beneath our feet.

Several years ago our family traveled to the Grand Canyon,

---

* *"We are taught that the Messianic era will begin in a generation with the power to destroy itself."* [485]

arriving at night. It is awesome to stand at the edge of deep, black silence and look outward. Who knows how vast is the chasm below? If there were no railing, you would be unwilling to take another step forward.

The next day, we walked out upon a rock outcropping. This time we could see the bottom. I imagined myself slipping over the edge. Perhaps I should not have allowed my imagination to run along on its own, but for a moment I did. I pulled back in fear. The bottom was a world below us!

Then, just a few years later, we all witnessed the impossible vision: bodies falling one hundred stories from the top of the World Trade Center.

Now, my friends, we all stand upon the edge of a precipice, but this has no bottom, no end at all. The silence is deep and the night is dark. Our feet are beginning to slip over the edge, an edge moistened with the blood of our brothers.

Look out over the edge, my friends. What do you see? The earth is astonishingly empty, with darkness upon the surface of the deep. The Divine Presence IS hovering upon the surface of the waters, but do we perceive It? These are the final hours before the process is complete, before chaos returns. All that is left now is light and darkness. We have destroyed almost every other aspect of G-d's Creation.* We have pushed G-d away from us so completely that only the barest indications of His presence are "permitted" in "our" world, and we are working diligently to eliminate them. We have banished G-d!

I was impressed several years ago by a book called Modern Times.[486] The author defines "modern times" with reference to Einstein's theory of relativity. In modern times everything has become relative, not just physics. Morality has also become relative;

---

* Newspapers inform us that each day many species of animal are disappearing forever from the world. What is happening to the Polar Ice Cap? What is happening to the Ozone Layer?

there is no right and no wrong. Moral standards, sexual standards, dress standards, behavior standards…. they are all relative. Do what you want; "if your conscience tells you it is right, then it is right."

I grew up in New York City in the "culture" of the Ethical Culture Society, a humanistic way of life founded in the late 19th Century. Here is a passage from The First Book of Ethics, by my former teacher at the Ethical Culture Schools.

"Every person becomes his own judge of right and wrong… You are the judge…. Everyone is a judge, and his court is his conscience. He must question and cross-examine himself as well as others. He must decide whether he is innocent or guilty. He may have to judge others, too. He may even have to judge the community he lives in, and the whole world… Ethics is a way of being a free person. It helps a person know what his choices are in life. It makes him his own judge all during his life-time. No matter what other people think and say and do, he is the one who decides for himself." [487]

Here we have the recipe for disaster and chaos that has pushed us to the edge of the precipice. This is the modern world! There is no right and no wrong, no G-d Who rules! There is no King!

I am the judge; I decide what is good and what is evil. So says every person on earth.

"*Every man did what was right in his own eyes.*"[488]

The process begun in the Garden of Eden is now almost complete; we have eaten every fruit on the Tree of the Knowledge of Good and Evil. We are full to bursting, nauseous with the satiety of our own moral perceptiveness. *I am like G-d! I make the rules!* We have created a world of billions of judges, each desiring to judge others.

G-d, get out of our world! We will push You out! We don't want You in our world! Leave! We make the rules here. "Ethics is *a way of being a free person!" I am a free person. You can't tell me how to live!*

The Divine Presence is hovering over the surface of the waters, but there is no place for G-d in this world. *"The dove could not find a resting place for the sole of its foot."*[489] Even light and dark is now gone, day and night have departed. We are living in a "twilight zone"[490] in which there is no distinction between right and wrong, hovering in the tiny slice of time before we drive the Presence of G-d from above His creation. Then the world will revert to total chaos. All creation is on the brink of destruction because we have driven the Creator out of His own world!

Do you understand what we are doing!

We have un-created the world! We are back almost to the Beginning. We have only a few seconds left, actually about six hours on the cosmic clock.

Let me explain. The Talmud informs us that history will last for 6000 years.[491] As I write these words, we are in the year 5763. Therefore, we have a maximum of 237 years until the end of history. If a thousand years is like a day in the eyes of G-d, as we have explained, then the Seventh Millennium is like the Seventh Day, when G-d's Presence will be tangible and visible to everyone. Messiah, the Son of David, must have come by then, because the Seventh Day is the Day of the Sabbath. The Sabbath begins on the eve of the Seventh Day, and similarly the Age of the Messiah must begin on the eve of the Seventh Millennium. We are now – in the year 5763 – just past three-quarters of the Sixth Millennium. In a twenty-four-hour day, we are at the equivalent of eighteen hours. In other words, on a day when the Sabbath begins at 6 pm, it is now just past twelve noon.

The week is almost over; history is almost over. It is time to prepare for the Sabbath. Sabbath is coming, whether we like it or not, whether we accept it upon ourselves or not. As we say in the Aleinu prayer, *"G-d will be king over all the world,"* meaning that He will be RECOGNIZED as King.

The question is whether we will complete our destruction of His world before the Sabbath comes. At any time, G-d can recreate His world. He does not need us. The world will be intact and pristine when the Sabbath arrives, but we may not be in it! If we succeed in destroying G-d's creation, the Sabbath will arrive but we will not be there to enjoy it!

This is the countdown. The clock is ticking backwards. Will we drive G-d completely out of His world? If we do, my friends, then at the exact moment His Presence departs from above the waters, the universe will be "astonishingly empty" and revert to chaos. We will have killed our beautiful world!

My friends, we must act now!

REPENTANCE

What can we do? How can we return the world to its purity and be worthy to live in that pure world? What practical steps can we take to survive?

It so happens that the very week I posed these questions to myself as I was writing this chapter, a most interesting commentary on the weekly Torah Portion came to me from the Holy City of Jerusalem.[492] The question was raised, why does Jacob's blessing to his first-born son Reuben sound more like criticism than blessing? Yes, Reuben was apparently wrong in some of his actions – and in fact his descendants lost the hereditary kingship and priesthood because of those mistakes – but didn't Reuben recognize his errors and spend years in sincere repentance?[493] And we know that *"repentance cancels the evil decree."*[494]

Why was he rebuked if he had repented?

On the other hand, if he really sinned so terribly, why was he rebuked in "delicate language"?[495]

The answer is that there are two types of repentance, repentance for the <u>action</u> and repentance for the <u>attitude</u> that caused the action.

When Adam and Eve sinned in the Garden of Eden, they repented intensely for the rest of their long lives.[496]

But they still did not merit to return to the Garden of Eden!

Great men have taught us how to repent, but how do we repent so completely that we eliminate the <u>attitude</u> that caused the sin, not just our actions? That is the question.

Jacob's sons repented for their ostracism of Joseph. That is why Joseph revealed himself to them in Egypt, paving the way for the reunion of the family and the eventual liberation of all the children of Israel from bondage in Egypt. Yet the children of Israel are still divided today, still unable to conquer the attitude that caused that conflict. We may have repented for our actions, but we have not yet erased the attitude that caused the problem in the first place. That attitude, that unwarranted hatred, is the cause of our exile today, and all the troubles that have befallen us over the past thousands of years.

How do we eliminate the attitude? How do we get down to the very core of our problems? How do we erase the sin and rebellion so completely that we can return to the purity of the world the way it was created? How do we clean ourselves out? How do we find G-d inside us? How do we navigate the inner geography?

THE SYMBOLISM OF THE TABERNACLE

There is a hint in the design of the Tabernacle that G-d commanded the children of Israel to build in the Desert. The

Tabernacle is the place where the children of Israel meet G-d. As such it is the basis for the Temple in Jerusalem. It is also the model for the "Inner Temple" that each of us should be building throughout our entire lives. [497] What does the design of the Tabernacle tell us about how to find G-d?

The Tabernacle contains the *"Chatzair,"* a rectangular court-yard enclosed by walls, but open to the sky. The entrance to the *Chatzair* is on the east. Within the *Chatzair,* on the western end, is another rectangular area called the *"mishkan,"* which is walled on all sides and covered with various hides and materials. With-in the *Chatzair,* to the east of the *mishkan,* is the Copper Altar, on which offerings[498] were brought. Between the Copper Altar and the *mishkan* is the *"kiyor,"* which contained water for the priests to purify their hands and feet.

The *mishkan* is divided into two compartments, the eastern one called "Holy," and, beyond it on the western side, the "Holy of Holies." The Holy is twice as large as the Holy of Holies. In other words the Holy occupies two-thirds of the *mishkan* and the Holy of Holies one-third.

Entering the *mishkan* from the east, one first comes to the Golden Altar, on which was burned incense, whose exact for-mulation is carefully described in the Torah. To the west of the Golden Altar are the *menorah* on the south, and the *shulchan,* or Table on the north, containing the twelve special loaves of bread placed there each week by the priests.

Beyond and west of the Holy is the Holy of Holies. This is where we find the Ark of the Covenant, which contains the Two Tablets that Moses brought down from Mount Sinai, as well as the fragments of the first tablets, smashed by Moses at the time the children of Israel built the Golden Calf. In addition, the Ark contains a Written Torah and a jar of the *Manna* that had been the food of the children of Israel in the Desert. Over the cover of the Ark and crafted out of the same piece of gold are the two *Cruvim*, angel-like figures facing each other over the Ark. The only person to enter the Holy of Holies is the High Priest, once a year on Yom Kippur.

What does all this mean to us, who are searching for Truth in a world that seems empty and G-dless? Please remember, the Sanctuary did not "have to" be built. It was built only in response to the sin of the Golden Calf.[499] Somehow, the existence of the Sanctuary is related to our rebellion against G-d and gives us a way to move toward Him and rectify the state of separation that exists between us.

What does the Sanctuary tell us about how to find G-d?

Outside the Sanctuary we are affected by wind and rain, daylight and darkness, heat and cold, the vicissitudes and difficulties of life. Today we might say that we are affected by all that we read in the newspapers and hear on radio and television: the stock market, war, disease and all kinds of social, family and personal problems. We are out in that difficult world and we wonder if there really is a G-d, really a possibility of life that is filled with satisfaction and protection from evil and pain. We want that kind of life but we are not sure it is real. So what do we do?

Just <u>wanting</u> to be closer to G-d is in itself a step toward Him. One who wants to come closer to G-d is elevating the world by having that desire. That desire, we might say, is symbolized by entering the *Chatzair*, the courtyard.

What do we see?

First we notice that we are surrounded in the courtyard by walls of the *Chatzair*. Although the *Chatzair* is open to the sky, the walls offer some kind of protection from the world around us. The wind cannot blow so hard against us; we are protected somewhat from the problems around us. The very fact that we are surrounded by a wall begins to give us a sense of shelter and protection.

Directly ahead is a great Altar, on which animal sacrifices are brought. The fate of those animals is in place of what our fate should be.[500] In other words, if I do something wrong and I should be punished for it, perhaps forfeit my life, an animal is slaughtered and burned on the altar in place of me, according the procedures spelled out in the Torah. I am to understand that I deserve the fate of that animal. If I take this to heart, then I am able to compensate for my sin and cleanse myself of the rebellion against G-d. The prototype for this procedure is the Biblical account of our Father Isaac, who was willing to be offered on the Altar as a sacrifice to G-d. But G-d did not want Isaac to be sacrificed, so He sent a ram, and G-d told our Father Abraham that the ram should be substituted for Isaac. G-d showed us how to achieve closeness to Him.[501]

Thus, the first thing that we accomplish in our journey toward G-d through the Sanctuary is that we are shown how to remove the burden of sin from ourselves. We don't have to run from the guilt any more and attempt to say it doesn't exist. Rather, we acknowledge its existence, but we do something about it. We do not have to be slaves to our past; we can actually remove our sins, cleanse our guilt and start to come closer to G-d.

In our secular society we have been taught to say, *"I don't have any sins."* We only say that because we are secretly hopeless about getting rid of the burden. But if we know that there is a way actually to remove the burden by acknowledging that G-d has standards for us and realizing that He will help us achieve His standards, then we can admit we have guilt and sin. At that moment we feel a tremendous relief.

So the Altar and the Sacrifices in the Sanctuary enable us to elevate ourselves and purify the attitudes that have separated us from G-d.

After we have begun to purify ourselves, then we can approach the *kiyor*, the vessel from which the priests washed themselves. When we know that it is possible to rise up from the effects of sin and rebellion, then we have hope and we feel we can become clean before G-d.

The *kiyor* resembles the *mikveh*, the ritual bath in which both Jewish women and men cleanse themselves spiritually. One must be physically clean to enter it and intend to purify oneself in order to come closer to G-d. As King David says, *"Turn from evil and do good."*[502] After we free ourselves of sin we can become spiritually clean. First we attempt to overcome the effects of sin, and then we try to overcome the attitude through which sin arises by cleansing ourselves and preparing to approach G-d.

As we enter the Holy area, we notice that we are now surrounded on all sides by coverings. Instead of being under the sky and protected only on the sides (by the woven materials in the Courtyard) we are now surrounded on all sides and above our heads by the protection of the Holy. Do you see what cleansing ourselves of sin has accomplished? We are no longer, as it were, exposed to the vicissitudes of life; we are no longer buffeted by outside forces that seem beyond our control. We are protected.

What do we find in the Holy area of the Sanctuary?

We first come to the Golden Altar, upon which the incense was burned.

There is something unique about incense, and we are going to find out that there is a deep reason why the Incense Altar stands at the entrance to the Holy Chamber. It all has to do with the sense of smell.

THE AROMA OF EDEN

Do you know where our Patriarchs and Matriarchs are buried? In the City of Hebron, in the Cave of Machpela, which our Father Abraham bought from Efron the Hittite for a very large amount of money.[503] Approaching the cave, Abraham inhaled a pure and beautiful aroma.[504] Our sages tell us that this cave is the entrance to the Garden of Eden; that aroma is all that remains to us from a world before sin.*

We have five senses: taste, touch, sight, hearing and smell. All – except the sense of smell —- were involved in the sin of Adam and Eve. Eve <u>saw</u> the fruit and desired it. She <u>heard</u> the snake convincing her. She <u>touched</u> the fruit and then she <u>tasted</u> it. But she did not smell it.

Smell is the innocent among the senses. It is pure, less sullied by sin. Even today, there are fewer objectionable influences aimed at the sense of smell than at other organs of sense.[505] There is something unique about the sense of smell.

"My G-d, the soul You placed within me is pure. You created it, You fashioned it, You breathed it into me..."[506]

G-d breathed the soul into us through our nostrils.[507] That is why, when we are saddened by the departure of our "extra soul" after the Sabbath, we smell pungent spices to revive us.[508] The same passage through which the soul originally entered, the same passage through which our extra soul departed after the Sabbath, through that same passage we are revived by the spices.

The sense of smell is our link to the Garden of Eden.

---

* The question presents itself whether the Garden of Eden is a physical or a metaphorical place. Let me answer that here by saying that I do not know any more than you, the reader. But this much I do know. The Torah teaches man how to make a bridge – or perhaps, a ladder – between the material world and the spiritual world. Let us just say for now, that without knowing all the answers, we are assuming that the process about to be described, in which we enter the Cave of Machpela and eventually emerge in the Garden of Eden, is in the nature of a bridge between the world of today and the world of tomorrow, whatever exactly that world is.

*"Among all the sacrifices that were offered in the Holy Temple,
none was as precious before G-d as the incense.... The incense...
was an enlightened remedy to purify people from sin. Whoever
smelled the fragrance of the incense*[509] *...would have thoughts of
repentance. His heart would be purified of all evil thoughts and from
the defilement of the Evil Inclination.... The incense had the power
to break and subjugate the power of the Evil Inclination... In the time
of plague there is no remedy better than the* ketores *(incense). This
was a gift that the Angel of Death gave Moses when he went on High
to receive the Torah."*[510]

"Incense is the dearest of all the offerings."[511]

When something we do is pleasing to G-d, the Bible frequently uses the language of aroma, as in *"a fire offering, a satisfying aroma to G-d."*[512] Rashi says that the words *"satisfying
aroma"* indicate *"a source of contentment before [G-d]."*[513]

In profile, the nose is the most forward part of the body. We
are supposed to guide ourselves from the head, and the leading
part of the head is the nose. The nose, so to speak, goes before
the brain, before the eyes, the ears, the mouth, and is above the
hands. The prosaic nose – perhaps it is still relatively pure
<u>because</u> it is prosaic – is in one sense the primary limb of the
body.

Our Father Abraham perceived a pure aroma emanating from
the Cave of Machpela. He followed that aroma, and discovered
the entrance to the Garden of Eden, as well as the burial place of
Adam and Eve. Hebron is also called *Kiriat Arba*, the City of
Four, referring to the four couples buried there, Adam and Eve,
Abraham and Sarah, Isaac and Rebecca, Jacob and Leah.*

Now here is our job: the way our ancestors at the time of

---

* This account is imaginary, but hopeful. There is in fact a tradition that we do not enter the
  actual areas where our Patriarchs and Matriarchs are buried. Who knows, however, what
  miraculous things will occur as the days of the Messiah come upon us!

Chanukah found pure oil buried in the defiled Temple, it is our job in this time of terrible darkness to find purity in this defiled world. How will we do it? We will follow our pure sense, our sense of smell, as Our Father Abraham followed his sense of smell. We will trace the aroma of purity back to its source, and that is how we will rebuild the world and with G-d's help prevent the ultimate catastrophe and bring Messiah the Son of David into the world for the rescue of all mankind and G-d's entire creation, which He entrusted to our care.

But why Hebron? Why does the pure aroma lead us to the place of burial?

We who are one with the Eternal G-d are beyond death. When we rediscover the purity of our ancestors we will once more be alive, because G-d, Who *"causes death,"* also *"restores life and makes salvation sprout."*[514] That is why the entrance to the Garden of Eden, which represents life without death, is through the Cave of Machpela.[515]

"Zion, lament to the Patriarchs [to seek] for the reestablishment of your House.... Go to the Cave [of Machpela], scream bitterly and cry [to the Patriarchs]...."[516]

What will we find in the Cave of Machpela?

ENTERING THE CAVE OF MACHPELA

In our contemporary world, we have a popular genre of literature and movie, the supernatural fable about innocence being attacked by pure evil. These stories' heroes are humble folk who embark on heroic quests that become epic battles to save the world from evil fanatics of apparently unlimited power. The heroes must pass through terrifying danger and adventure, confronting sorcery and wizardry. They engage in life-and-death battles against seemingly hopeless odds, and experience the intervention of powerful forces of good as well as evil.[517]

Sometimes the heroes are drawn into a kind of maze. The hero enters, but he is not sure where he must go or how to get there. He knows he has to confront the great evil, but where is the evil? And what is the evil? Finally, he is alone in a terrifying, silent place where no one will accompany him and no one can help him. Danger surrounds him, but what and where is it? Strange sounds are heard; unseen movements are sensed. Suddenly, at the rounding of a corner, or out of a seemingly smooth surface the enemy appears.

My friends, we are all living the great spiritual adventure. The reason the genre is so popular today is that there is so much of our yearning in it. We are in an epic battle to regain our lost paradise. Let us now enter the Cave of Machpela,* for this is the entrance to the Garden of Eden. Let us confront the sources of our alienation from G-d, the forces that confront us in the titanic battle of the soul.

And let us remember that the dawn is always preceded by darkness.

We are entering darkness, but it is the kind of darkness through which Moses passed as he ascended Mount Sinai to approach the Presence of G-d.

"Behold, I come to you in the thickness of the cloud."[518]

"G-d said that He would dwell in the thick darkness."[519]

"Moses approached the thick cloud where G-d was."[520]

---

* Hebron has become a scene of tragedy for the Children of Israel. Our enemies always challenge us at the holiest places, which – as we have discussed in Chapter Five – happen also to be the places our ancestors paid for in cash. Our ancestors knew that the holiest places would be the places over which the forces of evil would present the mightiest challenge, so they wanted to make our ownership doubly clear in the eyes of the entire world. To reiterate what has been stated in a previous chapter, Our Father Abraham paid for Hebron, Our Father Jacob paid for Shechem (which the Arabs refer to as Nablus), and King David paid for the Temple Mount. These are the places of greatest contention in the Holy Land!

After we pass through the darkness we will encounter the light of G-d.

The first question is, how do we enter the Cave of Machpela?

In Hebron today, we first must confront the danger of our enemies lying in wait to kill us before we even get there. At the actual Cave, despite the fact that G-d gave us the deed to the entire land of Israel and Our Father Abraham paid four hundred silver shekels for this exact property, we will have difficulty gaining admittance. After the Six Day War, the government of Israel gave our enemies jurisdiction over the Cave of Machpela, as if to say "those who are buried here are not important to us." We have given away the key to the Cave of Machpela!

How do we retrieve the key?

This is our first challenge: entering the Cave. Let us gird our spiritual swords upon our waists and approach the entrance.

How do we enter?

The key to getting into the Cave of Machpela is that the Children of Israel must <u>want</u> to enter, and that requires <u>unity</u>. Our fathers and mothers are in there! The children must want to be united with our Fathers and Mothers. We must all want to honor our Parents. We should all visit our parents together.

What, after all, do parents want? A parent wants unity among the children. To get back to our parents we children must be together. Please note what the Prophet says about the Final Days. *"Behold, I send you Elijah the Prophet before the coming of the great and awesome day of G-d. And he will turn back [to G-d] the hearts of fathers with [their] sons and sons with their fathers..."*[521] The sign of the coming of the Final Days will be when the children and the parents share one heart, and that heart is turned to G-d.

Our first step in returning to the Garden of Eden is to get close to our Fathers and Mothers, and that will be through unity among us children. That is what our Fathers and Mothers desire; that will allow us to enter their burial place, which will lead us back to the Garden of Eden.

The generation in which disunity began is the generation of the Tribal Patriarchs, the Children of Jacob (Israel): Joseph and his brothers. By unifying ourselves, we will have overcome their disunity.

PUSHING OUT THE ADVERSARY

I want to point out something rather amazing. Let us examine the <u>location</u> of the problem in each generation. Here is what I mean.

In the generation of the Tribal Patriarchs (the twelve sons of Jacob) our adversary resided within us. We weren't battling an outside enemy; we were battling ourselves! And that has been our problem ever since: we have been battling ourselves. That is what we call *sinas chinom*; causeless hatred of one Jew against another, the underlying reason for the destruction of the Second Temple and of all our problems since then, up to today. We are our own enemy.[522] This all started in the generation of Joseph and his brothers.

Was it always like that?

Oh no. Not in the previous generation. Let's go backwards one generation and examine the generation of Jacob.

In Jacob's generation, unlike the generation of the Tribal Patriarchs, our adversary was removed one degree from inside us. It was lodged in Esau, our twin brother. In Jacob's generation the adversary was no longer within us. It was close to us — our twin brother – but no longer within us. Esau had the same father and the same mother but he was our twin brother. So our adversary was pushed out of us one degree.

We will see that in each succeeding generation, going backwards, the adversary will be removed one further degree, until it is removed completely in the Garden of Eden. And that is where we want to go.

What happens in the next generation? In the generation of Isaac, the adversary – Ishmael – is pushed out one degree further. Ishmael was Isaac's half brother, not his twin brother. The father (Abraham) was the same, but the mother was different. Our adversary is further removed from us. As we go backwards, each generation brings one step of healing to us; we are progressively pushing the adversary away from us, and the generations become purer because the adversary is being pushed further away. In Isaac's generation it is no longer within us, nor is it our twin brother, but is now our half-brother.

And what about Abraham's generation? We find that our adversary has been pushed even further away. What was our Father Abraham's adversary? The entire outside world, something completely outside himself and his family. As we stated earlier, Abraham was so named because he was *"ivri,"* on one bank of the river and the entire world was on the other side. He was the only one in the entire world to speak up for G-d, to acknowledge and publicize the fact that G-d exists.

Thus, the adversary in the generation of Abraham was completely outside the family. When we emulate our Father Abraham, our adversary is no longer a half brother, no longer a twin brother, nor we ourselves.

Now let us jump back to the beginning of the world.

When we get to the generation of Adam and Eve, we see that the adversary was reduced to its primal form, a reptile, a non-human having nothing whatsoever to do with us. When the adversary is inside us (as in the generation of Joseph and his brothers and down to our time) one can understand how people are influenced by it, although the result is death. But in the case of the serpent, who can rationalize listening to a serpent? What does the serpent have to do with us? It is completely alien to us. It represents the nature of rebellion against G-d in its most graphic form, as a poisonous reptile who desires only to destroy us.

We see in the case of Moses how to handle the adversary when it assumes the form of a snake, for G-d turns Moses' staff into a snake and commands him to pick it up by the tail.[523] Moses under the command of G-d is able to push the adversary completely outside himself, pick it up by its harmless end, and then utilize it as his staff to assist him in carrying out the will of G-d. Moses' staff represents the adversary, transformed now into an instrument of power to assist us in carrying out G-d's will. It is like turning hatred of others into a powerful instrument for harmony and self-improvement. Moses is using the power of the adversary to serve G-d, and that is the model for us. That is how we will go back through the Cave of Machpela, backwards through the generations, to expel the adversary from within us until it is revealed as a snake that is completely outside us. Then, with G-d helping us, we will utilize its power to serve Him, until we regain the sanctuary of the Garden of Eden.

THE KEYS TO THE GARDEN OF EDEN

A "shattered nation,"[524] "an exhausted nation,"[525] we want to return to that primeval oneness with G-d that we once were privileged to experience in the Garden of Eden.

Tati, our Father. Please let us back! Please take us out of this torturous exile! Please save us from the hands of our enemies! Please remove sickness and tragedy! Please release us from pain! Please release our children from rebellion and from the corruption of a tainted society! Please let us live with You in purity! Please let us return to Your presence!

But the entrance to the Garden is guarded.

"Having driven out the man, [G-d] stationed at the east of the Garden of Eden the Cherubim and the flame of the ever-turning sword, to guard the way to the Tree of Life."[526]

How do we get back in? We are desperate! We are surrounded by the most cruel enemies, crushed by fear and pain, tormented by incomprehensible difficulties, sicknesses and tragedies.*

We have learned that the path to the Garden of Eden is through the Cave of Machpela. Now we stand outside; we want to enter. But how do we enter? Why can't we enter? We are locked out here in a hostile world and we are banging on the door, but we can't get in!

Let us think. We have discovered that there are keys, one corresponding to each generation of our Biblical ancestors. Each one will bring us one step closer to the Garden of Eden. What is the first key?

First we must gain entrance to the Cave.

How do we find the key?

Let us think. Who is in the Cave? Our Fathers and Mothers. What does every parent pray for? More than that their children will be good, all parents pray that their children will love each other! All parents pray that their children will never fight. If the children love each other, they will also love their parents. Then they will be good children!

That is the test. Let the children love each other. And let those of the second generation love those of the first generation,

---

* In America, and the Western World in general, we Jews may have forgotten that the last two thousand years have been an almost uninterrupted saga of fear and desperation. But especially since 9/11 we are being forcefully reminded, in Israel and in other countries, that the exile is not over and that hatred of the children of Israel is not dead.

and let the third generation love the second generation! Let the entire family be "loving friends"[527]! Throughout the generations, the fourth, fifth and sixth generations, let them also love each other, until the end of time. If my children love each other, then I know that I raised them the right way. I can die happy!

Isn't that what parents desire?

Inside the Cave of Machpela are our parents. Did they die happy? *"Rachel weeps for her children!"*[528] Why? Because we are fighting! Rachel's children are fighting!

That is why we cannot get into the Cave! Because we the children are fighting! The first key, the key that will open the Cave, is <u>peace among the children</u>! That is the first key. That will unlock the door to the Cave of Machpela! We must unlock the door <u>together</u>; we cannot unlock it separately!

Maimonides writes, regarding anger, *"It is a terrible trait, and a person must distance himself until the extreme, and teach himself not to become angry even when called for."*[529]

Anger is the one trait we do not accept even in moderation; it must be banished altogether. There is anger among the children of Israel. Our Fathers and Mothers have not slept since the days that their children became divided! Our Temple was destroyed because of causeless hatred among their children. Each day the Temple is not rebuilt it is because we continue to allow the ancient enmity to persist and even to increase![530]

That is why we have not been able to unlock the door to the Cave of Machpela! We cannot return to our parents when we are fighting! How can the children enter the parents' presence when we cannot speak to each other? How can we do that to our parents? How can we appear before them as a divided family?

The first key is Family Unity.

Stop fighting, children! Stop it I say! I don't care what the rea-

son is! I don't care! So there's a reason! So what? It's not worth it!
Close your mouth! Seal your lips! Open your heart! Your reason is
not a reason! If we open the door together, the door will open, but
only if we open the door together.

And we will do it!

We <u>will</u> enter together, because we must!

THE FIRST CHAMBER

ow let us imagine what will happen when we enter. Where
do we turn and what do we do? Our eyes are not used to the
dark. Shapes become visible, and we stumble in the darkness.
We are afraid in the dark, but there is a faint aroma that gives us
courage, a whiff of healing in the air, like the aroma that greets
us when we open the door on Friday afternoon, and the healing
aromas of *Shabbos* enter our nostrils, as the soul enters the body.

Suddenly, we stumble over a stone, and next to it is another
stone. We strike a match in the darkness. They are the grave-
stones of Father Jacob and Mother Leah. Beyond the two stones
is a door. From under the door comes the aroma. If we place our
face next to the door, the aroma becomes stronger, the aroma of
Shabbos foods cooking, the aroma of home, of comfort, of parents'
embrace, of peace and protection.

*Father Jacob, where is the key that unlocks the door? We want
to undo the damage that occurred long ago in your generation. How
do we unlock the door to go back, to undo the damage?*

And then, our Father Jacob speaks.

"*My Children, I have a brother named Esau. As I am alive, he
is alive.*[531] *Esau is the father of a nation named Edom, which has
dominated the world until today. Esau was unable to destroy me, but
Edom destroyed my House in Jerusalem, the House that my children
built to be a dwelling place for G-d in this world. Esau is trying to*

push G-d out of the world. He constructs tall buildings and great bridges, ships and planes, cars and trains, everything that is built under the sun. He strives to master the earth, but thinks he has no master. Esau lives in the world through his structures, through his commerce. If you want to open the door and come to my father's chamber, you must rebuild the House that Esau destroyed. In that House you will be reunited with Our Father in Heaven and He will give you strength. That is the key that will unlock the door to the chamber where my parents are buried."

And so, our Father Jacob has told us, the key to the next chamber in the Cave of Machpela is *Dveikus*, unity with G-d. The word *"dveikus"* is derived from the word *"devek,"* glue. Our survival in this world, our ability to open the next door in the path back to the Garden of Eden, our ability to follow that beautiful aroma to its source, is dependant upon sticking like glue to our Creator.

Now, my brothers and sisters, my dear friends, my family, let us reason. We hold one key in our hands, the key of Unity. We have opened the door to the Cave, using the key of Unity. The next key is *Dveikus*.

The time has come, my brothers and sisters, to put aside our fantasies so that we can survive. Let us acknowledge that *"not by bread alone does man live, rather by everything that emanates from the mouth of G-d."*[532] *"Some [trust in] chariots, and some [in] horses, but ... in the Name of our G-d we call out."*

Since Esau destroyed G-d's House in Jerusalem, we have lived in Esau's tall buildings, Esau's exile. We have forgotten what it is like to dwell in the Presence of G-d. That is the greatest tragedy of that terrible destruction; Esau has succeeded in wiping out our memory.

"One thing I asked of G-d, that shall I seek: That I dwell in the House of G-d all the days of my life; to behold the sweetness of G-d

and to contemplate in His Sanctuary. Indeed He will hide me in His Shelter on the day of Evil; He will conceal me in the concealment of His Tent."[533]

We think that we have advanced because we are competing with all the nations of the world in mastering the universe. Yes, we are great in business. Yes, we are great in commerce. Yes, we are great in law and medicine and science and literature and government.

But in whose eyes are we great?

In Esau's eyes?

Esau is not interested in our greatness. Esau is interested only in exploiting our contributions for his own advancement and eliminating our unique spiritual leadership role by drowning it in his world. We have lost our *Dveikus* with G-d.

That is the Second Key.

Let us grasp the Second Key in our hand, my brothers and sisters, and together open the door leading to the Chamber of our Father Isaac and our Mother Rebecca.

THE SECOND CHAMBER

The aroma of *Shabbos* grows stronger as we open the door to the next chamber. A bracing purity is becoming more noticeable. We have been breathing polluted air for so long that we do not even know what pure air is like. That is why we are all sick and why we are hurting so much. We have been breathing polluted air for centuries. In the last sixty years,[534] the air is thick with the stench of the smokestacks of Auschwitz. We have been choking on this air, dying from this air, becoming sick from this air. Every breath is poison. No wonder that strange sicknesses are creeping into the world. We cannot cease to breathe, but we cannot escape from sickness and death!

In the darkness of Machpela, we enter the Chamber of our
Father Isaac and our Mother Rebecca. We have grasped the
keys of Unity and Dveikus; they have opened two doors.

*Father Isaac, tell us please, how do we move further onward
toward the Garden, and complete our mission in this world? How
do we fulfill that for which you raised us, Father? You were willing
to sacrifice your life in order to fulfill the will of our Creator. Please
tell us, Father, how do we fulfill His will?*

"*My Children, I have a half-brother named Ishmael, the son of
our Father Abraham but not the son of our mother Sarah. He is, as
you know, the son of Hagar the Egyptian, the daughter of Cham, the
son of Noah. Ishmael has power, in that he believes in Our Creator
and cleaves to Him. With that power he is destroying you! He is
using the power and you are not! What is wrong with you, my Children! Wake up! My Mother Sarah drove Ishmael from our home
because he was trying to kill me. He was driven away, but his children never forgot and never forgave. Today he comes with his bow
and his arrows, his nails and his teeth to tear you limb from limb! He
is trying to undo what our Mother Sarah did. He wants to throw you
out of your home and take your place! He is trying to undo everything Our Holy Parents accomplished. He calls upon Our Father in
Heaven to help him destroy us! You, My Children, do NOT call
upon Our Father in Heaven!*

"*But Ishmael forgets that we are Our Father's favorite children.*

"'*Is Ephraim My most precious son or a delightful child that
whenever I speak of him I remember him more and more? Therefore
My inner self yearns for him. I will surely take pity on him...the
words of G-d.*'[535]

"*Ishmael learned about Our Father in Heaven from Our Father
Abraham, but he did not learn from Our Mother Sarah! Listen carefully, my Children, and I will tell you what you must know to unlock
the Third Chamber. Our Mother Sarah taught us loving-kindness*

and compassion. Hagar, however, taught her son the law of the sword, the knife concealed in the moonlight.

"Father Abraham and Mother Sarah taught me to sacrifice my life for our Father in Heaven, and so I learned Avoda, to build up this world, not to destroy it. I learned that if I devote myself to building up this world according to the laws given by Our Father in Heaven, then He will infuse this world with His Spirit and will give me of His strength. When I lay on the altar, willing to become a sacrifice, G-d substituted a ram for me. Later, Temple Services, where G-d taught us to substitute animals for ourselves, brought the presence of Our Father in Heaven into this world.

"My Children, the Third Key is Avoda, building up this world by doing G-d's will here. Not to destroy but to build up. Our Father in Heaven does not wish that His Name should be invoked using the sword and the knife. Our Father in Heaven wishes that His Name should be invoked through kindness and chessed, as our Mother Sarah taught us, not as Hagar taught Ishmael. That building up is our heritage, my Children, and that is the key by which you may enter the Chamber of Our Father Abraham and Our Mother Sarah! But hurry, my Children, because the hour is late and you are in great danger. Hurry to save us all before it is too late!"

THE THIRD CHAMBER

With the key of *Avoda* we open the door to the Third Chamber. The sweet aroma is growing stronger; our sullied lungs rejoice at the pure air, as we enter the Chamber of Father Abraham and Mother Sarah, who traveled in ancient days from distant lands to build the Nation that cleaves to G-d in the Holy Land of Israel.

And we encounter our Father Abraham. We ask him for the

key that will allow us to pass further on, to complete now, in the end of history, the mission that he began some 3700 years ago.

Father Abraham, please tell us how we may proceed. What and where is the key that will allow us to pass further on, and to return to that primeval world of purity to which it is our destiny to return?

Father Abraham answers us.

"My Children, I was willing to utter the Name of G-d in front of the entire world. I was not embarrassed. With the Name of G-d I overcame nations and kings. I was given the name "Avraham" because I stood on one bank of the River and the world stood across from me. I did not seek approval from the world; I did not ask permission from the idolaters to cleave to G-d. In the midst of corruption I walked with Him; I sought to know and to perform His will.

"That is the Fourth Key, my Children: Kiddush Hashem, the Sanctification of G-d's Name. If you are unafraid to utter G-d's Name in the world and to do His will, you will be able to open the door to the Chamber of Adam and Eve, and you will stand at the threshold of the Garden of Eden. But remember, to enter the Garden, you must carry all the keys with you, the keys of Unity, Dveikus, Avoda, and Kiddush Hashem and also what is given to you by our First Parents, Adam and Eve.

"May G-d bless you, my Children. But hurry! The hour is late. Shabbos is almost here, and the Angel of Death is seeking to destroy us, even here! You must enter the Garden before Shabbos! Please hurry, my Children. If you do not, then all our work will have been in vain! May G-d watch over you! May we all meet soon in the Garden! Hurry!"

Father Abraham's tears fall upon us as we leave his presence, and rush onward toward the Chamber of our First Parents.

THE LAST CHAMBER

A beautiful light filters in as we enter the last chamber with the key of Kiddush Hashem. This is the Chamber of Adam and Eve, who stood in the Presence of our Creator until sin broke their bond. Now we have come to redeem them, to re-enter the Garden. But we must obtain from them the secret of how to open the final door, the door that leads from the Chamber where they have been buried for almost five thousand years, back into the Garden of Eternal Sabbath and the place where we can bask in the presence of G-d. Already the aroma is strong, the pure air swirls around us, bracing and fortifying us with strength from beyond this world. But we are not yet free of death, not yet out of the grip of corruption. We must pass one more obstacle.

Father of Mankind, how will we enter the Garden?

"My Children, we have waited so long for you! Thousands are the years we have counted in this Chamber of Death! Even until our son Abraham appeared we counted the seemingly endless years! Now you have returned to us, children of the last generation! You have come to redeem the deeds we did long ago! How we bless you! You will save us from endless death! But still you must hurry on; your work is not yet done. The Angel of Death is pursuing you, even here, on the threshold of the Garden! Hurry my children. Take this. It is the Staff of Moses. I must explain to you how to use it.

"My son King David, Father of the Redeemer, said "Ivdu es Hashem b'simcha," worship G-d in happiness.[536] In order to serve G-d your heart must be filled with hope! You must trust G-d completely! But in the Garden, the snake tricked us, poisoned us by injecting his venom. Evil became a part of us! We entered a state of depression because we felt we could never eliminate the poison from our beings! It was not only the presence of rebellion within us, but

the conviction that we were forever at its mercy. This is the legacy of the serpent and tragedy of what happened to us in the Garden of Eden.

"Our son Moses, the greatest of all our children, taught us the antidote to the poison! When G-d told him to throw his staff upon the ground, the staff became a snake and Moses fled.[537] *But G-d called to him, "stretch out your hand and grasp its tail."*[538] *The snake once again became his staff. With that staff, Moses confronted Pharaoh, freed our Children from slavery and brought them to Mount Sinai!*

"With that staff, Moses freed our children from slavery to the poison of the snake!

"G-d taught Moses to take the source of the poison and convert that to the source of his strength. Moses turned and faced the source of evil, just as our son Jacob faced Esau's Angel and our Son David faced Goliath – all in the name of G-d. When Moses lifted the snake in the name of the Master of the Universe, he became master over the evil that had been within him.

"The sin that had been inside him became his servant. Moses taught us that sin can be subdued and turned to our service by following the commands of G-d. This was also reflected in the commandment concerning the red heifer, through which the internal corruption represented by the Golden Calf was externalized and removed through the medium of the Red Cow.

"The sin is removed! It no longer dwells within!

"My Children, know that the sin is now outside you, not within! You are free! Take this staff. You will now pass out of this Chamber and approach the Angel who stands at the entrance to the Garden. He will lay down the Ever-Turning Sword with which he guards the way to the Tree of Life. He will let you pass. But hurry, my Children! Shabbos is almost here, and you must enter the Garden before the Angel of Death stops you. All of creation is depending upon you!

All of the deeds of the holy people who have ever lived upon this earth
are upon your shoulders now. This is what they were preparing for!
Hurry my children! Take the Staff of Moses and run with it! Enter
the Garden and save us!

We ran out from the Chamber of Adam and Eve, grasping
the Staff of Moses. Ahead of us was the brightest light we had
ever seen, a light so bright that it banished all darkness. But it
did not hurt. It was a beautiful light that soothed our eyes and
reached into the depth of our souls. It was not just a physical
light; it was a spiritual light with healing on its wings.[539] The air
raced into our lungs! We had never breathed before! Our lungs
were filled with spiritual energy and all our organs were alive,
pulsing with desire to serve G-d! There was nothing between us
now and the Angel who towered before us, a flaming sword
swirling before him.

Suddenly I tripped; the Staff slipped from my hand. I was in
the dust and the staff had changed. A hissing sound filled my
ears, and a forked tongue flickered like lightning in a summer
sky. Huge jaws were opening in front of me. Fangs dripping
with poison were engulfing me. I saw the green eyes of the
Angel of Death!

I screamed!

SHEMA YISROEL!
HEAR O ISRAEL!
HASHEM IS OUR G-D!
HASHEM THE ONE AND ONLY G-D!

CHAPTER SEVEN

WE RETURN
TO THE GARDEN

"But as for you, do not be afraid, my servant Jacob, and do not be frightened, O Israel, for behold, I am saving you from afar, and your offspring from the land of their captivity.... Jacob shall return and be tranquil and complacent and none will make [him] afraid. You, do not be afraid, My servant Jacob — the word of G-d — for I am with you; though I shall make an end of all the nations where I have dispersed you, but of you I shall not make an end; I shall punish you with justice, but I shall not destroy you utterly."[540]

"When G-d will return the captivity of Zion, we will be like dreamers. Then our mouth will be filled with laughter and our tongue with glad song."[541]

The fangs were closing upon my face! Drops of poison fell before my eyes. Hissing filled my ears. I felt the cold embrace of eternal death! The green eyes paralyzed my body with fear!

I was dead.

Just before I died, time stopped.

In a distant corner of my petrified mind, I had a faint memory of almost forgotten words, the Torah of my Fathers: *"Hear O Israel. The L-rd our G-d, The L-rd is One!"*

I remembered that G-d had told Moses, "*Stretch out your hand and grasp its tail.*"[542] With my last atom of strength, I forced my hand to move. I could not reach far enough, but in a dream I saw Pharaoh's daughter standing by the river. She was weeping and reaching out, trying to grasp something that was beyond her. Her eyes were closed in a tremendous exercise of will. Her arm became longer and longer. I knew that if I tried the way Pharaoh's daughter had tried, I could also reach what was beyond my grasp.

I stretched out my hand, knowing that my life depended upon it. Suddenly my fingers wrapped around the tail of the deadly snake and closed tight. Instantly, the snake became a Staff again. I opened my eyes. Healing light entered my soul. My strength was returning. I held the Staff tightly in my hand, never to let it go!

I rose to my feet, leaning upon the Staff of Moses. I wiped off the dust of fifty seven hundred years. The Holy Angel laid down his flaming sword and we entered the Garden of Eden.

THE GARDEN OF EDEN

We saw before us a scene that took our breath away, a garden that was perfectly tended, with grassy meadows among swaying trees and flowers of every color and description. The sky was blue, with fleecy clouds, and the air was warm. Peace was in the air. Singing in the trees and flying above us were bright-colored birds. A beautiful mixture of aromas entered our nostrils and a soft breeze moved the trees, whose branches were laden with shining leaves of every shade of green. Everything was tended, but there was no sign of a gardener and no noise of machines. The only sounds were the songs of birds and the sounds of summer. The garden paths invited us. The ground was firm. The grass was soft, warm and healing beneath our feet.

But there was more than this. It wasn't simply physical beauty. The beauty we beheld with our eyes entered our souls.

Can I describe the Garden of Eden? I think I can, because I have a frame of reference. We are told[543] that the Sabbath is one-sixtieth of the World to Come. Granted that we don't know exactly what relationship the Garden of Eden will have to the Spiritual World that the righteous will inhabit forever in the presence of G-d, but the Sabbath gives us some insight into what to expect in the future.

There are two "islands" in the physical world, islands separated from the mainland of the striving and restless world that we had left behind. Those two islands are the Sabbath, which is an island in time, and the Land of Israel, which is an island in space.

They are each sanctified.

The Sabbath is an island in time. When the Sabbath begins, and we allow the Presence of G-d to enter, our souls expand with the addition of a "*neshoma yesaira*," an expansion of our "weekday" soul. We feel to a greatly heightened degree the presence of G-d. We feel liberated from the weight that has pressed us down for the previous six days. We are freed from slavery on the Sabbath by the uplifting presence of G-d within us. We are not threatened. We are not subdued. We are not enslaved by the pressures of time, money, competition, arrogant people, fear... all the spiritual enemies that beset us during the week. We know with complete certainty that G-d, our Father and our King, is with us to take care of us and that "*with His rod* and staff he will comfort us.*"[544]

---

* You might not think there is "comfort" in a "rod," but there is. If you know that even your difficult moments come from G-d and that He is your constant, most devoted Friend, then all of life becomes bearable.

During the week an army of pressures had surrounded us. We were intimidated and did not enjoy one moment of peace. Between difficulties with other people and illness and money and children and war and lost possessions and …an army of worries!

When the Sabbath arrives, then the army of troubles recedes. Why? Because we have a Champion. The Sabbath Queen enters, and the threatening army that surrounded us during the week is afraid. The Presence of G-d enters along with the Sabbath Queen, and He is standing next to us. All bow down in His presence, and those troublesome gnomes who so intimidated us during the week are nowhere to be seen. We remember that they existed and had besieged our body and mind, but the Majesty of G-d's Presence is so great that they have run away; they tremble in the presence of the Master of the World! They dare not bother us when He is standing next to us. He had also been there during the week, but we were not aware of it. As Our Father Jacob said, *"Surely G-d is present in this place and I did not know!"*[545] But on the Sabbath we know!*

On the Sabbath we know that He is standing with us, and everything in the universe trembles at His Presence. We are not afraid, because we are loyal to Him and we are following His commandments, and so we know He will not be angry with us. We are comforted by His presence, because all those forces in the world that threatened us are now subdued. Our hearts are at peace. Our Champion, our Father, our King is standing with us and all is good in the world.

Such is the feeling on the Sabbath, when we live according to the laws that our King has decreed for us. But there is one "flaw" in the Sabbath: it ends! Every Saturday night, when the

* As a great Chasidic Rebbe once said, "Don't tell the Creator how great your troubles are. Tell your troubles how great your Creator is!"

Sabbath departs, we smell sweet spices to revive our souls that are crushed at the thought that we must now return to the world of conflict and fear!   We don't want the Sabbath Queen to leave!

Now, in the Garden of Eden, at the end of time, when the Presence of G-d is visible in the world and the Master is clearly seen by all His servants, we know that the Sabbath is with us forever! We remember the old times, the times of fear and tragedy and suffering beyond comprehension, but like the weekday gnomes on the Sabbath, they have receded into the distance, this time never to return.

Now we will take those very sufferings and sing about them to Our G-d! *"Then Moses and the children of Israel chose to sing this song to G-d, and they said, ... 'I shall sing to G-d for He is exalted above the arrogant, having hurled horse with its rider into the sea. The might and vengeance of G-d was salvation for me. This is my G-d and I will build Him a Sanctuary; the G-d of my father and I will exalt Him.'"*[546]

We will use the memories of the past to comprehend the greatness of the present, the salvation that our G-d has brought about for us! The Judge rules the world! All evil has been crushed. All who sought to destroy G-d's world have been dealt with as they wished to deal with those who were faithful to G-d. There is no one left to speak words of evil and falsehood, no more hidden daggers embedded in smooth phrases and no more poisoned smiles. There is no one left to threaten us physically or spiritually, to wound our hearts with brutal words, to separate brother from brother or children from parents.

The "deficiency" of the Sabbath no longer exists, because now the Sabbath is forever. It will never end. G-d is standing at our side and He will never leave us, or – to put it more accurately – we will never leave Him.

THE WORLD OF THE MESSIAH

The Prophet Ezekiel writes about the world in the time of the Messiah:

"I shall take you from the nations and gather you in from all the countries, and ...bring you to your Land; and I shall sprinkle pure water upon you, [and] you [will] be cleansed. ... I shall give you a new heart; I shall put a new spirit within you; I shall remove ... [your] heart of stone ...and give you a heart of flesh; and I shall put My spirit within you, ...I shall cause you to go by My decrees and guard My laws and perform them; and you shall dwell in the land that I gave your fathers; and you shall be a People to Me and I shall be your G-d ....I shall not place famine upon you; and I shall increase the fruit of the tree and produce of the field so that you no longer accept the shame of hunger among the nations. On the day when I cleanse you from all your sins, and cause the cities to be inhabited and the ruins to be built, and the ...land to be tilled instead of being desolate; then they shall say, 'This very land that was desolate has become a Garden of Eden, and the cities that were destroyed and...desolate and ruined shall be inhabited!'"[547]

Maimonides also writes about the world of the Messiah.

"In the future, the Messianic King will arise and renew the dynasty of David, returning it to its initial sovereignty. He will build the Temple and gather the dispersed of Israel. In his days, [the observance of] all the statutes will return to their previous state. We will offer sacrifices [and] observe the Sabbatical and Jubilee years according to all the particulars mentioned by the Torah. Anyone who does not believe in him or does not wait for his coming denies not only [the statements] of the other prophets, but [those of] the Torah and Moses, our teacher. The Torah testified to his [coming], as it states:[548] 'G-d will bring back your captivity and have mercy

upon you. He will gather you [from among the nations].... Even
if your diaspora is at the ends of the heavens, [G-d will gather you
up from there]... and [G-d] will bring you [to the land].' These
explicit words of the Torah include all the statements made by all the
*prophets."*549

"If a king will arise from the House of David who is learned in
Torah and observant of the mitzvos, as prescribed by the written law
and oral law, as David, his ancestor was, and will compel all of Israel
to walk in the [way of the Torah] and reinforce the breaches [in its
observance], and fight the wars of G-d, we may with assurance con-
sider him the Messiah. If he succeeds in the above, builds the Temple
in its place and gathers the dispersed of Israel, he is definitely the Mes-
siah. He will then improve the entire world, [motivating] all the
*nations to serve G-d together as the Prophet states,*550 *'I will make the*
peoples pure of speech that they all will call upon the Name of G-d and
*serve Him with one purpose.'"*551 *"One should not presume that the*
Messianic King must work miracles and wonders.... [Proof may be
brought form the fact] that Rabbi Akiva... considered [King Bar Koz-
ibah] ... to be the Messianic King until he was killed because of sins.
*Once he was killed they realized that he was not [the Messiah.]"*552

"Do not presume that in the Messianic age, the nature of the
world will change or there will be innovations in the work of creation.
*Rather, the world will continue according to its pattern."*553

"There will be no difference between the current age and the
Messianic era except [the emancipation] from our subjugation to the
*[gentile] kingdoms."*554

"The sages did not yearn for the Messianic era in order to have
dominion over the entire world, to rule over the gentiles, to be exalt-
ed by the nations, or to eat, drink and celebrate. Rather, [they
desired] to be free [to involve themselves] in Torah and wisdom with-
out any pressures or disturbances so that they would merit the World
*to Come."*555

"In that era, there will be neither famine nor war, envy or com-petition, for good will flow in abundance and all delights will be [as common] as dust. The occupation of the entire world will be solely to know G-d. Therefore the Jews will be great sages and know hidden matters, attaining knowledge of their Creator to [the full extent] of human potential as the Prophet states,[556] 'The world will be filled with the knowledge of G-d as the sea fills the ocean bed.'"[557]

"For G-d comforts Zion. He comforts her ruins, and He will make her wilderness like Eden, and her wastes like a garden...Glad-ness and joy shall be found there, thanksgiving and the sound of music."[558]

TOWARD JERUSALEM

We walk on green paths north from Hebron, from where we entered the Garden of Eden, drinking along the way from clear streams. Walking with us are our holy parents, Adam and Eve, Abraham and Sarah, Isaac and Rebecca, Jacob and Leah. We walk in the yellow sunshine of eternal summer. We come to Bais Lechem (called "Bethlehem" by others in another time) and there, standing at the door to a white domed building, is our Mother Rachel. *"And Rachel weeps for her children."*[559] But this time her tears are tears of joy! Your children have come home!

Now all Israel is together; our Fathers lead us. We march northward to Jerusalem! From the East we hear the sound of the *Shofar*. Our Teacher Moses is approaching from across the Jordan River! And ahead of us, standing to welcome us to the Holy City, is David our King! From his ruined tomb arises our Father Joseph; he is coming southward toward Jerusalem. Samuel the Prophet arises upon his hilltop and is walking toward the Temple Mount. Rabbi Akiva has stood up in Tiberias and is coming to meet us. From Meron comes Rabbi Shimon bar Yochai!

All Israel is coming to the Holy City!

Ahead of us, high on a hill, is a shining edifice. Around it, throngs of people are approaching, dressed in white. The edifice is perfectly proportioned, but has room for all, and we enter through the Eastern Gate. No one is pushing; no one is in a hurry. There is enough time and space for everyone. No one is afraid that he or she will not hear or see or find room and comfort. Time and space have become our servants; they are no longer our masters. All are walking onward, content with their lot.

Every child of Israel is here, all the sons and daughters who loved our G-d and served Him through all the years of history. Since space has been subdued, there is room for everyone. We look at faces and find that we know each other: here is the *Chofetz Chaim* and here is the *Baal Shem Tov* and here is the *Baba Sali!* No one is arrogant and no one is angry; all are united in serving our G-d.

Before us stands David our King, robed in white, his face shining in purity. Behind him are his fathers and mothers, Adam and Eve, Abraham and Sarah, Isaac and Rebecca, Jacob with Rachel and Leah. Surrounding them are the Tribal Patriarchs, Reuven, Shimon, Levi, Yehuda, Yissacher, Zevulun, Dan, Naftali, Gad, Asher, Yosef, Ephraim, Menashe and Binyamin. Moses and Aaron stand together. Joshua and the Judges and Prophets surround them. The Rabbis from all the generations and all corners of the world stand in their holiness, not bowed nor bent, but with the vigor of eternal youth, the light of Torah illuminating their faces.

King David speaks, and all hear his voice rising on tremors of emotion.

"My children, our sufferings are over now. We have passed all the tests. We have survived the fiery furnace. We have clung to our

G-d and His Commandments despite the flames and swords of those who tried to destroy us. We have testified to eternity that Truth is beyond this material world, because we have clung to our G-d and His Commandments in the face of all that our enemies could heap upon us.

"Since we brought these trials upon ourselves, we were called upon to purify ourselves and to cleanse the world that we had sullied. But even our mistakes were a glorification of G-d's Name. Because we rebelled, we who love our Father in Heaven were anxious to atone for our sins and inadequacies, and, like a child who begs his father for forgiveness, we spent our lifetimes in the deepest devotion to Him. The world was amazed at us. They could not believe that such a Nation could exist, despite all that they themselves did to destroy us! And so, we made a Name in the world for our Father in Heaven.

"So many of us lived and died lives of torture and tragedy beyond comprehension. So many of us drowned in tears. So many sacrificed and fought to purify ourselves in order to be good children to our Father in Heaven. My children, everything we sacrificed to serve our Father in Heaven has been returned to us and infinitely more. All the prayers that we thought could never be fulfilled have been fulfilled, and all our efforts will be rewarded. We will live with our families in peace forever and we will never be troubled. Our sacrifices are recorded in a book written with our tears. Because it is written with tears we did not read it during our lives and the world could not read it; the nations did not know that it existed. But our Father in Heaven, Who is above the material world, read the book every day.

"Standing here today are all our children whom we never thought we would see again. Standing here today are all our parents whom we never thought we would see again. Now, my children, we are all together forever, and we will never have to be afraid again."

King David's voice broke, and he could no longer speak. He broke down and wept, his body shaking. All of us wept tears of deepest emotion and thanksgiving, and words were beyond us. King David continued.

"There are an infinite number of heroes here. Everyone standing here is a hero in the eyes of our Father in Heaven. All of us will find our families here; there is no one missing among the loyal children of our Father in Heaven.

"ALL THE LOST CHILDREN ARE RETURNED!"

Once again, King David broke down and wept! He could speak no longer!

Then, there was a tremendous murmur flowing like a wave upon us, and we all turned toward the East. A man of enormous height in flowing white robes had entered and a path was being made for him. Moses, our Teacher, our Leader, our Prophet, was entering the Sanctuary of G-d! He walked steadily and with great dignity. Never had we seen a face like this, never had we seen a man who glowed with the fire of Heaven as the face of Moses glowed. With him, his face also shining like the summer sun, was Moses' brother Aaron, in the garments of the High Priest.

They stopped as they walked to speak and to embrace us. They were our fathers, our teachers! We wept as we saw their kindness and their love for us. And tears flowed from their eyes as they beheld their loyal children!

Moses stood before us and these were his words.

"My children, you know that I never set my foot in the Land of our Destiny. It is recorded in the Torah how I begged our Father in Heaven to allow me to enter this Land. But I had to be content to see the Land from afar; my prayers were not fulfilled ... UNTIL TODAY! We are a very patient Nation; we know that our Father will answer us, but sometimes it seemed that there was to be no end to our trials and our exile. I waited and waited, in exile along with you, my children, knowing that someday our Father would answer

my prayers. I waited for you, my children, so that we could enter the Land of our Destiny together. I waited in silence; you did not hear from me for over three thousand years. But you knew I was with you. Although you did not see my face, you read and followed the words that our Father in Heaven had taught me. Today, my children, our redemption has come; today we stand together in our Holy Land and from this moment onward we will never be parted."

And then, in the silence – for there was an uncounted multitude standing together, but all were quiet – suddenly a pure voice was heard, singing. It reminded me of Friday night in the synagogue. After a week of tension and worry, fear and anxiety, suddenly, on a Friday night, the pure voice of the one who leads the prayers sings out, "Lecha Dodi, Come my Beloved, to greet the bride, the Sabbath Queen. Let us welcome her. Enter, O bride! Enter, O bride." Suddenly, all fear and anxiety are banished in the presence of the Sabbath Queen.

Out of the mouth of Moses, our Teacher, was coming a song that stirred my soul and brought soothing tears to my tired eyes. It was a song from the depths of time and the beginning of Creation, a song from the souls of those who have survived and those who have endured, a song of devotion to G-d, eternal allegiance to the One Who sustains the world, the One Who has saved us in every generation when we clung to Him.

"Then Moses and the children of Israel chose to sing this song to G-d and they said…"[560]

"I shall sing to G-d, for He is exalted above the arrogant, having hurled horse with its rider into the sea. G-d is my might and my praise, and He was a salvation for me. This is my G-d and I will build Him a Sanctuary, the G-d of my father, and I will exalt Him. G-d is Master of war, through His Name. Pharaoh's chariots and army He threw into the sea, and the pick of his officers were mired in the Sea of Reeds. Deep waters covered them; they descended in the *depths like stone. Your right hand, G-d, is adorned with strength; Your right hand, G-d, smashes the enemy. In Your abundant grandeur You shatter Your opponents; You dispatch Your wrath, it consumes them like straw. At a blast from Your nostrils the waters were heaped up; straight as a wall stood the running water, the deep waters congealed in the heart of the sea. The enemy declared, 'I will pursue, I will overtake, I will divide plunder; I will satisfy my lust with them; I will unsheathe my sword, my hand will impoverish them.' You blew with Your wind – the sea enshrouded them; the mighty sank like lead in water. Who is like You among the heavenly powers, O G-d! Who is like You, mighty in holiness, too awesome for praise, doer of wonders! You stretched out Your right hand – the earth swallowed them. With Your kindness You guided this people that You redeemed, You led with Your might to Your holy abode. Peoples heard – they were agitated; terror gripped the dwellers of Philistia. Then the chieftains of Edom were confounded, trembling gripped the powers of Moab, all the dwellers of Canaan dissolved. May fear and terror befall them, at the greatness of your arm may they be still as stone; until Your people passes through, G-d, until this people You have acquired passes through. You will bring them and implant them on the mount of Your heritage, the foundation of Your dwelling place that You, G-d, have made – the Sanctuary My L-rd, that Your hands established.*

"G-d shall reign for all eternity!

"When Pharaoh's cavalry came with his chariots and horsemen into the sea and G-d turned back the waters of the sea upon them, the children of Israel walked on the dry land amid the sea."

"That, my children, was the song I sang on the 21st day of the month of Nissan in the year 2448. At that time, we escaped from the water that drowned our enemies and through which we emerged to safety and the road to Mount Sinai.

"We escaped from the water, but we plunged into fire! The Torah

was given in fire and G-d descended in fire.[561] My Brother Aaron's
sons died in fire when they brought strange fire.[562] *The House of*
G-d built on this very spot was burnt in fire. And then we built
another House on this Mountain, which Mattisyahu and his sons
purified with fire that burned for eight days. But when we rebelled
against the Torah that was written in letters of fire, that Second
House was also burnt in fire and then we as a People descended into
an Exile of Fire. Throughout those seemingly endless years, we were
pursued by fire and the murderers burned our houses, our books and
our bodies in fire. Rabbi Chananya was burned in fire and the Torah
in which they wrapped him flew up in letters of fire. Throughout the
centuries they pursued us with fire. The Inquisitors burned us in fire
and the Dictator whose name will be consumed in fire even as he
burns forever in fire, burnt us in fire. Toward the end of history, men
who rebelled against the Torah of Fire built weapons of fire as strong
as the sun. Men who hated G-d and His fiery Torah set themselves
and the world on fire, and their fire went out of control.

"But we who walked through fire held the fiery Torah in our
hearts, and that enabled us to survive the fires of our enemies. It stood
as a pillar of fire between us and those who fought to destroy us. We
followed that pillar of fire throughout the long night of fiery Exile. We
followed it to this Mountain, and now it will never depart from us, just
as we will never again depart from this sweet and exalted Land. Those
who perished in flames, sanctifying the name of G-d, are here with us
today. Now the fire is inside our hearts forever, burning with a pure
and bright flame. It is no longer burning out of control; it is contained
in the Holy Menorah that you see before your eyes! It is burning on
the Altar that provides our atonement. And smoke – instead of blind-
ing and choking us – rises from the Golden Altar in healing incense
that will renew our souls and banish death forever. The fire will burn
in eternal Shabbos candles and in our hearts."

Moses our Teacher then turned and left the Sanctuary. We

followed, all in deep emotion, with tears of gratitude and praise to G-d in our hearts for our salvation, which was coming about just as the words of the prophets had assured us it would. No one was speaking; all hearts were full of emotion, too much praise and too much emotion to allow words to come forth. Two thousand years of gratitude, or was it three thousand, or four thousand or five? We followed our Teacher Moses, and before us was a *sukkah* so great in size that we could not see the end of it. Its walls were a silvery animal skin and it was supported on old and majestic trees, on top of which were placed bows of leafy branches. Inside was the most perfect atmosphere of dappled sunlight and shade, sparkling upon majestic tables laden with the most inviting foods.

We sat by families, and as far as the eye could see, there were tables and tables filled with devoted and holy children of our Fathers Abraham, Isaac and Jacob, in awe of the great salvation that had come upon us and upon the world. Our hearts were so filled with gratitude that there was barely room for words to emerge. But the words of our sages we did speak, *"Blessed are you, Our G-d, King of the Universe, Who creates the fruit of the vine."* We poured from silver pitchers into silver goblets and drank chilled wine that brought cheer to our hearts.

As we refreshed our souls, our father Abraham arose. I am not going to tell you how it was that we could all see and hear him, because the nature of this time and place exceeded the boundaries of nature as we had known them previously. I will say to you that throughout history there were countless, an infinite number of miracles that defied what the world considered the laws of nature. For those who did not want to think, they were simply accepted. But for a Jew who kept the Sabbath to experience each week the miracle of gaining an additional soul, a soul that lifted him above the grinding tragedy and despair of that pain-filled world, there is no need to explain the miracles of going beyond time and space. We knew it each week, as Shabbos carried us above and beyond what the world called reality.

Our survival itself was beyond logic. There is no way the children of Israel should have been able to survive as a distinct and discrete nation, scattered among our enemies throughout the world and apparently powerless to resist their cruelty. How did we survive? If you will contemplate these miracles, then you will understand how it is possible that an infinite number of the children of Israel could be sitting together in a boundless *sukkah* and all be seeing our Father Abraham and hearing his voice.

"My children, we bequeathed to you endless patience. My holy wife, Sarah, your Mother, and I were very old when your Father Isaac was born. It was impossible that we could become parents at our age, and yet all the rules of our world are made by our Father in Heaven, so nothing is impossible. But the waiting we endured, the seemingly endless years, the constant questionings – "Will it be? Will it be?" — even though our Father in Heaven had promised that "only he that shall come forth from within you shall inherit you"[563] *still no one had come forth from within us, and we were drying up and becoming old. Our entire life was a test. We knew that G-d had promised us a redemption, but it was not coming! Day after day passed, year after year. We kept on in our work of discovering the Torah and trying to live as the Master of the World wanted us to live, but each year passed and still G-d's promise was not fulfilled. With each passing second we got older, and the way of the world was that with each passing second it became less possible, until it seemed to become impossible. Only after it seemed to become impossible, the angels came to us and announced that it was happening.*

"My children, that is what sustained you. Our years of waiting, our years of hanging on to that promise even when everything logical

told us that it could never materialize. Just as we waited an eternity for our redemption, so you waited an eternity for your redemption. Just as we should have lost all hope, so you should have lost all hope, but you did not lose hope. You who sit here today never gave up, despite all the tragedies, the tears, the sights and sounds that tore our hearts apart. I know that so often you felt as if you were being buried under a mountain of despair and exhaustion! The savagery in the world, the brutality, the poison, the daggers of hatred, the lies, the mental agony, the feeling that 'I cannot endure one more atom of pain!' How did we survive? Indeed, Mount Sinai was resting upon our heads! The only reason we survived was that our Merciful Father was suspending it above us and holding it so that we would not be crushed. And in your hearts we knew it!

"My children, thank you for remembering the lesson of your Father Abraham and your Mother Sarah. Our Father in Heaven loves you so much! You have remained true to Him through endless years of pain. You have glorified and sanctified His Name in the world. You have demonstrated that He exists to a world that continually tried to run away from Him. And now, my children, you have earned your rest. Now we are together forever, and you will never have to be afraid again. You will never have to worry about your children, and you will never have to worry about your parents! Your work is done, my dear children; you have passed all your tests. You can breathe now children. You can smile; you can laugh; you can sing; the world is yours in its perfection. You have earned your rest. Shabbos is yours for eternity!"

As Our Father Abraham finished his emotional words, a tall man stood up. You could see that his majestic figure had once shined with perfect innocence and purity, but that millennia of the burdens of the entire world had etched upon his brow the deepest burdens of any man. His features glowed with a distant light reflected from the Presence of G-d and the purity of His creations as they had been at the first dawn. Adam spoke, the father of all mankind.

"*I am your first father. I am the father of the world. The Creator gave me and my beloved wife the honor and weighty privilege of having been present at the dawn and birth of the world. Oh, what a time that was. The earth glistened with the dew of creation. Everything was fresh with eternal hope. The Almigh-ty placed all His trust in us, His children, to preside over His perfect world and to raise eternal generations of children dedicated to tending the perfect Garden He had planted in Eden.*

"*We failed! We did not justify Our Creator's trust in us! We failed in our first and greatest test! We were forced to leave our beautiful home, and wander, homeless, in the cruel and frightening world outside the Garden. We were banished from the presence of our Creator! An angel stood with twirling sword at the entrance to what had been our Garden. We could not return! Our home! Our G-d! Our life in eternal ruins! Can you imagine the tears we shed! Can you imagine the rivers and oceans of tears we shed at our unbearable guilt! What had we done! We had condemned all our uncounted offspring to a life of slavery and suffering in a cruel and savage world!*

"*I could not stop weeping, but my beloved wife comforted me. She told me that we must now dry our tears and go onward. She told me that G-d would help us if we made a sincere effort to come back to Him and to atone for our terrible mistake and rebellion. She told me that our job in the world was to raise children who would return to our Father, our Creator. Our job was to tell our story to our children, and imbue them with love for Our Father, our Creator and the desire to return to Him with all their heart and all their soul and everything that they possess.*

"*I thank G-d Who gave me such a wife**, *who comforted me*

---

* Rashi says (in his comment on Genesis 3:12) that Adam was not grateful to G-d for his wife and blamed her for the sin at the time G-d confronted them in the Garden. Perhaps Adam, however, upon reflection over thousands of years, may have looked differently at the past and realized how indebted he was to Eve.

and allowed me to go on in life. I tried to dry my tears and do as my wife said. Not all our children understood our message, but one of them did, and that blessed child passed the message down through history. Sometimes, at certain periods in history, there were only a few in the entire world who remembered the secret of life and hope. Sometimes those few were so threatened by the evil in the world that it seemed all would be lost! But Our Father in Heaven hid and protected those few, and in every generation the thin, vulnerable, almost invisible thread winding through history was saved from destruction. In the very end, in the terrible Sixth Millennium, the tiny thread was almost lost, saved only because the water of tears protected it from the flames of destruction!

"But now, my brave and devoted children, you have prevailed! You have carried the thread of Truth home to Hebron; you have unlocked the door to the Cave of Machpela. You have passed through the Cave where we slept, and you have awakened us! My beautiful children, you have saved your ancient parents! You have redeemed us! You have saved the world! You have saved your parents from eternal tears and you have brought the light of G-d's Face once again into our world. You have allowed us to return to our Garden, our home! And now, my children, we have returned to our G-d! His Face will once again shine upon us! And now <u>His</u> tears will be dried. The children have come home forever! You have redeemed us, our children! You have saved the earth! Thank you, my children! Thank you, my children! You have fulfilled the ancient words, 'he will turn back [to G-d] the hearts of the fathers with [their] sons and the hearts of sons with their fathers!'"[564]

Adam, the first man, broke down completely, and tears consumed him! He sat down, shaking and sobbing, unable to speak. As our eyes were fixed upon him, suddenly we were aware that we were in the Presence of G-d. He was here, in our midst; He surrounded us; He was next to us, within us, all around us. Our insides quivered with life. Unspeakable fulfillment filled every part of our heart, mind, and body.

Suddenly, it was night. A full moon shone in a sky surrounded by stars that seemed to be sparkling and twinkling like fireworks of every color in the spectrum. But the moon was different! It shone in the dark sky with the light of the sun! And yet it was night, but the moon shone with the light of the sun!

And then we heard the voice of G-d. Every person in that vast sukkah was shaking, crying and laughing, singing and sobbing inside. Every person in that vast assembly was gripped by a force of life so powerful that we saw all creation before us. We saw the spiritual and we saw how it prevailed over the material. We saw how every single action in Creation emanated from the Creator and how every breath of wind and fall of a leaf emanated from Him and was part of His eternal plan and design. Nothing was an accident! All the earth and all history were His. All our actions were in His plan. Even our mistakes and rebellions were foreseen by Him and led inevitably to the end that He had directed. Everything had led toward this moment. Nothing was left out. All who had remained with the Creator were alive at that moment, and all who had denied His existence were as if they had never existed. Only that which was attached to Him existed; all else had ceased to exist.

That vast multitude began to sing an eternal song, and the whole earth echoed with that song.

Lecha dodi likras kalla, pnai Shabbos nekabla!

Come my Beloved to greet the bride! Let us welcome the Sabbath Queen!

"Safeguard" and "remember" in a single utterance the One and Only G-d made us hear; G-d is One and His Name is One, for renown, for splendor and for praise.

To welcome the Sabbath, come let us go. For it is the source of blessing; From the Beginning, from antiquity she was honored, last in deed but first in thought.

Sanctuary of the king, royal City, Arise and depart from amid the upheaval. Too long have you dwelled in the valley of weeping. He will shower compassion upon you.

Shake off the dust! Arise! Don your splendid clothes, My People. Through the son of Jesse, from Bais Lechem, draw near to my soul... redeem it!

Wake up! Wake up! For your light has come, rise and shine. Awaken, awaken, utter a song. The glory of G-d is revealed on you.

Do not feel ashamed. Do not be humiliated. Why are you downcast? Why are you disconsolate? In you will My people's afflicted find shelter as the city is built upon its hilltop.

Your oppressor will be downtrodden and those who devoured you will be cast far off. Your G-d will rejoice over you like a groom rejoicing over his bride.

Rightward and leftward, you shall spread out mightily and you shall extol the might of G-d, through the man descended from Peretz, then we shall be glad and mirthful.

Enter in peace, O crown of her husband. Even in gladness and good cheer. Among the faithful of the treasured nation. Enter O bride! Enter O bride!

And then King David arose, and took up his harp, and began to sing in a voice that was heard even by the stars twinkling above.

Mizmor Shir l'yom Ha Shabbos!

"*It is good to thank G-d and to sing praise to Your Name, O Exalted One, to relate Your kindness in the dawn and Your faith in the nights, upon ten-stringed instrument and lyre, with singing accompanied by a harp. For You have gladdened me, G-d, with Your deeds; at the works of Your Hands I sing glad song. How great are Your deeds O G-d, exceedingly profound are Your thoughts. A boor cannot know, nor can a fool understand this; when the wicked bloom like grass and all the doers of iniquity blossom – it is to destroy them till eternity!   But You remain exalted forever, G-d.   For behold! – Your enemies, G-d, for behold! — Your enemies shall perish, and dispersed shall be all doers of iniquity. As exalted as a re'im's shall be my pride, I will be saturated with ever-fresh oil.   My eyes have seen my vigilant foes; when those who would harm me rise up against me, my ears have heard their doom.   A righteous man will flourish like a date palm, like a cedar in the Lebanon he will grow tall.   Planted in the house of G-d, in the courtyard of our G-d they will flourish.   They will still be fruitful in old age, vigorous and fresh they will be — to declare that G-d is just, my Rock in Whom there is no wrong!*[565]

NOTES

1 Isaiah 11:9

2 By Rabbi Bachya ben Joseph ibn Paquda. (This passage is from the Introduction. I used the translation in the Feldheim Torah Classics edition.)

3 Psalms 116:12

4 From the Morning Service.

4a Sefer HaChinuch, Mitzva #2

5 In this book, I follow the convention of using the word "man" to stand for all of mankind, including women. I know that this has become unpopular in today's world, but no slight is intended.

6 Psalm 115

7 Rashi on Genesis 1:27, based on accounts in the Talmud and Medrash (a rabbinical explanation of the Torah), explains how Adam and Eve were created as one entity and separated from each other.

8 Rabbi Bachya ibn Pakuda in the classic Duties of the Heart (Chovos Ha L'vavos, Shaar ha Bechina) tells us that we must reflect on the wonders of creation, in order to gain an appreciation of the One who created these things.

9 Deuteronomy 30:19

10 Isaiah 1:3-4

11 Psalm 81:9

12 Without earning our Eternity through free will our reward would not be complete. This concept is found in Magid Maisharim (by R. Yosef Caro) Beraishis.

13 Proverbs 24:16

14 Psalm 55:23

15 Talmud Tractate Avoda Zarah 3a

16 Deuteronomy 8:17

16a Duties of the Heart (Shaar Habitachon, Chapter Five, Par. 2) ascribes such an attitude to lack of trust in G-d.

17 Exodus 20:14

18 Genesis 6:5-6

19 Isaiah 51:3

20 I heard this story from Rebbetzin Esther Jungreis.

21 Genesis Chapter 38

22 Boaz, the great-grandfather of King David, was the descendant of Perez, who was the child of the "illicit" union of Judah and Tamar. Ruth, the great-grandmother of King David, was the descendant of the royal family of Moab, the corrupt nation that descended from the "illicit" union of Lot and his daughter (Genesis 19:37). (The word "illicit" has been placed in quotation marks because, although these unions were outside the normal course of accepted behavior, they were clearly arranged by G-d as a means of hiding the seed of the future salvation.)

23 Psalm 12:8-9

24 Maimonides, Mishneh Torah, Hilchos Avodas Kochavim (Laws Concerning Idolatry), Chapter One, Halacha 1 (Moznaim Publishing Corp, 1990, translated by Rabbi Eliyahu Touger)

25 See Kuntres Hachesed of Rav Eliahu Dessler (Michtav M'Eliyah, Volume One) where the concept of "givers and takers" is discussed.

26 Talmud Tractate Sanhedrin page 108a. Robbery "destroys the fabric of society and poisons the atmosphere among people." (Radak).

27 Medrash Rabbah Genesis 26:5ff.

28 Genesis 1:11

29 See Medrash Rabbah Bereishis 2:5 and Meam Loez on Bereishis 2:3.

30 Isaiah 60:1-2

31 This motivation for anti-Semitism is mentioned by the Rambam (Maimonides) in Iggeres Taiman.

32 According to Rashi (on Genesis 7:2), Noah studied the traditions handed down to him from Adam. He also apparently knew by prophesy details of the Torah that would later be given to the Children of Israel at Mount Sinai. That is how he knew which animals were pure and therefore should be

taken into the Ark in groups of seven rather than groups of two. (Medrash Rabbah Bereishis 26:1)

[33] The word "Torah" refers to the Written and Oral Law handed down by G-d to Moses at Mount Sinai. He taught it to the children of Israel, through whom the Written Torah (The Bible) became known to the entire world.

[34] Jonah 1:4

[35] Talmud Tractate Chulin 7b

[36] In each period in history G-d makes His laws very clear to us. Adam and Eve were instructed precisely what the rules were (Genesis 2:16). Likewise, Noah was informed (Genesis 9:1 ff), as were the Jewish People at Mount Sinai.

[37] According to the Me'am Lo'ez (on Genesis 9:20-23) Noah was "deeply depressed because he was alone in the world, surrounded by wild beasts."

[38] See Rashi on Genesis 6:9

[39] Talmud Tractate Shabbos 33b

[40] There is a reference to this in Talmud Tractate Sotah 17a.

[41] Apparently, fire and water are two "warring" elements. According to their basic natures they would destroy each other if G-d did not "force" them to make peace and coexist in nature. We recognize this when we say in Kaddish, the prayer that describes the greatness of G-d's powers, "G-d makes peace in His heights." This is said to refer to G-d's control over the warring elements of fire and water. Just as G-d makes peace between these eternal enemies, so He will make peace between the warring elements in the soul of man, if we allow Him to enter. (See Rashi on Job 25:2)

[42] Genesis 1:2

[43] Genesis 1:6

[44] Genesis 1:7

[45] From the morning prayers.

[46] Psalms Chapter 1:3

[47] Talmud Tractate Avoda Zara 5b

[48] As it says in the Evening Prayer, "Torah and commandments, decrees and ordinances have You taught us... They are our life and the length of our days." Incidentally, by using the term "Torah" I am not excluding non-Jews; non-Jews are obligated in the Seven Mitzvos given by G-d to all mankind.

[49] From the Kaddish prayer.

[50] I heard this concept from Rebbetzin Esther Jungreis

[51] Jeremiah 2:2

[52] Genesis 8:22

[52a] Quote from "Yom Ze Mechubad," a traditional Shabbos song

[53] Talmud Tractate Sanhedrin 56b, Rambam Yad Hachazakah, Hilchos Melachim 9:1

[54] It is important to note that once a commandment is given it is not revoked. The Seven Laws promulgated at the beginning of creation are still in effect. The are applicable to the entire world to this day. Additional commandments have been added by G-d at Mount Sinai, but they have not nullified the previous commandments.

[55] The rule concerning the Tree of the Knowledge of Good and Evil is obviously not applicable outside the Garden, although the lessons from it are eternally relevant.

[56] The Kuzari discusses the universality of the seven-day week in Part One, Paragraph 57.

[57] Of course, both the Roman and the Islamic cultures have adopted from us the idea of one day that is different from the other six. But what did they not adopt from us?

[58] Permission to slaughter and eat the flesh of animals

[59] At Mount Sinai.

[60] Psalm 117

[61] Radak says that its simplicity, Psalm 117 reflects how the world will be in the time of the Messiah.

[62] Rashi on Exodus 13:18 says "one out of five (Israelites) departed (from Egypt); the (other) four fifths died (in Egypt) during the three days of darkness."

[63] G-d says of Israel in the Desert, "[they] have tested Me these ten times and have not heeded My voice" (Numbers 14:22).

[64] Proverbs 3:18

[65] Genesis 9:26

66 See Derech Hashem of R. Moshe Chaim Luzzato (Ramchal), Section 2,Chapter 4

67 Genesis 9:25-27

68 Genesis 9:22

69 Talmud Tractate Sanhedrin 70a

70 I have heard this concept explained by Rebbetzin Esther Jungreis.

71 Koheles (Ecclesiastes) 10:20

72 Genesis 19:30-37, which describes how Lot impregnated his own daughters.

73 Genesis 9:14

74 The Gemorah tells us that the rainbow is also a sign of "din," judgment. This is not inconsistent with what I am saying. To recognize that G-d is standing over nature and over history and over our lives reminds us that we must adhere to His commandments. That is essentially a positive concept, for if it were not for G-d's enforcement of His laws, the world would dissolve into chaos.

75 Psalm 115

76 During the construction of the Tower, if a brick broke everyone wept, but if a man died, no one looked at him. (Pirkei d'Rabbi Eliezer, Chapter 24.)

77 As Rebbetzin Esther Jungreis says, most people go through life without ever thinking. In her classic phrase, "some people are so open-minded that their brains fall." Open-mindedness and not thinking may not be exactly the same, but they are connected.

77a Psalm 53:3

78 Ecclesiastes 1:3

79 Talmud Tractate Gittin 56b

80 Until this time all men in the world spoke one language, but G-d broke their unity by making them unable to understand each other (Genesis 11:7). Thus, the project was doomed. This was the beginning of many languages in the world.

81 Genesis 6:5

82 Psalm 20

83 Rashi (the great commentator on the Written and Oral Torah, who lived from 1040 to 1105 in France) wrote this comment on

Genesis 11:9

84 Talmud Tractate Yoma 9b

85 Psalm 81

86 Rashi on Genesis 14:13

87 Genesis 12:1ff

88 Medrash Bereishis Rabbah 42:8

89 Numbers 23:9

90 Numbers 13:33

91 Genesis 1:26

92 Psalm 81

92a Deuteronomy 4:37-8

93 Shem, the son of Noah, revealed the Torah to Abraham. (Bereishis Rabbah 43:6)

94 This means that the Torah, the Bible and its commentaries, the revelation that G-d gave to Moses on Mount Sinai, contains the "instructions" that G-d used in constructing the world. Therefore, one cannot understand the world without understanding the Torah. (Bereishis Rabbah 1:1, Zohar, Parashas Terumah, page 161a)

95 According to Bereishis Rabbah 39:1, Abraham asked how the world could run without someone running it.

96 Rabbi Elchonen Wasserman states that G-d's existence should be obvious to anyone of average intelligence (Biurei Agados al Derech Ha Pshat, Chapter One, subsequently published in Kovetz Maamorim, Chapter One.)

97 Psalm 19

98 Talmud Tractate Brachos 64a

99 Adam and Eve repented, and as a result they were able to pass down to their descendants a spiritual heritage. There are traditions that Cain repented (Tanchuma Beraishis, 9).

100 Talmud Tractate Sanhedrin 56b

101 The upper worlds animate the lower worlds as the soul animates the body. Each world is the garb of the world above it and is moved and shaped by it. (Rabbi Chaim of Volozhin, Nefesh HaChaim, Part One, Chapter Six, based on the Zohar and writings of Rabbi Yitzchak Luria Ashkenazi, the Ari'zal.)

102 See Talmud Tractate Eiruvin 100b. Avos

d'Rebbe Noson 32:1 seems to say that Abraham received knowledge prophetically.

[103] Genesis 8:22

[104] The second blessing of the Shemoneh Esrei prayer reads, *"The King who causes death and gives life!"* Why in that order? Shouldn't it be the other way around? Obviously not. Clearly, life comes after death! Michtav M'Eliyahu, Volume 1, Page 177 compares the death and rebirth of a seed to the Resurrection of the Dead.

[105]This phrase is used throughout the account of Creation. We learn from it a general rule that we should regard night as preceding day (Talmud Tractate Berachos 2a).

[106] Psalm 30

[107] Despite the fact that the essence of their life was to be the parents of the holy Nation of Israel, they had only one child together, and that child was conceived by a miracle, after decades of prayer and supplication.

[108] Ecclesiastes 7:1

[109] In the song *"Chad Gadya,"* when G-d slaughters the angel of death.

[110] Talmud Tractate Yoma 28a, Mishna Tractate Kidushin 4:14

[111] Verses from the Torah, reminding us about our relationship to G-d, that Jews are commanded to say twice daily.

[112] The commandment to attach fringes to the corners of a four-cornered garment. The fringes are tied in a way that reminds us of the existence of the 613 commandments. The specific text is as follows: "G-d *said to Moses, saying 'Speak to the children of Israel and say to them that they are to make themselves tzitzis (fringes) on the corners of their garments throughout their generations.'"* (Numbers 15:37)

[113] The use of the word "mask" in this context is suggested by the book "Worldmask," by Rabbi Akiva Tatz.

[114] According to Sefer ha Chinnuch (Vol 4, pp 105, Feldheim Edition), *"the root purpose of the mitzvah [of tzitzis] ... is in order that we should remember all the mitzvos ... constantly.... The Sages of blessed memory said further that the word 'tzitzis' hints at the 613 mitzvis [which a Jew is obligated to follow] in conjunction with the eight threads in*

the tassel and the five knots in it."

[115] Numbers 15:39

[116] A common four-cornered garment is the poncho, for example.

[117] Shulchan Aruch, Orech Chaim 24:1

[118] Psalm 16:8

[119] The earth is frequently referred to this way, even though we know it is a sphere. The four directions, "north, east, south, west," are universal. When the Messiah comes, G-d will gather the dispersed *"from the four corners of the earth."* (Isaiah 11:12)

[120] A mezuza is a parchment scroll written by a scribe containing certain Biblical verses, that the Torah commands us to affix to our doorposts.

[121] Rambam, Yad HaChazakah, Hilchos Mezuzah 6:13

[122] Maharal, Ner Mitzvah

[123] Deuteronomy 6:8

[124] Deuteronomy 6:8

[125] Deuteronomy 6:9

[126] Deuteronomy 6:9

[127] The word "Hashem" stands for the Name of G-d.

[128] See Rambam Hilchos Mezuzah 6:13

[129] See Rashi on Genesis 9:3

[130] See Rabbi Yosef Albo's Sefer Halkarim 3:15.

[131] One could object to this logic and say that vegetables, for example, should have the same status as milk. In other words, why are vegetables permitted with meat but milk prohibited? Vegetables and milk are both "pre-Flood" foods. There is an interesting and logical answer: when you kill the cow to eat the meat you kill the source of milk. Eating the meat is a direct contradiction to drinking the milk; they are mutually exclusive. Such is not the case with vegetables. Killing a cow does not kill the source of the vegetable.

[132] As we pointed out before: the Creator and the Lawgiver.

[133] The Talmud says that sleep is one-sixtieth of death (Talmud Tractate Berachos 57b), and in death the soul is reunited with G-d.

Rabbi Moshe Chaim Luzzato in Derech Hashem 1:3:11 describes the "soul world" as a place where souls get reward. In section 3:1:6 he says that, during sleep, aspects of the soul move about in the spiritual realm, being somewhat detached from bodily restraints.

134 In Sefer ha Chinnuch (Feldheim, Vol 4, page 161/Parshas Chukas) it says, *"Our sages of blessed memory spoke at length of the profundity of its mystery [this mitzvah] ... until they said that King Solomon attained knowledge... of all the reasons of the Torah except for this; for he declared about it, 'I said 'I will get wisdom,' but it is far from me.'"* The same passage relates that G-d told Moses, *"To you I will reveal the reason for the heifer, but not to others."*

135 Which shows that when the nations ridicule us, they are really ridiculing G-d, because we certainly did not invent this apparently illogical commandment. G-d gave it to us, along with all the others.

136 From Rabbi Yehoshua Kalish

137 When my book "From Central Park to Sinai: How I Found My Jewish Soul" was being prepared, I was told by the Bostoner Rebbe in Lawrence, N.Y. that, if the process of having my book published and accepted was difficult, that would be a sign of its value. These words encouraged me.

138 See Rashi on Genesis 16:4

139 Our patriarchs and matriarchs prepared us for this phenomenon. The lives of Abraham, Isaac and Jacob and their wives all consisted of one trial after another.

140 The Talmud in Tractate Berachos 7a discusses this, referring especially to Exodus Chapter 33.

141 I am indebted to Rabbi Yehoshua Kalish for explaining this concept at length in his discussion on Shavuos night (about 3 a.m.) on May 17, 2002.

142 If the President of the United States, however, uses his powerful position to sanctify the name of G-d and to recognize the spiritual greatness of the Jewish People, then he has used his G-d-given position in a way that will bring him blessing. And the converse would of course also be true.

143 Arabs danced in the streets when the World Trade Center was destroyed, and they dance in the streets whenever Jews are killed – G-d forbid. But the Arabs make a mistake when they think their apparent "success" is a positive sign from G-d. Of course, not every Arab indulges in this behavior. But we all have genetic traits transmitted from our ancestors, the earlier the ancestors the more powerful the traits. That is why the Biblical accounts are so vital to understand, because they educate us as to our earliest and most basic traits. If we are to improve ourselves and rise above our weaknesses, then we must be aware of our origins, so that we know what we are working with.

144 Genesis 12:1-2

145 Genesis 17:21

146 Genesis 25:32 ff

147 Genesis 27:18

148 Exodus 19:6

149 Rabbi Shaul Dov Miller points out the fascinating fact that in Hebrew the numerical value of the name "Ishmael" is equal to the combined numerical values of "Abram" and "Hagar," his parents. (Ishmael was born before the name "Abram" was changed to "Abraham." Thus it is clear that Ishmael is a composite of his parents. But following Ishmael's birth, G-d elevated Abram by adding the Hebrew letter "hey" to his name. Thus Isaac's father was a different person spiritually from Ishmael's father. Clearly, the mother was a different person.

150 Genesis 16:12

151 Targum Onkelos, Genesis 2:7

152 See Pirkie d'Rebbe Eliezer 32. Ishmael ("G-d hears") is thus called because G-d will hear the cries of the children of Israel over what Ishmael has done. See also Baal Ha Turim on Deuteronomy 31:29. In general the descendants of Ishmael are characterized by a tendency to act violently without explanation, to substitute loudness for lucidity and arrogance for articulateness.

153 Psalm 20

154 "Torah scholars increase peace in the world." Talmud Tractate Berachos 64a

155 Genesis 21:9

156 Genesis 21:10

157 Genesis 21:12

158 Genesis 16:12

159 Numbers 15:39

160 Genesis Chapter 22

161 "Please take your son, your only one, whom you love – Isaac … and bring him up there as an offering upon one of the mountains…"

162 Jeannette Friedman brought this point to my attention.

163 Leaving aside for the moment the question of whether it was ever his to begin with.

164 Rabbi Shimon bar Yochai as quoted by Rashi on Genesis 33:4

165 Genesis 27:34

166 Talmud Tractate Succah 52a

167 See below, the comparison with a tube into which two peas have been placed.

168 Genesis 25:33

169 Ramban, commentary on Parshas Vayishlach

170 Borrowing the phrase of Rabbi Dovid Cohen.

171 Genesis 25:22-23

172 Rashi on Genesis 25:23

173 See Rashi on Genesis 1:1

174 Deuterononmy 14:2, 26:19

175 Rashi on Genesis 25:26

176 There is an amazing hint about what will happen in the end of history, in the blessing that Jacob gives to his son, the Tribal Patriarch Dan. "Dan" means "judgment" in Hebrew. Jacob's blessing to Dan is as follows: *"Dan will avenge his people, the tribes of Israel will be united as one. Dan will… bite the horse's heels so its rider falls backwards. For Your Salvation do I long, O G-d."* (Genesis 49:16-18) This remarkable statement seems to prophesy that at the time of judgment and salvation – *may it come soon, in our days!* – our "lowly" position, our proximity to the heel – not even of our enemy but even lower… to his horse! – will enable us to overthrow him forever.

177 As Rebbetzin Jungreis would say, using a favorite Yiddish expression, "Esau didn't *'fergin'* Jacob anything." Esau wanted everything for himself, even something he didn't value, just so Jacob wouldn't have it.

178 Rabbi Shaul Dov Miller points out: The Sfas Emes [Rabbi Yehuda Leib Alter of Gur, 1847-1905] explains that Esau could have been the provider of physical needs, and the nation would have been a duality of Jacob and Esau. That was Isaac's plan, but Rebecca rejected Esau's tainted input to Jacob's pure devotion [similar to Sarah's rejection of Ishmael's tainted input]. Hence Jacob assumed the role of Esau as well. That's how he could TRUTHFULLY proclaim to Isaac, "I am Esau." That is why the blessing that Isaac uttered with Esau in mind in fact to Jacob. That also explains why Leah, when confronted by Jacob regarding her masquerade [on the first night of their marriage], responds, "I learnt from you. Didn't you say to your father, 'I am Esau'?" What Leah meant was "I was Esau's destined soul-mate, suited to complement his life's mission. Now that you have assumed his life's mission, it's a package deal, I come along!" That's why the marriage was indeed valid and not simply a mistake.

179 *"Rabbi Yaakov said: This world is like a lobby before the World to Come; prepare yourself in the lobby so that you may enter the banquet hall."* (Ethics of the Fathers 4:21)

180 Even though Isaac had in fact instructed Esau to come to him for a blessing, it had been Esau's lifetime effort to convince his father that he deserved that blessing. This deceit is what alarmed Rebecca.

181 Genesis 27:1

182 "Zevulun would engage in commerce and provide food for the Tribe of Issachar, while [the Tribe of Issachar] would engage in the [the study of] Torah." (Rashi on Genesis 49:13) Each tribe benefited, supported and complemented the other in a mutually beneficial relationship.

183 See Rashi on Bereishis 33:4

184 See Genesis 25:22

185 Genesis 32:25ff

186 Joshua 24: 2-4

[187] Rabbi Yehuda Leib ben Betzalel, 1512(?)-1609

[188] From Gevuros Hashem by the Maharal of Prague, as found in the Hagadah shel Pesach Le ha Maharal.

[189] Joshua 24: 5-13

[190] Genesis 49:1ff

[191] Proverbs 3:12

[192] "Moses' face was like the sun; Joshua's face was like the moon." (Talmud Tractate Bava Basra 75a, repeated by Rashi in his commentary on Numbers 27:20.)

[193] G-d spoke directly to the Children of Israel when He gave the first Two of the Ten Commandments. But after that, they were unable to listen directly to G-d and asked Moses to transmit G-d's commands to them. (Talmud Tractate Makkos 24a)

[194] In fact, the road ahead would not be smooth precisely because the Covenant is eternal! In other words, if we don't keep our part of the bargain, we open ourselves up to the corrective action specified by G-d if we stray from our responsibilities under the Covenant!

[195] Deuteronomy 31:29

[196] Judges 3:7 and other places. It is important to keep in mind when discussing the lives of our ancestors that we are so far below them in greatness that we do not even understand the nature of the trials they faced. But there is a reason that G-d has revealed these incidents and stories in the Bible. Our rabbis have discussed certain things and therefore we may take certain conclusions from these Biblical incidents in order to learn lessons for our own lives. But, as the next section explains, it would be a great mistake to judge our ancestors or to think we approach their level.

[197] Genesis 3:14. Do snakes actually eat dust? Whatever the exact meaning of that phrase, it is clear that the snake has been cut off from a relationship with G-d, that he travels on his belly in the dust and eats things that crawl in the dust.

[198] This interpretation I heard from Rebbetzin Jungreis.

[199] Genesis 3:17-19

[200] "G-d said to Moses, 'Go to Pharaoh in the morning.'" (Genesis 7:15) Only in the morning did [Pharaoh] go out to the water, because [he] used to boast that he was a god and did not need to relieve himself; therefore he used to go early in the morning to the water (to relieve himself secretly there). (Medrash Shemos Rabbah 9:8)

[201] Proverbs 3:12

[202] Psalm 84: 5-6

[203] Genesis 12:3

[204] Judges 21:25

[205] Deuteronomy 17:15

[206] I Samuel 8:6

[207] I Samuel 8:7

[208] I Samuel 8:19-20

[209] "Saul said to Samuel, 'I have sinned, for I have transgressed the word of G-d and your word, for I feared the people and I hearkened to their voice.'" (I Samuel 15:24)

[210] I Samuel 15:17

[211] I Samuel 13:13

[212] I Samuel 13:14

[213] Judges 21:25. I found an amazing if unwitting reference to this passage in a book that emanates from my own childhood. I grew up in the Ethical Culture Schools and the Ethical Culture Society, an organization founded by a German reform Jew in the late 19th Century. In my book "From Central Park to Sinai: How I Found My Jewish Soul," I discuss the paralyzing effect that growing up with such non-belief had on my sensitive Jewish soul. I recently found a book by a former leader of the Ethical Culture Society that used almost these exact words from the Book of Judges to describe what he considers the ideal moral society. Here is a quote. "With ethics… every person becomes his own judge of right and wrong." (The First Book of Ethics, by Algernon D. Black, Franklin Watts Publishers, 1965, page 1) This catastrophic situation, in which there is no morality because everyone makes up his own version of what is "ethical," is described here perfectly, and the existence of this attitude is a confirmation that the prophetic words found thousands of years ago in the Book of

Judges are applicable to our own times perhaps more than ever before.

214 Speech delivered in Parliament May 13, 1901 as quoted in "Winston Churchill: An Intimate Portrait," by Violet Bonham Carter (Harcourt Brace & World, 1965) pages 68-69

215 Deuteronomy 17:18-20

216 This is the basic prayer said three times every weekday.

217 Judges 21:25

218 When I refer to the period of the Judges, I mean the approximately 400 years between when the children of Israel entered the Land under Joshua's leadership until the time when Saul became king over Israel.

219 Judges 2:14

220 Judges 5:11

221 Abarbanel. See II Samuel 23:13.

222 Ramban on Genesis 12:6.

223 Genesis 15:13

224 Genesis 49:10

225 Perhaps the miracles occurred precisely because of Joseph's self-control.

226 See "The Riddle of the Bowing Moon," by Rabbi Moshe M. Eisemann (2003)

227 Genesis 37:32

228 Talmud Tractate Yoma 9b

229 Granted that the Ten Tribes were lost during the age of prophecy and so technically during the Biblical era, yet those ten tribes remain lost to this day.

230 The outstanding example of this is his refusal to be tempted by Potiphar's wife (Genesis 39:7ff)

231 Exodus 1:8

232 Genesis 45:1-3

233 "You will say on that day, 'I thank You, G-d, for You were angry with me." (Isaiah 12:1)

234 Talmud Tractate Sota 36b; Medrash Bereishis Rabbah 86:7

235 Genesis 48:20

236 "Rav said, 'Our Father Abraham fulfilled the entire Torah.'"(Talmud Tractate 28b)

237 Psalms 1:2

238 Every day we say in our prayers, "through our sins, the Holy Temple is destroyed."

239 Maimonides writes that in the era of King David's descendant, the Messiah, "the occupation of the entire world will be solely to know G-d." (Yad Hechazakah, Hilchos Melachim 12:5)

240 Psalm 3:2

241 Psalm 27:1

242 Talmud Tractate Sukkah 52a

243 Talmud Tractate Sukkah 52a

244 Isaiah 11:9, quoted by Maimonides in Mishna Torah in his description of the days of the Messiah.

245 Deuteronomy 34:5-6. Ironically, Moses is buried in the land of Moab, the same degraded country from which emerged Ruth, the great grandmother of King David and the paragon of chessed, kind-heartedness.

246 Sefer Ha Yashar, Parashas Vayigash

247 But significantly not its females; David's great-grandmother Ruth thus was permitted to convert and enter the House of Israel.

248 I Samuel 16:10-11

249 I Samuel 16:11-12

250 Psalm 118:22

251 Targum on Psalm 118:22

252 In Deuteronomy 31:17-18, G-d says "I will conceal My face from them... because of all the evil that [they] did."

253 Genesis 3:8

254 Exodus 2:11-12

255 Numbers 22:3

256 Psalm 69:9

257 Book of Our Heritage, by Eliahu Kitov, Vol. 3, pages 850-1 (Feldheim Publishers)

258 Genesis 19:30-38

259 Numbers 22:2ff

260 The Book of Our Heritage by Eliahu Kitov, Feldheim Publishers, pages 845-6

261 The Book of Our Heritage, page 852. This is not to imply that we should go out into the desert and separate ourselves from our

brethren. In fact, Ethics of the Fathers (2:5) tells us, *"do not separate yourself from the congregation."* We should not embrace isolation, but, if it comes, we should utilize it for good.

262 Deuteronomy 18-19

263 Numbers 12:3

264 Mount Sinai

265 "You are the fewest of all the peoples." (Deuteronomy 7:7)

266 Proverbs 19:21

267 Genesis 38:6 ff

268 II Samuel 12:10.

269 II Samuel 12:13

270 Tractate Taanis 8b

271 II Samuel, Chapter 24, tells the story of how King David wrongfully counted the people, after which he said, *"I have sinned greatly in what I have done."* (II Samuel 24:10)

272 Genesis 32:25 ff

273 See Medrash Lekach Tov, Genesis 32:25.

274 Exodus 19:5

275 Genesis 32:25

276 "The Torah is light." (Proverbs 6:23)

277 Rashi on Genesis 1:1

278 Joshua 1:1-4

278a Deuteronomy 19:8-9

279 Numbers 33:55. That prophecy has proven true to the letter, for indeed today our enemies load their bombs with pins!

280 Deuteronomy 12:11 and other places

281 I Kings 8:44

282 Talmud Tractate Makkos 24b

283 Deuteronomy 11:16-17

284 I Kings 5:1-14

285 I Kings 10:1-5

286 I Kings 8:1-5

287 Yom Kippur Machzor, Chazzan's repetition of the Mussaf Prayer, Artscroll translation

288 I Kings 11:29-33

289 I Kings 12:21

290 I Kings 15:26 and many other places in the Book of Kings

291 II Kings 17:7-23. This, by the way, is the moment at which we became known as "Jews" (from "Judah") because all that remained of the children of Israel was the tribe of Judah, with remnants of the tribes of Benjamin and Levi. It is important to realize in today's world that the term "Jew" does not refer to our entire nation. It is like the contemporary misnomer in which a house of worship is called a "temple." There is no such thing as a Temple today; we are waiting for the Temple to be rebuilt in the time of the Messiah. The use of that term implies a misconception. Similarly, the word "Jew" does not encompass our entire nation. In the time of the Messiah, when we will all be reunited in our Holy Land, we will once again be known as the children of Israel, not simply as Jews. The tragedy of Exile is not only what has happened to the Jews for the past two thousand years, but the fact that we Jews are only part of our nation, and that untold millions of our brethren have been completely swallowed up into other nations and are invisible today.

292 Rashi on Genesis 9:21 says the word "Samaria" means the Ten Tribes of Israel

293 II Kings 18:9-12

294 II Kings 25:1-21

295 Stones on the High Priest's breastplate that lit up in a way that signified G-d's guidance in a particular situation.

296 The "Presence of G-d" did not rest on the Second Temple, according to the Talmud (Tractate Yoma 10a). See also Rashi on Genesis 9:27.

297 Isaiah 42:6

298 After Moses, later books of the Written Torah were dictated to the prophets and added to the complete set of 24 books of the Bible.

299 Pirkei D'Rebbe Eliezer 46.

300 Malachi 3:22. I am grateful to Rabbi Naftali Jaeger, Rosh Yeshiva of Yeshiva Sh'or Yoshuv, for pointing this out to me.

301 In our day some people might not be aware that our Rabbis are the leaders of our people, yet they really are, for without them,

G-d forbid, we would not survive. Our existence, as we are seeing, is entirely dependant upon our "*dveikus*," glue-like adherence to G-d and His laws.

302 Talmud, Tractate Taanis 8b

303 In the Sukkah it is our tradition to invite our ancestors, Abraham, Isaac, Jacob, Joseph, Moses, Aaron and King David, to join us as guests.

304 Psalm 20

305 I am indebted to Rabbi Meshulam ha Levi Jungreis, may he rest in peace, for this story.

306 Name is fictitious.

307 Psalm 20

308 Talmud Tractate Yoma 9b

309 Genesis 37:5

310 The Talmud tells us that their motives were pure. Nevertheless they were based on a misconception, and the situation was very dangerous.

311 See the "*Eilah Ezkarah*" prayer in the Yom Kippur Mussaf; the Roman murderer kills the Ten Martyrs using the pretext of "revenge" for the sale of Joseph by his brothers.

312 Genesis 37:19

313 Genesis 37:22

314 Rebbetzin Jungreis says that G-d created the world in Technicolor. Or, in another metaphor, the beauty of orchestral music is the harmony of different instruments.

315 Kitzur Shulchan Aruch, Chapter 12, Section 2 (Translation from Metsudah Edition, by Rabbi Avrohom Davis)

316 In the story of Tamar (Genesis 38:1-30) Judah embarrasses himself and admits his guilt rather than letting Tamar take the blame for his actions.

317 King David humbled himself when he was rebuked by the Prophet Nathan (II Samuel 12:1-13).

318 Tragically, that belief is still very much in evidence among some of our brethren to this day.

319 Mishna Midos 3:4. Rashi on Exodus 20:22

320 Like every mitzvah, this requires constant work.

321 Jeremiah 2:2.

322 October, 2002

323 Genesis 4:13

324 I am indebted to Rabbi Ephraim Wachsman for explaining this concept.

325 Ethics of the Fathers, Chapter Four, Mishnah 1

326 I Samuel 20:27

327 I heard this from my son, Aharon Yaakov, who learned it from the book "M'ain Bais Hashoeva" by Rabbi Shimon Schwab

328 Each of these exiles will be further subdivided, according to Torah sources, and that is the basis for our tradition that the final part of the Exile of Edom will be the Exile of the Children of Ishmael, the era in which the Moslem/Arab nations will accumulate power. This is what we are seeing in our own times. (See the last comment of the Baal HaTurim on Parashas Chayei Sarah, also Rashi on Genesis 15:14 and Daniel, Chapters 7 & 8.)

329 Genesis 15:13-14. In fact the word "also" (in Hebrew "*v'gam*" in the Biblical text) is precisely the hint of all the future exiles in addition to the Egyptian Exile. Such is the way of the Torah! A word of three letters encapsulates some three thousand years of exile! (Perhaps each letter hints at one thousand years!) See Rashi on Genesis 15:14. (The figure "three thousand," referring to our cumulative period of exile, was stated in a lecture by Rabbi Yisroel Reisman on the Book of Daniel.)

330 Chapter 8

331 Daniel 8:22

332 Artscroll edition of the Sapirstein Edition of the Book of Genesis with the commentary of Rashi, page 150, note 1.

333 Numbers 1:51

334 Isaiah 8:2

335 Micah 3:12

336 Zechariah 8:4

337 Talmud Tractate Makkos 24b

338 Passover Haggadah

339 Numbers 15:39

340 Psalm 126

341 Leviticus 26:14ff and Deuteronomy 28:15ff

342 See The Ramban on Leviticus 26:16

343 As Rebbetzin Jungreis – who was there – points out, it is more often the ones who were not there who say this than the ones who were there.

344 Deuteronomy 11:16-18

345 Here is how a well-known commentator describes the efficacy of the Temple sacrifices. "The death and burning of the animal presented a strong visual symbol of the punishment that unmitigated justice might exact from a sinner. In this way, sacrifice gave the sinner a vicarious taste of death, and vividly portrayed the tenuousness of mortal life… [But] no sacrifice could atone for sin unless it was accompanied by repentance…Now that the Temple no longer stands, study and prayer take the place of sacrifice." (Handbook of Jewish Thought, by Aryeh Kaplan. Moznaim Publishing Corp. Vol. 2, page 168-9)

346 When I was young, I attended a school whose "humanistic religious" philosophy was expressed in the words "the place where men meet to seek the highest is holy ground." But if the "highest" is not G-d, then the "holy ground" is quicksand.

347 Psalm 121:1

348 Psalm 121: 2

349 Ethics of the Fathers, Chapter Two, Mishna 1.

350 Psalm 23

351 Isaiah 2:3

352 Jeremiah 33:10-11

353 Jeremiah 33:14-16

354 Psalm 113

355 Lamentations 3:29

356 The Biblical Exile in Egypt is the prototype; it is not one of the Four. We have noted that it sprang directly from the bitterness between Joseph and his brothers, and we have noted that the destruction of the Second Temple is also ascribed to bitterness among the brothers. Our rabbis tell us that the Egyptian Exile was written into our history by the prophesy Abraham received (in Genesis 15:13); future exiles, however, were contingent upon our behavior. The circumstances leading up to the Egyptian Exile were a lesson to us as to where brotherly conflict could lead.

357 Rashi to Zechariah 5:11 cites a Medrash (Shocher Tov 6:1) that states that the four kingdoms that rule over Israel during its four periods of Exile were actually eight. (I saw this in the Artscroll Selichos (Nusach Ashkenaz), footnote on pages 69-70.) The last of the eight (the final part of the final exile) is the exile in which the descendants of Ishmael will rule.

358 See last Baal HaTurim in Parashas Chayei Sarah and Chapter Six below.

359 Genesis 25:25

360 Geneis 36:19

361 Lekach Tov on Genesis 36:19.

362 As discussed in Chapter Two. Isaac's idea in giving the blessings of the material world to Esau was that Esau should excel in this world so that he could protect and supply the physical needs of Jacob, who would dedicate himself to spirituality. Rebecca realized, however, that Esau would not use the physical world to help Jacob, but rather to try to hurt him (Malbim on Genesis 27:1 and 27:5)

363 There are other cultures, for example in the Far East, with a calendar similar to that of the Children of Israel. The similar calendars may indicate that those others cultures were connected to Israel in the distant past. (See the discussion of the children of Abraham and Keturah below.)

364 Exodus 12:2

365 Exodus 13:10 and Deuteronomy 16:1

366 Talmud Tractate Chullin 60b; Rashi on Genesis 1:16

367 Rashi on Genesis 1:16

368 I am NOT extending the application of this Talmud account of the moon attacking the sun to the moral sphere. In other words, I am not saying that since the moon attacked the sun and not the other way around the moon (the children of Ishmael) are guilty and the sun (the children of Esau) are innocent. I am simply using this account to show that there is a Biblical

basis for the attack by the children of Ish-mael against the children of Esau as a result of jealousy. I am not, however, saying that the children of Esau are innocent regarding the Jews. If anything, they have a worse record against us than the children of Ish-mael, although the latter are making a mighty effort to catch up.

369 See Maimonides, Mishneh Torah, Law of Kings, Chapter 8, Halachah 11.

370 I am reminded of the powerful story I heard on a tape from Rabbi Efraim Wachs-man, about one of the earlier Lubavicher Rebbes, who, when he was arrested in Rus-sia, told the KGB agents to put away their guns. He said something to this effect: "You have many gods and one world; I have One G-d and two worlds. Do you think I am afraid of your toy?"

371 Deuteronomy 28:13. Incorporated into the Rosh Hashana "simonim".

372 Exodus 12:2

373 The Mishna in Talmud Tractate Rosh Hashana page 25a, quotes the verse from Leviticus 23:4, "these are the appointed festi-vals of G-d, the holy convocations which **you shall designate** in their appropriate time," and comments, "you shall designate… whether or not they are proclaimed at their proper time."

374 Joshua 10:12

375 "[G-d] took [Abraham] outside, and said,'Gaze, now, toward the Heavens and count the stars…" (Genesis 15:5). Rashi on that verse refers to the Medrash that says when G-d took Abraham "outside," it means that He took him "outside" nature, bequeathing to him and his descendants the ability to exist beyond the limitations of nature (Genesis Rabbah 44:12). See also Talmud Tractate Shabbos 156a.

376 Genesis 25:6

377 Rashi on Genesis 25:6 describes these gifts as "a name by whose pronunciation they would be able to perform sorcery." (See Talmud Tractate Sanhedrin 91a.)

378 Deuteronomy 4:27-28

379 The Vilna Gaon (Aderes Eliahu on Deuteronomy 29:16) refers to "their abomi-nations and detestable idols… of wood and stone" (Deuteronomy 29:16) as a prophesy of the idols we would encounter in our pre-sent exile, the wood referring to the reli-gion of Rome and the stone referring to the religion of Mecca.

380 This was pointed out to me by Rabbi Shaul Dov Miller.

381 Yes, David killed Goliath with a stone, but David says to Goliath, "You come to me with a sword, a spear and javelin – but I come to you with the Name of … the G-d of the battalions of Israel that you have ridiculed." (I Samuel 17:45) David's stone was thrown by a child of Israel in the name of G-d; Moslem stones are thrown against the children of Israel and against the name of G-d.

382 Interestingly, the day whose name is asso-ciated with the moon is not Friday, but Monday, the day after Sunday. In the Roman weekly calendar, it is only logical that the day of the moon comes after the day of the Sun, because the moon is subservient to the sun.

383 Each month we pray (in the Sanctifica-tion of the Moon) that "the light of the moon be like the light of the sun," based on the pas-sage in Isaiah 30:26.

384 Isaiah 2:4, Michah 4:3

385 Genesis 32:25

386 Deuteronomy 4:4

387 Psalm 81

388 See Sefer Chassidim 191, the Mekor Chesed, commentary by R. Margolis #3, Beis Medrash (a collection of medrashim edited by Aharon Yellinek) Vol. 6, Page 9. I heard these ideas originally on a tape by Dr. Sid Leiman of Queens College.

389 Encyclopedia Judaica, Vol 13, page 191

390 Encyclopedia Judaica, Vol 13, page 190

391 Isaiah 49:6

392 Genesis 12:3

393 Genesis 15:13 and other places

394 I referred to this remarkable statement in my book, From Central Park to Sinai: How I Found My Jewish Soul.

395 From the essay, "Concerning the Jews," Harper's Magazine, September 1899.

396 Rebbetzin Esther Jungreis has said that this is the first generation in Jewish history in which it is **COMMON** for children to be more religious than their parents! This seems to be a fulfillment of the last prophecy in the Torah, regarding the era before the coming of the Messiah, in which it says, *"before the coming of the great and awesome day of G-d...[Elijah the Prophet will come and] he will turn back [to G-d] the hearts of fathers with their sons and the hearts of sons with their fathers"* (Malachi 3:23-4).

397 Talmud Tractate Megilah 29a

398 Genesis 32:12

399 Genesis 32:25-32

400 Medrash Bereishis Rabbah 77:3 and Rashi on Genesis 32:25.

401 Rashi on Genesis 33:4. "Rabbi Shimon bar Yochai said: "It is a given fact, it is known that Esau hates Jacob.""

402 Rebbetzin Esther Jungreis' classic comment.

403 Ethics of the Fathers 5:5 (In the Prayer Book 5:7)

404 Israel is called "Eretz Tzvi"; the land is compared to a deer, whose skin stretches to accommodate the deer. (Talmud Tractate Gittin 57a)

405 Deuteronomy 19:14, 27:17

406 Genesis 25:30

407 G-d tells Moses to tell Pharaoh, "My first-born son is Israel" (Exodus 4:22).

408 Rashi compares them to two stones in a tube: first one in is the last one out. Jacob was the first conceived and the first one "in the tube," so naturally Esav was ahead of him when it came to getting out, but that only proves Jacob was first. (See Medrash Bereishis 63:8 and Rashi on Genesis 25:26)

409 Genesis 23:3

410 The Arabs call Shechem "Nablus." The destruction and looting of Joseph's grave there was the first act of the recent wave of Arab violence. See Joshua 24:32 regarding the burial of Joseph's bones.

411 And not just land. Tragically, how many thousands of times in our long history have we tried – sometimes successfully and sometimes not – to purchase our own people from our enemies' prisons!

412 Did you think "identity theft" is a modern phenomenon? *"There is nothing new under the sun."* (Ecclesiastes 1:9)

413 Rashi on Genesis 25:27

414 Genesis 28:6

415 Rashi on Genesis 28:9

416 Rashi on Genesis 32:25

417 Zechariah 14:7

418 The late Rabbi Shlomo Rottenberg, of blessed memory, said that one reason European gentiles held out such hope for the "New World" was because they thought they had finally found a place in which there would be no more Jews. How disappointed was their hope!

419 Genesis 32:29

420 Genesis 32:29

421 Genesis 32:26

422 Genesis 32:32

423 It is interesting but not surprising that the word "heel" in English has come to mean a "hateful person."

424 Lamentations 3:29

425 When we mourn for our lost Temples.

426 We also walk in bare feet on Yom Kippur, which is not a mournful day, and so did the Priests in the Temple. The reason for these practices is perhaps somewhat different.

427 Genesis 17:1

428 Genesis 24:65

429 Rashi on Genesis 32:32

430 Psalm 113 (Hallel)

431 Zechariah 3:1-7

432 Genesis 35:10

433 Malachi 3:20, quoted by Rashi on Genesis 32:32

434 Obadiah 1:10-14; 1:18

435 Deuteronomy 32:21

436 Deuteronomy 32:21

437 Isaiah 41:14-15

438 "Sword of Islam", by John F. Murphy, Jr. (Prometheus Books, 2002) page 113

439 Kinna 7, stanza "*Ayin,*" Tisha b'Av

Machzor (page 161 in Artscroll Edition)

440 Genesis 1:1

441 Genesis 1:3

442 According to the Medrash (Bereishis Rabbah 11:9), He also created Gehinnon ("hell") and the angels on the second day.

443 See Rashi on Genesis 1:7

444 The Medrash (Bereishis Rabbah 11:9) differentiates between the creation of trees and other plant life on the Third Day. Additionally, G-d created the Garden of Eden on this day.

445 Genesis 1:14-15

446 Genesis 1:16

447 Genesis 1:20. According to the Medrash (Bereishis Rabbah 11:9), the creations of the Fifth Day are birds, fish and the Leviathan, the great sea creature whose presence will be revealed at the End of Days.

448 Genesis 1:24. According to the Medrash Bereishis Rabbah 11:9, man, woman, creeping creatures, domestic animals, wild beasts and harmful spirits were all created on the Sixth Day.

449 Genesis 1:26

450 Genesis 1:28

451 Genesis 2:2-3

452 Genesis 2:3

453 Genesis 2:1

454 Psalm 90:4 The Ramban states in his commentary on Genesis 2:3 that there is a concept in the Torah that a day is equivalent to one thousand years.

455 Medrash Bereishis Rabbah 11:9

456 There is an apparent proof for the nature of the relationship between man and animals where the Torah states that G-d will remove our enemies in the Land of Israel "little by little," so that "the beasts of the field [will not] increase against you." (Deuteronomy 7:22) Rashi explains that G-d is telling us, regarding the children of Israel, "if they perform the will of the Omnipresent they do not [have cause to] fear beasts." Conversely, if we do not perform His will, we do have cause to fear.

457 See Talmud Yerushalmi Tractate Brachos 5:1.

458 Genesis 6:11-12

459 Rashi on Genesis 6:11-12.

460 Although the birds died as a result of the Flood, the fish did survive. But their entire environment and habitat was altered and disrupted, as we will see below.

461 Moses said to Korach, "[G-d] divided His world with boundaries. Can you turn morning into evening?" (Rashi on Numbers 16:5)

462 Derived from Psalm 136:6

463 Genesis 37:9

464 Genesis 37:10

465 Genesis 15:5

466 Medrash Rabbah on Genesis 21:9

467 Proverbs 26:18. According to the above Medrash, the verse in Proverbs 26:18 refers to the actions of Ishmael as described in Genesis 21:9.

468 The famous Rashi on Genesis 33:4

469 Talmud Tractate Chullin 60b; Rashi on Genesis 1:16

470 Genesis 37:9

471 In those days Egypt was the dominant power in the entire world.

472 During the years of plenty Joseph governed Egypt wisely, preparing it for the oncoming famine; which is the other side of the coin of "saving Egypt during the years of famine." He was the prototype of the respected Jewish adviser who guided powerful foreign countries in future centuries, like R. Yitzchak Abarbanel in fifteenth-century Portugal and Spain.

473 The creations of the Third Day included, according to the Medrash (Bereishis Rabbah 11:9), the Garden of Eden itself, which was the epitome of trees and plant life upon the earth.

474 Exodus 3:8 and other places

475 Leviticus 18:25

476 Deuteronomy 11:16-21

477 Isaiah 11:12

478 Medrash Bamidbar Rabbah 8:9

479 Genesis 37:16

480 I want to emphasize that the actions of the Jewish People are not the only defining traits of each millennium, but the fact is that the actions of the Jewish People reflect the actions of the other nations of the world and vice versa. During the Second World War, for example, Hitler's overriding ambition was not only to enlarge German hegemony but to destroy – G-d forbid – the Jewish People. When hatred of the Jew increases, so does war and tragedy in the world as a whole. When there is a benevolent attitude toward the Jews, peace and tranquility increases, as for example in the years of the Talmudical Academies of Babylonia or the Golden Age of Spain. When Jews are respected in a given country, their presence always brings blessings. This has certainly been true in the United Sates. The history of the children of Israel reflects the history of the rest of the world.

481 Isaiah 2:3

482 Medrash Bereishis Rabbah 11:9

483 Source: The Jewish Timeline Encyclopedia by Rabbi Mattis Kantor, an invaluable source I have used for many dates throughout this book.

484 Genesis 1:1-5

485 Handbook of Jewish Thought, Vol. 2, page 364, by Rabbi Aryeh Kaplan.

486 By Paul Johnson, a distinguished non-Jewish British historian. (Harperperennial Library; Revised edition, June 1992)

487 First Book of Ethics by Algernon D. Black, Franklin Watts, Inc., New York, NY, 1965 (Pages 1-2)

488 Judges 17:6, 21:25

489 Genesis 8:9

490 There is an implication in Rashi's comment on Genesis 1:4 that at first light and dark were not completely separate. Also, interestingly, the Prophet Zechariah says (Zechariah 14:7) that in the days before the coming of the Messiah there will be a time when it will be "neither clear light nor heavy darkness."

491 Talmud Tractate Sanhedrin 97a

492 This was the weekly Torah commentary from Rabbi Avigdor Nebenzahl, Rabbi of the Old City in Jerusalem. That week we were reading the last portion of the Book of Genesis, Parashas Vayechi, in which our Father Jacob gives blessings to his sons, the Tribal Patriarchs. (Weekly Sicha for Parshas Vayechi 5763)

493 Talmud Tractate Sotah 7b, Beraishis Rabbah 84:19, Medrash Hagadol Beraishis 49:3

494 Yom Kippur Services

495 Reuven was characterized as having "water-like impetuosity" (Genesis 49:4)

496 Zohar Chadash Rus 79b

497 The verse in the Torah (Exodus 25:8) says, "They shall make a Sanctuary for Me, so that I may dwell among them." It does not say "dwell in it." Why? Because the Presence of G-d can dwell in the heart of each individual. See Alshich on Exodus 25:8 and Nefesh HaChayim 1:4 (the note).

498 Animal, as well as meal offerings and libations.

499 This is the approach of the Seforno. See for example his words on Vayikra 11:2

500 According to the Sefer ha Chinuch, a reason for the sacrifices is, "so that a man will consider... that he sinned toward G-d with his body and his spirit, and he deserves that his blood shold be spilled and his body burned – if not for the kindness of the Creator that He has taken from him the offering as exchange and ransom... one life in lieu of another" (Mitzvah 95). See also Ramban to Leviticus 1:9.

501 See Nefesh HaChaim 2:14.

502 Psalms 34:15

503 Genesis 23:14

504 Medrash Hagadol 23:9

505 Which does not mean that we are free of possible corruption from that source. We must guard against improper impulses from the sense of smell as well as from any other sense. The perfume industry, for example, is trying to influence us through aroma.

506 From the Morning Prayer Service

507 Genesis 2:7

508 As part of the Havdallah Service.

509 At permissible times. Torah Law regulated when it was permitted to smell the incense.

510 Yalkut Meam Loez, Volume 9, pages 307-8,

Moznaim Publishing Co. (Translated by Rabbi Aryeh Kaplan)

511 Rashi on Numbers 16:6

512 Numbers 28:8

513 Rashi on Numbers 28:8. See also Sefer HaChinuch, commentary on Mitzva 97.

514 From the Prayer Service.

515 See Zohar Beraishis 81

516 Kinna 39 in the Tisha b'Av Service.

517 Contemporary examples of these epic stories are *Harry Potter, Lord of the Rings* and *Star Wars*.

518 Exodus 19:9

519 I Kings 8:12

520 Exodus 20:18

521 Malachi 3:23-24

522 Quoting Pogo, "We have met the enemy and he is us." Sometimes, in our mixed-up world, cartoon characters say the most profound things.

523 Exodus 4:2-4

524 From *"Yom Ze L'Yisroel,"* a *Shabbos Zemer*

525 Lamentations 5:5

526 Genesis 5:24

527 This phrase is part of the Seven Blessings said at a wedding.

528 Jeremiah 31:14. And Rachel is not even buried in Machpela! That is even more tzouris! Our Mother Rachel is all alone, and somehow we are to blame! We must fix it.

529 Hilchos Deos 2:4. Maimonides' total condemnation of the trait of anger is particularly striking in light of the fact that he advocates moderation in every other character trait.

530 Talmud Tractate Yoma 9b

531 Rashi says of Jacob, "'Dying' is not said of him. Our Rabbis of blessed memory said that our father Jacob did not die." (Rashi on Genesis 49:33; see also Talmud Tractate Taanis 5b)

532 Deuteronomy 8:3

533 Psalm 27

534 I owe this, as so many thoughts, to the words of my teacher, Rebbetzin Esther Jungreis

535 Jeremiah 31:19, the Haftarah for the Second Day of Rosh Ha Shana.

536 Psalm 100

537 Exodus 4:3

538 Exodus 4:4

539 Malachi 3:20

540 Jeremiah 46:27-8

541 Psalm 126

542 Exodus 4:4

543 Rashi, Talmud Tractate Berachos 57b

544 Psalm 23:4

545 Genesis 28:16

546 Exodus 15:1-2

547 Ezekiel 36:24-35

548 Deuteronomy 30:3-5

549 Maimonides, Laws of Kings, Ch. 11, Halacha 1

550 Zephaniah 3:9

551 Maimonides, Ch. 11, Halacha 4

552 Maimonides, Ch. 11, Halacha 3

553 Maimonides, Ch. 12, Halacha 1

554 Maimonides, Ch. 12, Halacha 2

555 Maimonides, Ch. 12, Halacha 4

556 Isaiah 11:9

557 Maimonides Ch. 12, Halacha 5

558 Isaiah 51:3

559 Jeremiah 31:14

560 Exodus 15:1-19

561 Exodus 19:18. The Torah itself is compared to fire (Jeremiah 23:29).

562 Leviticus 10:1-2

563 Genesis 15:4

564 Malachi 3:24

565 Psalm 92